Medieval Philosophy & Theology

Volume 1 (1991)

Medieval Philosophy & Theology

VOLUME I (1991)

EDITORIAL BOARD
Norman Kretzmann (chair)
Mark D. Jordan (managing editor)
Stephen F. Brown, David B. Burrell, Kent Emery, Jr., Eleonore Stump

EDITORIAL ADVISORS
Marilyn McCord Adams, Jan A. Aertsen, E. J. Ashworth, Thérèse-Anne Druart, Stephen Dumont, Sten Ebbesen, Alfred J. Freddoso, Charles H. Lohr, Scott MacDonald, Luca Obertello, Edith Sylla, Avital Wohlman

EDITORIAL ASSISTANTS
John William Houghton, Randall B. Smith

Editorial correspondence and manuscripts should be addressed to Mark D. Jordan, Medieval Institute, University of Notre Dame, 715 Hesburgh Library, Notre Dame, IN 46556. Authors should send two copies of their manuscripts, which should conform to the *Chicago Manual of Style*, 13th edition, and which should be suitable for anonymous reviewing. Prepaid orders (for individuals) and standing orders (for libraries) should be addressed to the University of Notre Dame Press, Notre Dame, IN 46556.

Medieval Philosophy & Theology

VOLUME 1 (1991)

University of Notre Dame Press
Notre Dame & London

Copyright © 1991
University of Notre Dame Press
Notre Dame, IN 46556
All rights reserved
Manufactured in the United States of America

ISSN 1057-0608
ISBN 0-268-01386-1

Medieval Philosophy & Theology

Volume 1 (1991)

Abbreviations		vii
Augustine on Original Perception	Luca Obertello	1
Odo of Tournai's *De peccato originali* and the Problem of Original Sin	Irven M. Resnick	18
Signification and Modes of Signifying in Thirteenth-Century Logic: A Preface to Aquinas on Analogy	E. J. Ashworth	39
Beauty in the Middle Ages: A Forgotten Transcendental?	Jan A. Aertsen	68
Aquinas on Aristotle on Happiness	Don Adams	98
Aquinas's Parasitic Cosmological Argument	Scott MacDonald	119
Peter of Candia's Hundred-Year "History" of the Theologian's Role	Stephen F. Brown	156

Abbreviations

AHDLMA	Archives d'histoire doctrinale et littéraire du moyen âge
AL	Aristoteles Latinus
BGP(T)M	Beiträge zur Geschichte der Philosophie (und Theologie) des Mittelalters
CCL	Corpus Christianorum, Series Latina
CIMAGL	Cahiers de l'Institut du moyen âge grec et latin
CPDMA	Corpus Philosophorum Danicorum Medii Aevi
MGH	Monumenta Germaniae Historica
PL	Patrologiae cursus completus . . . , Series Latina, ed. J.-P. Migne
PM	Philosophes médiévaux

Augustine on Original Perception

LUCA OBERTELLO

The image of God in the human person is to be found, according to St. Augustine, in the "highest part" of the human mind, to which he reserves the name *mens*.[1] "One's mind [*mens*]," he says, "is not of the same nature as God. Nevertheless the image of that nature which transcends all others must be searched for and found in us, in

---

1. *Mens* is the superior part of the rational soul. *Animus* or *anima* is the vital principle that gives life to the body (*De Trinitate* 4.1.3). The human soul shares with other souls a capacity for sensible knowledge and a certain degree of consciousness (8.6.9) but is distinguished from animal souls as *substantia spiritualis* (12.1.1 [CCL 50:356.17–18]). The human mind is the seat of knowledge, memory, and imagination. Mind embraces reason and intelligence ("mens, cui ratio et intelligentia naturaliter inest," *De civ. Dei* 11.2 [CCL 48:322.21]). It adheres to the intelligibles and to God (see *Enarr. in Psalmos* 3.3; *De diver. quaest.* 83 7). In some passages, *mens* is identified with *animus* (e.g., *De Trin.* 15.1.1: "quae mens vocatur vel animus" [CCL 50A:460.6]), but Augustine generally considers it as the "caput [animae] vel oculus vel facies" (15.7.11 [50A:475.11–12]). While Plotinus distinguished between *psyche* and *nous* and regarded them as two hypostases, the one deriving from the other through emanation, Augustine firmly maintains the unity of the soul. It is the same spiritual principle, he maintains, that in turn perceives, animates the body, imagines, reasons, and intuitively knows the eternal truths. There is thus considerable warrant for rendering *mens* as "soul" in modern English, but I shall usually retain a distinction between "mind" and "soul" in order to remind readers of Augustine's distinction between *mens* and *animus*.

that than which our nature has nothing better."[2] This does not mean, of course, that the Trinity can be demonstrated from created things, even the highest of them—such as the human mind. It does mean that a hint, an echo, a reflection can be traced from some creatures to the most perfect nature, and that this tracing in some way brings the very notion of the divine nearer to us.[3]

Despite some loose, or even ambiguous, passages, a central thesis in Augustine is that the human being was created in the likeness of the creator, "not according to the body nor to any part of the soul, but to the rational mind [*rationalis mens*], where alone there can be acquaintance [*agnitio*] of God."[4] It is certainly plausible that only the rational mind should have knowledge of God, and that such knowledge should not be had by the body or the lower parts of the soul (which are in touch with what is sensible and so participate in the sensible's blindness towards what is spiritual). But this plausibility does not seem to justify the conclusion that the image of God is present only in the highest part of the soul.

It might indeed seem more logical to think that God, in creating the human person, should have impressed on the whole being, both body and soul, both sensibility and rationality, God's own mysterious image. God's self-exhortation in Genesis, "Let us make humanity in our image and likeness," cannot be readily translated as, "Let us make *the human soul* in our image and likeness." It would seem that this restrictive translation should be rejected not just because "Moses" (or the first author of Genesis) had no knowledge of Platonic thought but, more radically, because the creative action of God relates to global entities, to the totality of beings and not to their constituent elements, however high and embracing.

2. *De Trin.* 14.8.11 (CCL 50A:436.4–7). Compare 12.7.12, in which some texts from St. Paul are brought forward in support of this thesis, not without a bit of forcing. A parallel passage (14.3.6) says, "There ought to be found in man's soul, namely in reason and intellect, that image of the Creator which is immortality inscribed in its immortality" (CCL 50A:428.62–63). Here the immortality of the soul must be understood in the sense that "in every condition of life, even the most miserable, the soul never ceases to live. In the same way, although reason and intelligence may now appear to be quenched in it, now small and now great, the human soul is never other than rational and intellectual" (50A:428.4–8).

3. For instance, *De civ. Dei* 11.26. As it is easy to see in this passage, Augustine implies that the whole human person is the image of the Trinity.

4. *De Trin.* 12.7.12 (CCL 50:336.82–84).

In answering this objection, which explicitly opposes the metaphysics of the Bible to that of Plato and the Neoplatonists, we do indeed have to resort to a Neoplatonic doctrine that carries a particular theoretical weight and that had an extensive historical diffusion.[5] In *De libero arbitrio* 2, in his discussion with Evodius, Augustine establishes three basic levels: the level of being (*esse*), of living (*vivere*), and of thinking (*intelligere*).[6] He asks Evodius, "Which of these three seems to you superior to the others?" Evodius answers, "Intelligence." Augustine asks, "Why do you think so?" Evodius's response is synthetic and articulate, providing a compendium of the Neoplatonic point of view. These are his words:

> These things are three: being, living, thinking. A stone exists, and a beast lives, but I do not think that a stone lives or a beast thinks. It is most certain, however, that one who thinks both exists and lives. So I have no doubt in judging more excellent that being in which all these states are present than the being that is wanting one or another of them.

The three basic qualities of reality, of every possible reality, interact with each other in a way that I would call *telescopic*. I mean that the one inheres in, or leads to, the other, in a scale from pure nothingness to that most complex and integrated reality which is the human being. Evodius thus proposes a synthetic, but quite precise, vindication of the superiority of the subject in which all these qualities are simultaneously present. In this subject itself, again, the relative superiority of thought is established so far as it "implies, in those who possess it, being and living."

It is important to observe that the superiority of thought over the other qualities or states is justified, not on the grounds of its specific excellence over living and being, but rather because the presence of thought indicates the fullness of the being to which it belongs.

---

5. Two examples must suffice. Proclus gives the principle a place of importance in his philosophical teaching. See, e.g., *Elements of Theology* theor. 101–103, 138, and 198; and *Platonic Theology* 3.9, edited by Saffrey and Westerink (Paris, 1978) 35.19–24. And Michael Psellus, in the eleventh century, proposes exactly the same distinction between being, living, and thinking that we are about to state, stressing the excellence of thought as summing up the other qualities or levels of reality. See, e.g., the third opusculum in Westerink ed., *De omnifaria doctrina* (Nijmegen, 1948) 105.18–24.

6. *De lib. arb.* 2.3.7.21–22 (CCL 29:240.18–25), from which the immediately following quotations are also taken.

Thought is excellent because it is the sign and proof of a fullness, not because it in itself is a sufficient fullness. Thought is the embracing principle for the whole of the present world, in which all lower beings—the inanimate and the animate but unintelligent—are held together and transcended.

As thought brings together being and living, so we can assume that the mind is the synthesis (not only potentially, but also actually) of all the qualities that are scattered in the present world. It is only natural, then, that the likeness to the world's creator should be sought in it, a likeness recorded as image or imprint in the beings called to existence by God. Another central theme of the Augustinian vision, in many ways dependent on Neoplatonic theories about the mind's self-knowledge, casts even more light upon this important speculative principle of hierarchical inclusiveness.

Augustine maintains that we do not perceive our being, our knowing, and the love that unites us to both of them,

> with any bodily sense, as we perceive things outside: colors by seeing, sounds by hearing, odors by smelling, flavors by tasting, hard things and soft by touching. Rather we treat images of these sensible things—images very similar to them, but no longer bodily—by thought, retain them by memory, and by their means are solicited to desire them. But my being, my knowing, my loving is most certain to me, not with any images or visions of a deceitful imagination, but certain and free from the deceptions of an imagination.[7]

But how do we perceive these interior realities or subjective facts? Do we perceive them through "reason" or whatever else we may wish to call the higher faculty of the human soul? Augustine does not say or suggest that the original human certainties are known by means of reason alone. All of his arguments, on the contrary, stress that the certainties in question here are immediate, self-evident, indisputable—that they carry in themselves their own foundation and final verification.

According to Augustine every act of existence is self-assertive. The skeptics of the Academy may object: But what if you are mistaken in this foundational certainty of yours? What if you do not exist, while believing that you do exist? After all, you know that your faculties deceive you and make you take one thing for another. To them,

---

7. *De civ. Dei* 11.26 (CCL 48:345.9–17).

Augustine replies simply, "If I am mistaken, I *am*."[8] The basic certainty about the self's existence is unshakable and inconfutable. Another Augustinian formulation of the same principle is perhaps even more effective:

> If you do not discern what I am saying and doubt whether it is true, discern at least whether you doubt about whether you are doubting these things. If it is certain for you that you are doubting, then ask how it is certain. The light of no other sun will appear to you there but *the true light that shines upon every human being who comes into this world.*[9]

Some may argue, says Augustine, that the certainty of their and my existence is groundless and erroneous, and that I in fact do not exist even while I am sure of existing. But to be sure (even erroneously) of existing, I must exist.[10] In a more general form, we could say, "Every being that acts in a certain way, even erroneously, must exist in order to act." In the hands of Augustine, who fully exploits its dialectical, rhetorical, and existential aspects, the argument from doubt becomes a refined demonstration of the vacuity of objections that have been, and still are, made against humanity's basic certainties, the certainties of being, living, knowing, wanting, loving.[11] These certainties do not need any additional check before being accepted. Their validity is absolute and indisputable in itself, as the Augustinian argument makes decisively clear.[12]

---

8. *De civ. Dei* 11.26 (CCL 48:345.18), to which compare the ample, important passage in *De Trin.* 15.12.21.

9. *De vera relig.* 39.73 (CCL 32:234.25–235.30), with the allusion to John 1.9.

10. Compare the accurate analysis in Bruce Bubacz, *St. Augustine's Theory of Knowledge: A Contemporary Analysis* (New York: E. Mellen, 1981), pp. 39–55.

11. See *De Trin.* 10.10.13–14, particularly 10.10.14.

12. A pregnant passage in the dialogue between Augustine and Evodius states the problem clearly (*De lib. arb.* 2.3.7.20 [CCL 29:239.6–240.10]). Augustine addresses Evodius: "In first place I ask you . . . whether you exist. Do you perhaps fear to be led into error by this request? But, certainly, if you did not exist, you could not be mistaken in any way." Evodius simply answers, "Proceed to other problems . . . ," as if to say that Augustine's considerations are obvious. But the reading required by such a text, as by *De civitate Dei* and *De Trinitate*, is very different from the pragmatistic reading by Bubacz. He likens Augustine's teaching in one passage to a "cognitive Darwinism" (*St. Augustine's Theory of Knowledge*, p. 218). But in place of a fortuitous outcome of interactions between experience and the world, Augustine offers a theory of the soul and its knowledge based on the naturalness of consciousness, that is, on the facts that its testimony is anterior to any other and that the ensuing certainty is indisputable.

The same certainty that presides over the self-assertion of being presides over knowing and loving and whatever other states may be singled out as belonging to the original human self-experience. In every case, it is a question of immediate perceptions that cannot be contradicted. Together these make up the ontological "platform" of human nature, which Augustine identifies with the mind. The knowledge of minds, our own and those of others, is connatural and immediate to us.

We love the Apostle Paul, Augustine says, when we get to know him by reading his letters. We make for ourselves a sensible image of him in imagination. This image differs from reader to reader and is always different from the Apostle's true visage. But that is not what really matters to us. What matters is to know that Paul participated in our human nature. We do not know what his actual features were, even when we try to imagine them. But we know what a human being is because we ourselves are human. "We do of course believe about him what we know of ourselves in species and genus," that is, according to the logico-metaphysical definitions of human nature elaborated in the ancient philosophies. But there is a kind of knowledge even more natural and original than that. We love the mind of Paul, not because we have recourse to the conceptual instruments of genus and species, but because we "know" what a mind is.

> And we do not say inappropriately that we know what a soul is, since we too have a soul. We do not see the soul at all with our eyes, nor create for ourselves a notion of soul according to genus or species by comparing many of them as seen by us, but we know it rather . . . because we too have a soul. What is so intimately known, and perceives its own existence [*seque ipsum esse sentit*], as that by means of which all other things are perceived, the soul itself?[13]

Augustine's punctuating question, which is less rhetorical than philosophical, suggests briefly what the following passage of *De Trinitate* gradually unfolds. In order to understand it, one false impression must be set aside at once. It might seem obvious to a modern reader that when Augustine speaks of the soul's knowledge of itself and of other similar souls, he must be speaking of an evidential knowledge. But the "intimate knowledge" that he is describing is in truth a sort of perception or apprehension. In fact, in Augustine's language it is

13. *De Trin.* 8.6.9 (CCL 50:279.9–15).

always joined, as in a hendiadys, to the "perception of its own existence." This fundamental complementarity is taken up again and again, being explained and specified by the whole context.

All animals, both rational and irrational, partake of a natural and spontaneous advertence to the vital principle that animates other living beings. There is a perception of likenesses between the movements of our body and those of others. In fact, we move our bodies in ways that we see other bodies move. We might imagine that when another living body moves, an interior channel or "window" (different from the sensible faculty, though naturally involving it) opens for the living observer, who feels that in the body that he or she perceives there is something similar to what moves his or her own body, namely, life and soul.

This perceiving faculty, interior and exterior as it is, and exterior insofar as it is interior, is a common endowment of all animals. It consists in perceiving the act of being and living both of oneself and of others. One does not see the other's soul but, rather, is led back from exterior movements to the transcendent principle that gives rise to them. Such a principle is not articulated with rational clearness and distinctness, but is perceived immediately and "with utmost ease by means of a natural affinity" ("statim et facillime quadam conspiratione naturali"). And not only do we "perceive" the souls of other people by analogy with our own, but we can also know what they are by considering our own soul.[14]

Such are the naturalness and immediacy of this inner act of perception, and so great is its difference from formal and explicit thinking, that it may well escape our attention and lie hidden in our minds. There are dimensions of knowledge ignored by the mind itself, in the sense that they are present in it but obscure and not made evident in the light of actual consciousness. Augustine asks himself, How is this possible? "What do we know, in fact, if we do not know what is in our own minds, since we can know all that we know only by means of our mind?"[15]

The specific power of thought is so great that the mind itself, through which all that is being thought is thought, could not face

---

14. See, again, *De Trin.* 8.6.9 (CCL 50:280.25–30), here paraphrased.
15. *De Trin.* 14.6.8 (CCL 50A:430.29–31), from which the immediately following quotations are also taken (431.5–8 and so on).

itself with itself in any other way than by thinking itself. "How the soul is not in its vision [*conspectus*] when it does not think itself—since it can never be separated from itself, as if it were both itself and the vision of itself—this I cannot discover."[16] Augustine here asks himself how it could happen that the mind should not have a cognitive vision, a full apperception of itself, except when in the act of thinking. That may cause some astonishment, because everything in the mind is unitary, and the mind's "vision" or "sight" is not different from the mind itself.

The most immediate answer, which is also the most incorrect, supposes that the mind sees a part of itself with another part, that an "active" or "actualized" part of the mind sees others that are "passive." Augustine objects:

> Can anything more absurd than that this be thought or said? From where is the mind brought out, if not from itself? And where is it put in its own vision, if not in front of itself? It was not where it was, then, when it was not in its own vision, because if it has been put here, then it has been removed from there. But if it has to be moved to be seen, where shall it stay to see itself? Or does it come to be twinned in some way, so that it is here and there—here to see, there to be seen—in itself contemplating, in front of itself contemplated?[17]

Whoever thinks in this way, thinks according to material imagery. Yet the mind is not a material thing but an incorporeal reality. There is nothing to be said, at least in principle and in view of the mind's kind, except that "it belongs to the nature of the mind to have sight of itself [*conspectus eius*]. When it conceives itself, it turns to its own nature, not as if by a spatial passage, but with an incorporeal turning." But what happens, then, when the mind does not explicitly and actually conceive itself? At such times, which are frequent, the mind does not see itself and is not present to its own sight, but even so it "knows itself as if it were its own memory for itself" ("tanquam ipsa sibi sit memoria sui"). Augustine adds a concrete example: it is like what happens to one who knows many things. What such a person

---

16. The difficulty is real, and it points clearly to a limit on the Augustinian doctrine about the will, a limit that can be overcome only through a rethinking of body-soul dualism.

17. *De Trin.* 14.6.8 (CCL 50A:431.18–24).

knows is placed "in arcana quadam notitia," that is, in a hidden knowledge called memory.

This example, like every other, holds only so far. Memory is *notitia* not only of images, notions, or ideas held in the mind and stored there but also of the mind's intimate reality, of its pure and essential being. As such, memory is the backdrop, so to speak, for the appearance or manifestation of the mind to itself, which constitutes the mind in some functional way at least, because it is there that the mind lays its own foundations. But while it is a manifestation, and the originating manifestation, the *memoria sui* is also an *arcana quaedam notitia*, that is, a hidden knowledge, mysterious and remote from the knowledge that persists on the surface of explicit consciousness. With seeming contradiction, we can say that memory is at once revelation and concealment, knowledge and ignorance. Memory is that dawnlike contact of the mind with itself and the world kept in itself, where everything is present, but nothing is already explicated.

All this should tell us "that we have within ourselves, in the recess of mind, some knowledges [*notitiae*] of things. And then, when they are thought, they somehow come forth and place themselves as it were more openly in the mind's vision. Then the mind itself finds that it remembered, knew, and loved them even when it did not think them, when it thought of other things."[18] Emerging from the obscurity of the original identification with itself, from the immediacy of perception and the latency of memory, the mind moves towards an ever-growing consciousness of itself and comes ever nearer to the measure of its own specific perfection. At first it has, or better is, only memory of itself. When it begins to think reflexively, it comes to have intelligence of itself and to love itself as well.

With expressions that cannot fail to perplex by their strangeness to the everyday, Augustine says, quite rhetorically: "Let the mind not seek itself as if it were absent from itself. What is there, indeed, so present to understanding [*cognitio*] as what is present to the mind? Or what is so present to the mind, as the mind itself?"[19] The mind, we may conclude, must not leave itself in order to know and love itself. It must remain in itself.

---

18. *De Trin.* 14.7.9 (CCL 50A:433.19–434.24).

19. *De Trin.* 10.7.10 (CCL 50:323.41–44), to which compare the analogous expressions of 14.5.7.

There are many possible alternative theses about the mind's inward perception of itself, but none is very satisfactory. It might be that the mind loves and desires to know itself by having conceived from external opinions some ideas about itself and its desirability. Or it might be that it makes up a mental representation similar to itself, so that in order to reach itself it must first pass through notions about other minds. Or, finally, it might be that it happens with mind as with bodily eyes, which "know" other eyes better than themselves. But if this is true, then the mind, seeking itself, will never find itself. "The eyes in fact never see themselves without a mirror. Nor should one ever think that such a thing might be used in the contemplation of incorporeal things too, as if the soul could know itself *in a mirror*."[20] Unlike bodily eyes, which must become objects for themselves in order to be able to see themselves, the mind must not go out from itself if it will know itself.

The body's eyes see other eyes, not themselves. Whatever power it is that enables them to see, we do not see that power through the eyes. We see by means of the power, but precisely because of that we cannot see it as such. It is the mind that allows us to understand that the act of vision is accomplished through the intervention of a specific power—and consequently the mind allows the sense of sight to become conscious of itself, not as such, of course, but so far as it belongs to the mind and is immersed in the mind's light of understanding.[21]

Augustine distinguishes three kinds of knowledge, to which there correspond as many kinds of love. In doing so he once again takes over and recreates Neoplatonic doctrine.[22] If knowledge is inferior to what

20. *De Trin.* 10.3.5 (CCL 50:317.15–18).

21. Following a complementary line of consideration, we can also say that if the soul knows itself, it does not know itself as it knows the objects of ordinary experience. Augustine states quite clearly that "if anyone says that the soul believes itself to be like the other souls of which it has experience, on the grounds of a knowledge [*notitia*] made up of genera and species, and that it loves itself in consequence, he speaks most foolishly" (*De Trin.* 9.3.3 [CCL 50:290.2–5]).

22. The trichotomy of knowledge is clearly to be related to the doctrine about the *medietas* of the soul between the intelligible and perceptible or sensible worlds. As is well known, Plotinus teaches that the soul "occupies a middle rank [*taxis*] among the things that exist, for while it shares in the divine, it also finds itself at the lowest point of what is intelligible. In this way, bordering on perceptible nature, it gives to it something of what it has in itself, and receives something in exchange" (*Enneads* 4.8.7 [Henry and Schwyzer 2:246.5–9]). That does not amount in any way to saying

is known (which in itself is fully knowable), it is of course imperfect knowledge. If it is superior, the knowing nature is superior to the known. The knowledge that the mind has of the body, for example, is superior to the body itself. But the mind, knowing itself, "does not exceed itself with the knowledge [*notitia*] that it has of itself, since it both understands and is understood [*ipsa cognoscit, ipsa cognoscitur*]. Since it understands the whole of itself, and nothing else together with itself, its knowledge is equal to itself, nor does its understanding derive from another nature."[23]

In other contexts, Augustine states that

> every thing understood by us coengenders in us the knowledge of itself; the knowledge is indeed begotten by both, by the understander and the understood. Therefore when the mind knows itself, it is the only begetter of its knowledge. It is at once understander and understood. It was knowable by itself, even before it knew itself. But when it did not know itself, the knowledge of itself was not in it. From the fact that it knows itself, then, the mind generates a knowledge of itself equal to itself, since it does not know itself less than what it is, nor is its knowledge another essence, not only because it is the knower, but because it knows itself.[24]

What exactly does it mean to say that the mind, the knowing

---

that the soul is an intermingling of corporeal and incorporeal. It is said to be intermediate because, in laying down what is sensible, it pervades and permeates it with itself, without deflecting in any way from the unity of its being. "Remaining wholly in itself, it is divided relatively to the bodies according to their own divisibility, because they are not capable of receiving it in a unitary way. Therefore the division is an affection of the bodies, not of the soul." (*Enneads* 4.2.1 [Henry and Schwyzer 2:6.73–76]).

23. *De Trin.* 9.4.4 (CCL 50:297.19–23). The same concepts are illustrated at greater length in 9.11.16. On the intermediate position of soul, see also 12.11.16. The doctrine of the threefold relation or proportion between knower and known is a constant of Neoplatonism. Ammonius of Hermias reiterates it in his commentary on *On Interpretation*, very much under the influence of Proclus, but attributing it to "the divine Iamblichus." He exemplifies the three possible cases of this relationship by saying that (1) when the intellect knows what is particular in the events, referring it to the universal, its knowledge is better than what is known; (2) when it turns to itself and considers its own substance, the knowledge is of the same kind as what is known, and therefore homogeneous with it; (3) when at last, ascending to the summit of its own capacities, it considers the divine ordering of things, the knowledge is without doubt inferior to what is known. See Ammonius, *In De interp.*, ed. Busse (Berlin, 1897) 135.14–32.

24. *De Trin.* 19.12.18 (CCL 50:309.29–34).

principle, does not descend below its own nature when knowing itself, that it remains in knowledge equal to itself? If we compare this remark to others already quoted, according to which nothing can be more present to the mind than the mind itself, we may be tempted to conclude that the mind has a knowledge totally exhaustive of itself, so clear and distinct as not to leave blind spots or uncertainties, a knowledge that possesses itself immediately and totally, that is transparent to itself, a full revelation of itself to itself. The first and most obvious answer to this superficial reading of Augustine is that, if this were so, the mind would be God or equal to God.

Of course, some crucial points of Augustine's speculative thought might be adduced in support of such an interpretation. There is, for instance, the radical transcendence of mind over body, with the corollary that mind is thus necessarily "impermeable" to body. This is the principle that Etienne Gilson calls the "interiority of thought." He explains it in these terms: "Since everything comes to the mind from within, nothing antecedent can be given to it: the mind is therefore its own first object. At the same time, the mind finds in the act by which it immediately takes hold of itself an invincible certainty, the warrant for the possibility of a certainty in general. It is then a principal characteristic of metaphysical Augustinianism that the evidence through which the mind apprehends itself is the first of all evidences and the criterion of truth."[25]

Apart from the fact that the first evidence and criterion of truth do not depend for Augustine on a subjective fact but on the truth's manifestation and illumination within the mind,[26] it can rightly be objected to Gilson that everything depends on how the act of the mind's self-apprehension is conceived. Is it simultaneously an intellectual and vital act (as we have tried to show), that is, a perception of real existence in which being, life, and thought are so intimately united as to mirror in a mysterious, but true, manner the unity-in-distinction of

---

25. Etienne Gilson, *Introduction à l'étude de saint Augustin* (Paris: J. Vrin, 1949), p. 321.

26. It is not out of place to recall *De vera relig.* 39.72–73, one of the profoundest passages in the whole Augustinian corpus. The truth of which Augustine speaks is "summa et intima" (*De vera relig.* 20.38 [CCL 32:210.2]). It is neither a creature nor a projection of consciousness, but an objective reality established and shone forth by the sovereign being (compare *Confess.* 8.10.16).

the Trinity?²⁷ Or is this act to be conceived as a "pure" thought, in which the quality of thought logically and really precedes being?

It seems that this second reading has been adopted by Gilson on the grounds of a historiographical assumption that sees a historical and theoretical continuity from Augustine to the various Augustinianisms that have flourished so abundantly in modern thought, especially near its beginnings.²⁸ But what Augustine really says in the passages quoted above, as in others that could be brought forward, in no way permits a Cartesian or subjectivist reading. Augustine only maintains that, when the mind knows itself, its knowledge is on a par with its self—namely, is endowed with a nature and a dignity at the level of the mind's own being.

We must not forget that the mind's operations are consubstantial with itself, given its incorporeal nature. In Augustine's own words, "These things subsist in the soul and somehow unfold, having been enfolded, so that they are now perceived and enumerated substantially or, so to speak, essentially."²⁹ The knowledge that the mind has of itself is thus an actualization of its own substance. The preceding thesis, that the mind's self-knowledge is at the level of its nature and essence, must be construed in the context of this second statement. The mind becomes equal to itself in knowing itself. This does not mean that it knows its own metaphysical substance as if it were one of

---

27. On this suggestive theme, which confirms Augustine's friendly adherence to the realistic tradition of ancient philosophy, see, for example, *De Trin.* 9.5.8. It follows that thought (a substance of its own kind) is melted into substantial unity with being and love. That thought is substantially united to being in the distinction of the relative "persons" (if we can adapt theological language to a philosophical theme) is a principle not to be found in Descartes nor in many other modern thinkers. According to Augustine, being is on par with thought and love (as conversely) in the created trinity that forms the human soul. This Augustinian thesis might be considered subordinate and instrumental to his theological reflection on the Trinity. But it is better to consider it as a philosophical principle *pleno jure* that meets a theological position, correlated if independent.

28. On the very page quoted above, Gilson states that the metaphysical principle of the transcendence of the soul over the body has given origin to a whole series of strictly connected theses: "[They] will seldom dissociate in the course of history, and [their] necessary connection will not appear anywhere with greater evidence than in the doctrines of Descartes or Malbranche" (*Introduction à l'étude de saint Augustin*, p. 321).

29. *De Trin.* 9.4.5 (CCL 50:297.28–298.30).

the objects that constitute the formal world of thought and experience. Augustine insists many times on this point, and with good reason.

The knowledge that the mind has of itself is completely *sui generis*. It belongs to an anomolous dimension outside the usual modes of knowledge. Speaking loosely, we can say that the mind "feels" itself—though the expression is inaccurate, not only because we are here dealing with what eludes any strict specification, but also because "feeling" must not be interpreted as connected to corporeality or sensibility. The "feeling" is general; it is specified in several fundamental ways. The mind in fact perceives itself as existing, living, thinking, and loving. It knows itself, not in its own objective nature or essence (which would require an external observer endowed with some higher and more comprehensive nature than the mind itself has), but rather in its states and operations, while and so far as it exercises acts of being, living, thinking, loving. The mind takes hold of itself at the very roots of its own being, and it does so dynamically, not statically.

The mind's perception of itself in its own interior activity cannot be said to have only a pragmatic meaning, as if one could not look beyond the operations and the being that grounds them to some dimly seen metaphysical level.[30] Augustine often repeats that the mind has a kind of vision (*conspectus*) of itself—an inward and nonsensible vision, of course. The metaphor should not be understood literally. Augustine wants to say that, as eyes see an object, so the mind sees itself as if "in front of itself" (*in conspectu*)—not as an object, but as being identical with itself. It does not have to go out of itself in order to know itself but need only stay within itself. Staying in itself, it turns towards itself with a "movement" (*conversio*) made possible by its incorporeal nature. It must be said, of course, that these descriptive terms suggest spatial states and interactions and so are unfaithful to the reality that they attempt to describe.

A being that is free from bodiliness does not stay in itself strictly

---

30. This simple description of internal states and the structures of self-consciousness does not yet imply any particular theory about the soul's nature or, alternately, about the meaninglessness of the concept "nature" and its replacement by a concept of disposition to action. Existential perception and natural self-consciousness are, not theories, but original inner realities, preceding, and having priority over, every possible theory.

speaking (that is, physically speaking), nor does it put itself into its own presence, or see itself, or turn towards itself. The mind has no parts, and cannot double itself into an "in-itself" and an "out-of-itself." These and other spatial images are used only to suggest that spiritual realities have the capacity to see themselves without mediation, that is, to come into direct cognitive contact with themselves, to apprehend and perceive themselves. But this assertion must not be understood to mean that these realities, whatever they are, are able fully to realize their own substances. Divine nature, whose intimate knowledge coincides with its own substance, and in which there is no discrepancy between being, knowing, living, loving, or any other essential determination, is obviously quite different from the human mind, which is a creature, however much it is also a spiritual one.

We have said that the mind does not know "what" it is as a reality, but knows itself as a principle of activity or actuality before and beyond the circuit of objective knowledge, in an intimacy rich with meanings but void of restricted connotations. Being, living, knowing, loving are qualifications to the mind's original perception of itself and so are the authentic roots of human being. As such, and at the same time, they are also the highest perspectives upon reality, within the frame of which objects and their relations appear to the mind. The mind's knowledge of itself is indeed only formal, because it does not display objective contents that would constitute it as such and make its substance accessible.

If we want to say that the original and founding consciousness has contents, let us say (with an appropriate oxymoron) that they are subjective contents, inner determinations of the subject that identify themselves with the subjective principle as knowing and perceiving itself. The mind's self-knowledge is not inferior to objectifying knowledge, as if in lacking objects it lacked something essential. As the very moment of the foundation and opening of consciousness's horizon, self-knowledge is prior to the world and so different from it.

If we wish to understand more exactly the speculative potential of this Augustinian teaching, we must read it in its natural connection with reflection on the Trinitarian mysteries. This reflection suggests an analogical similarity between the structural elements of the mind, which appear in the acts of its self-perception,[31] and what Christian

---

31. Augustine enumerates various "created trinities" that exemplify this likeness,

revelation tells us about the mystery of the Trinity, one God in three consubstantial persons. The analogy is real. It does not derive from forced assimilations or fictitious convergences, but from natural references and consonances between the two parallel lines of investigation that reciprocally confirm each other.

The mind's insight first meets itself—not as an intelligible object, but as an opaque, indecipherable mirror of itself that perceives more than it knows and knows by perceiving. In turning toward itself and reflecting upon itself, the mind discovers that its own substance is interwoven with essential orders rooted in itself—indeed, identical with itself. Its interior space, void of objects, is vivified from within by the merging of these articulations of its own consciousness. The mind is conscious of itself so far as it perceives existing, thinking, loving. These forms of perception or apperception qualify the consciousness in its inner reality as identical with and constitutive of it, not as elements joining it from without. The mind is one, but it is also modulated in its unity by figures that define its essential virtualities. Aristotle remarks of the mind's nature, "If its own form is made manifest alongside another, what is inside will hinder and intercept it."[32] For example, if there were a color inside the eye's pupil, that internal color would impede the perception of external ones, because the only color to be perceived would be that internal to the eye. If the mind, similarly, should participate in the nature of any of the substances that it knows, this participated nature, being internal to the mind, would prevent it from knowing any other thing.

Turning the Aristotelian thesis upside down, we might say that it is what is inside the mind that coincides with its own essence, characterizing it and making possible its self-manifestation. The mind can set itself as principle, and understand itself as such, so far as its inside is not empty or undifferentiated but, rather, is framed according to forms with an individuality of their own. Of course, the forms cannot be thought to have the status of objects, and consequently to be in need of definition according to categorical schemes. They are, in fact, precategorical. And even so (or perhaps just for that reason), they

---

under different points of view and as ordered to different speculative requirements. See the very precise inventory in *De Trinitate*, vol. 1, Bibliothèque Augustinienne 15 (Bruges and Paris: Desclée de Brouwer, 1955), p. 571.

32. Aristotle *On the Soul* 3.4.429a20–21.

really do distinguish the mind as it is in itself, just as they also constitute it.

In this way, the vision of the inner eye, glimpsing itself, also glimpses in itself these metaphysical powers. Its communion in them discloses the setting for its reality. This reality, on the other hand, is wholly present in every one of the principles as well as in their totality, because none of them subsists in and for itself, in isolation from that fullness, but in and for it, as it subsists in and for them. For these consubstantial principles of the mind, the name "transcendentals" may perhaps be proposed.[33] Their function and ontological stature are indeed analogous to the familiar transcendentals of being, one, truth, goodness, and beauty. Coessential to the mind, these new transcendentals form its very substance. In the personal subsistence of the mind's transcendentals, in their reciprocal implication and inherence within the common substance that is present in all and unifies everything in itself, the mysterious image of the Trinity shows itself in the human mind.

Augustine says, "When the soul knows and loves itself, the trinity of soul, love, and knowledge remains. And these are not confused by commingling, although each one is in itself, and all are mutually in all, and each one in the other two, and two in one. Therefore, 'all in all.'"[34] In this flowing spiritual life, "the mind loves and knows all of itself, and knows all its love, and loves all its knowledge, when these three are perfect in relation to themselves. In an admirable way, the three are inseparable from each other, and yet each one of them, considered in itself, is substance, and all together one substance or essence, when they are said in relation to each other."[35]

Università di Genoa

---

33. On the role of the transcendentals in our always obscure and imperfect comprehension of the mysteries of the Trinity, see the important paper by Norman Kretzmann, "Trinity and Transcendentals," in *Trinity, Incarnation, and Atonement*, edited by Ronald J. Feenstra and Cornelius Plantinga, Jr. (Notre Dame: University of Notre Dame Press, 1989).

34. *De Trin.* 9.5.8 (CCL 50:300.1–5), with the allusion to 1 Cor. 15.28.

35. *De Trin.* 9.5.8 (CCL 50:301.26–31). This passage and the one just quoted are taken from the beginning and end of the chapter, but the whole text that they enclose—not to say, its context in the whole book—must be kept in mind in order to understand what Augustine will teach about the created unity/trinity of soul, knowledge, and love in the human person.

Odo of Tournai's *De peccato originali* and the Problem of Original Sin

IRVEN M. RESNICK

AUGUSTINE AND THE EARLY CHURCH

Although there were early disagreements over the right understanding of original sin and its consequences, a consensus gradually emerged in the Western Church as the outcome of the debates between St. Augustine and the followers of Pelagius early in the fifth century. Pelagius's disciple Celestius was condemned for the view that Adam's sin affected only Adam, not the entire human race. Other Pelagians (or semi-Pelagians) reasonably inferred that "If sin is natural, it is not voluntary; if it is voluntary, it is not inborn. These two definitions are as mutally contrary as are necessity and [free] will."[1] Since the Pelagians insisted on the voluntary character of sin, it seemed to them impossible that one might be born with sin. Augustine, on the other hand, affirms that original sin is both voluntary and free for Adam, while it is natural and necessary for us. In part this view stems from Augustine's efforts to safeguard the practice of infant

---

1. See Augustine *Contra secundam Juliani responsionem opus imperfectum* 1.78 (PL 45:1002) and 4.93 (PL 45:1303), quoted by Jaroslav Pelikan, *The Christian Tradition: A History of Development and Doctrine*, vol. 1: *The Emergence of the Catholic Tradition (100–600)* (Chicago: University of Chicago Press, 1971), p. 313.

baptism in the Church, which certainly makes sense if there is some inherited sin of which infants must be cleansed. In part it stems from his reading of one Vulgate version of Romans 5.12, which identifies Adam as the one through whom sin and death have entered the world, the one in whom all have sinned.[2] Because all humanity has participated in the sin of the first man, Augustine avers, all humankind constitutes now a *massa perditionis* or a *massa damnata*,[3] a single lump of sin,[4] a lump of filth.[5]

Augustine insists that every person participates in and inherits Adam's sin and its consequences but is not very clear about precisely how this sin is transmitted to subsequent generations or to the whole of human nature. Augustine had often been asked to explain the origin of the soul and the transmission of original sin. In reply, he eliminates the views of the Pythagoreans and the Origenists, who claim that the soul fell from heaven and entered a body as a punishment for previous sins.[6] He refutes also the Stoics, Manichaeans, and Priscillianists, who argue that the soul is an emanation from the divine substance. Finally, he attacks Tertullian's view that the individual soul is produced from a material seed or rootstock (*tradux*) of the parent. But Augustine himself is unable to decide between two remaining options: creationism and spiritual traducianism.[7] Creationism, a view Augustine attributes to Jerome,[8] maintains that God creates *ex nihilo* each new individual soul and infuses it in the body

---

2. Augustine *Epistle* 177.11 (PL 33:769). On the influence of Rom. 5.12 on the development of the doctrine of original sin, see S. Lyonnet, "Le péché originel et le exégèse de Rom., 5, 12–14," in *Recherches de science religieuse* 44 (1956): 63–84.

3. Augustine *Enchiridion* 27.

4. Augustine *De diversis quaest. ad Simpl.* 1.2.16.

5. Augustine *De diversis quaest. ad Simpl.* 83.68.3.

6. See especially R. J. O'Connell, "The Origin of the Soul in St. Augustine's Letter 143," *Revue des études augustiniennes* 28 (1982): 239–52. For a good survey of views in the patristic era on the origin of the soul—and their later influence—see J. M. da Cruz Pontes, "Le problème de l'origine de l'âme de la patristique à la solution thomiste," *Recherches de théologie ancienne et médiévale* 31 (1964): 175–229.

7. On these two views, see especially A. Michel, "Traducianisme," *Dictionnaire de théologie catholique* 15:1351–1366. For a general discussion of original sin, creationism, and traducianism in the early Church, see J. N. D. Kelly, *Early Christian Doctrines*, 5th ed. (New York: Harper and Row, 1978), pp. 174–183, 344–374.

8. Augustine *Epistle* 166.3.8 (PL 33:723). Whether this is actually Jerome's view is unclear. See Gerard O'Daly, *Augustine's Philosophy of Mind* (London: Duckworth, 1987), p. 19.

generated from sexual intercourse. This infusion occurs either at the moment of conception or forty days later, in the womb. Spiritual traducianism maintains that the individual soul is generated from a parent soul or spiritual principle: "As light is kindled from light and from it a second flame comes into existence without loss to the first, so a soul comes into existence in a child from the soul of the parent, or is transferred to the child."[9] Both positions, Augustine maintains, can be defended by an appeal to the canonical scriptures.

In a letter addressed to Jerome, Augustine reveals his uncertainty, but seems to follow Jerome's preference for the creationist solution.[10] Still, Augustine elsewhere confesses that so long as we are agreed that all suffer from original sin and require God's grace in order to be freed from this sin and its consequences, the question of the origin of the soul and the transmission of original sin can remain undecided without danger. "Someone once fell into a well where the water was deep enough to hold him up so that he did not drown, but not deep enough to choke him so that he could not speak. A bystander came over when he saw him and asked sympathetically: 'How did you fall in?' He answered: 'Please find some way of getting me out and never mind how I fell in.'"[11] So it is not as important to know how we fell into the well of sin as it is to find the way out.

Later Christian tradition, at least until the thirteenth century, reflected Augustine's uncertainty when reviewing the creationist and traducianist alternatives. Gregory the Great, Isidore of Seville, Prudentius,[12] Cassiodorus, Rabanus Maurus,[13] Agobard of Lyon,[14] and

---

9. Augustine *Epistle* 190.15 (PL 33:862): "Tamquam lucerna de lucerna accendatur et sine detrimento alterius alter inde ignis existat, sic anima de anima parentis fiat in prole, vel traducatur in prolem."

10. Augustine *Epistle* 166.8.26 (PL 33:731).

11. Augustine *Epistle* 167.1.2 (PL 33:733): "Cum quidem ruisset in puteum, ubi aqua tanta erat, ut eum magis exciperet ne moreretur, quam suffocaret ne loqueretur; accessit alius, et eo viso admirans ait: Quomodo huc cecidisti? At ille: Obsecro, inquit, cogita quomodo hinc me liberes; non quomodo huc ceciderim, queras." For this translation, I have relied on Augustine's *Letters*, vol. 4 (letters 165–203), translated by Wilfrid Parsons, The Fathers of the Church 12 (New York, 1955), p. 33.

12. Prudentius *Carmen Apotheosis* 780–990.

13. *Tractatus de anima* 2 (PL 110:1112C). Rabanus Maurus does not share Augustine's hesitancy but declares himself strongly in favor of creationism. See also his *Liber de corpore et sanguine Domini* 3.3.

14. *Liber contra objectiones Fredegisi abbatis* 14 (PL 104:168).

others generally preferred the creationist solution but often hesitated to condemn traducianism altogether.[15] In the eleventh century, Odorannus of Sens defended creationism, after reviewing the views of Gregory, Prudentius, and Isidore.[16] He was joined by Werner of St. Blaise.[17] In the twelfth century, Hugh de Ribemont took up the defense of creationism.[18] In the twelfth and thirteenth centuries, traducianism began to appear not only as a less probable solution but also as false, impious, and, ultimately, heretical one. This change appeared in Peter Lombard,[19] Thomas Aquinas,[20] Robert Pullen,[21] and others. Finally, the Fifth Lateran Council, under Pope Leo X, defined as Catholic doctrine the infusion of a soul—created from nothing—to each new body.[22]

THE ELEVENTH- AND TWELFTH-CENTURY DEBATE

It is especially in the eleventh and twelfth centuries that one finds new interest expressed in the origin of the soul and the transmission of original sin. The reasons behind this new interest are difficult to determine. Perhaps popular religious movements during the eleventh century, which contemporary critics associated with Manichaeanism,[23] revive the emanationist theory of the soul's origin, a view that Augustine had condemned in his own century. Perhaps renewed encounters with a Neoplatonic explanation of the origin of

---

15. For additional citations, see especially Michel, "Traducianisme," pp. 1355–1358.

16. *Ad Everardum monachum, de tribus quaestionibus* 4, in *Opera omnia*, edited by Robert-Henri Bautier et al. (Paris: Editions du Centre national de la recherche scientifique, 1972), pp. 134–151.

17. *Deflorationes SS. Patrum* 2: *De origine animae* (PL 157:1161–1162).

18. *Epistola ad G. Andegavensem* (PL 166:833–836).

19. *Sententiae* 18.8, 31.2.

20. For a discussion, see Jean-Marie Dubois, "Transmission et rémission du péché originel: Genèse de la réflexion théologique de saint Thomas d'Aquin," *Revue des études augustiniennes* 29 (1983): 283–311.

21. *Sententiarum libri octo* 2.8 (PL 186:731A).

22. See Michel, "Traducianisme," p. 1358.

23. For example, Adhemar of Chabannes. For a translation of some of the relevant texts, see especially R. I. Moore, *Birth of Popular Heresy* (New York: St. Martin's Press, 1976), pp. 9–10, 93–94.

the soul, conveyed to the twelfth century especially by Macrobius, contribute as well to this new interest.[24] Perhaps the appearance of a nominalist challenge to Christian Platonism can explain the resurgence of debate.[25] Perhaps encounters with the Jewish community in northern Europe encourage it; or, perhaps the development of the *quaestio* from the *lectio* in the schools may help explain the new efforts directed toward a systematic examination of the problem of original sin.[26] Whatever the causes, there is a new willingness among Christian theologians to appeal to philosophy in order to examine this question, together with a confidence that dialectic could treat it with some success.

Anselm is perhaps the best-known example of an orthodox dialectician from the late eleventh century. He discusses the reception and consequences of original sin in his *De conceptu virginali et originali peccato*.[27] In the process, he employs a philosophical vocabulary that will become common in these discussions—a vocabulary that distinguishes nature from person, and natural sin from personal sin. He fails to decide between the virtues of traducianism or creationism, how-

---

24. Macrobius defends the view that there is single World-Soul that is the source of all other souls. See his *Commentarii in Somnium Scipionis* 1.6.20, edited by Jacob Willis (Leipzig: Teubner, 1970). For complaints against those who have received the Platonic doctrine from Macrobius in the late eleventh century, see Manegold of Lautenbach, *Contra Wolfelmum Coloniensem*, edited by Wilfried Hartmann, MGH Quellen 8 (Weimar: 1972), pp. 1–2. For a study of Manegold's work, see Wilfried Hartmann, "Manegold von Lautenbach und die Anfänge der Frühscholastik," *Deutsches Archiv für Erforschung des Mittelalters* 26 (1970): 47–149.

25. See especially Joseph Reiners, *Der Nominalismus in der Frühscholastik*, BGPM 8 (Münster, 1910). This work includes the Latin text of the letters of Abelard and Roscelin. For Roscelin of Compiegne, see Francois Picavet, *Roscelin: Philosophe et théologien* (Paris: Felix Alcan, 1911).

26. Jewish medieval philosophers also accepted the view that God infuses the soul into the body at the moment of creation. See, for example, Saadia Gaon, *Book of Opinions and Beliefs*, treatise 6. Still the doctrine of the soul's preexistence persists in aggadic literature. See Louis Ginzberg, *The Legends of the Jews*, translated by Henrietta Szold, 7 vols. (Philadelphia: 1938–1946), 1:56. On the development of the *quaestio*, see especially Bernardo C. Bazán, "Les questions disputées, principalement dans les facultés de théologie," in *Les questions disputées et les questions quodlibétiques dans les facultés de théologie, de droit et de médecine*, edited by Leopold Genicot, Typologie des sources du moyen âge occidental 44–45 (Turnhout: Brepols, 1985), pp. 21–40.

27. See especially *De conceptu virginali* 23.

ever. This failure evidently disturbed him for the rest of his life. Eadmer, in his *Vita Anselmi*, notes that when Anselm was awaiting death, he hoped at the end to have a little more time in this world so that he might solve the problem of the origin of the soul, which he had been turning over and over in his mind and which he feared no one after him would solve.[28]

Whether Anselm's ultimate solution would have supported creationism or traducianism is difficult to settle. His works leave an impression of uncertainty.[29] Any determination in favor of creationism is complicated by the fact that his student, Gilbert Crispin, supported the traducianist position. It is often assumed that Gilbert was representing his master's view.[30] By contrast, the creationist view seems to have been defended by the school of Laon, to judge from some fragments treating original sin that are sometimes attributed to Anselm of Laon.[31] The most complete eleventh-century treatment of these questions, however, which discusses both traducianist and creationist alternatives, comes not from Laon or Bec but from Tournai. In a little-known work, *De peccato originali*, Odo of Tournai presents the first theological treatise written expressly on original sin since Augustine.[32] This work represents, then, an important part of a long theological struggle that was moving to define the origin of the soul and the transmission of original sin.

---

28. Eadmer, *The Life of St. Anselm*, edited by R. W. Southern (London: T. Nelson, 1962), p. 142: "Et quidem si voluntas ejus in hoc est. voluntati ejus libens parebo. Verum si [Deus] mallet me adhuc inter vos saltem tam diu manere, donec quaestionem quam de origine animae mente revolvo absolvere possem. gratanter acciperem, eo quod nescio utrum aliquis eam me defuncto sit soluturus."

29. For a discussion, see Jasper Hopkins, *A Companion to the Study of St. Anselm* (Minneapolis: University of Minnesota Press, 1972), pp. 206–210.

30. Gilbert Crispin's *De Anima*, found in British Library MS Add. 8166, ff. 37–39, has recently been published in *The Works of Gilbert Crispin, Abbot of Westminster*, edited by Anna Sapir Abulafia and G. R. Evans (London: Oxford University Press, 1989), pp. 157–164. For his apparent defense of traducianism, see especially *De Anima* 16, p. 159.

31. For a translation of some of these, see *A Scholastic Miscellany: Anselm to Ockham*, edited by Eugene R. Fairweather (Philadelphia: Westminster Press, 1956), pp. 261–266.

32. For this claim, see also da Cruz Pontes, "Le problème de l'origine de l'âme," p. 191.

ODO OF TOURNAI AND THE PHILOSOPHICAL LIFE

Since it is often assumed that toward the end of his life Odo abandoned philosophy after he entered a monastery, it may be useful to provide a few biographical details in order to establish the position that his *De peccato originali* enjoys in his literary corpus. Odo was born about the middle of the eleventh century. During the 1080s he became a popular master at the cathedral school of Notre Dame at Tournai.[33] There Odo's reputation as a dialectician and master of the liberal arts attracted students from Flanders, Normandy, Saxony, Burgundy, and Italy.[34] Unfortunately, Odo's earliest, and perhaps most philosophical, works—*Sophistem*; *Liber complexionum*; and *De re et ente*—have not survived.

Odo's extant works must be dated from after his conversion to the religious life—a conversion precipitated by a reading of Augustine's *De libero arbitrio*. His biographer, Herman, explains that Odo was overcome with grief when, attempting to explicate the fourth book of Boethius's *Consolation of Philosophy* for his students, "he came to read the third book [of *De libero arbitrio*] in which the aforementioned Doctor [Augustine] compares sinful souls to a slave struck down from his prior dignity for his crimes and [compares these souls] to the filth of this world, who have lost celestial glory for their crimes."[35] Almost immediately, Odo took a small group of disciples, departed the cathedral school of Notre Dame, and established an eremitic community at the abandoned abbey of St. Martin of Tournai in 1092.[36] Odo became the first abbot of this new foundation. He ended his life (d. 1113) as bishop of Cambrai.

Before this abrupt renunciation of the life of the secular scholar,

---

33. On the cathedral chapter, see Jacques Pycke, *Le chapitre cathédral Notre-Dame de Tournai de la fin du XIe à la fin du XIIe siècle*, Université de Louvain: Recueil de travaux d'histoire et de philologie 6/30 (Brussels, 1986).

34. Herman *Liber de restauratione monasterii sancti Martini Tornacensis* 1, MGH Scriptores 14 (reprint, 1963), p. 274.

35. Herman *Liber de restauratione* 4, p. 276: "Cum ecce legendo ad tercium librum pervenitur, in quo prefatus doctor servo criminibus suis de priori dignitate pulso et mundande cloace deputato comparat peccatrices animas, que celestem quidem gloriam pro sceleribus suis perdunt."

36. See my "Odo of Tournai and Peter Damian: Poverty and Crisis in the Eleventh Century," *Revue Bénédictine* 98 (1988): 125–152.

Herman remarks that Odo had taken more pleasure in the works of Plato than the writings of the Fathers. Boethius's *Consolation of Philosophy* was only one text that communicated to the Middle Ages Platonic doctrines of participation and the hierarchy of being. Odo may have owed his understanding of universals to this text. His philosophical realism distinguished him from more innovative masters in the eleventh and early twelfth centuries—such as Roscelin of Compiègne and Raimbert of Lille—who began treating universals as a mere *flatum vocis*.[37] Yet Odo did not shrink from defending his view.

Odo's commitment to a realist doctrine of universals is visible in his principal work, *De peccato originali*.[38] It was written sometime between 1095 and 1110.[39] Even the earlier date, however, establishes that this work was written after Odo had abandoned the cathedral school at Tournai for the monastery in Tournai that had been rededicated to St. Martin. Odo may have left the school, but he did not leave behind his interest in philosophical questions.

Odo's text may thus have been written before or after Anselm's *De conceptu virginali et originali peccato*, composed between the summer of 1099 and the summer of 1100.[40] Both authors share the view that original sin is the result of the loss of original justice that Adam enjoyed.[41] Moreover, Odo shares Anselm's understanding of adequate

---

37. For Odo's competitive relationship with Raimbert of Lille, see Herman's *Liber de restauratione* 2, p. 275. This portion of Herman's text, which discusses school debates on universals at Tournai and Lille, is reproduced in Picavet's *Roscelin*, Appendix. For a good discussion of the twelfth-century debates on universals, see John Marenbon, *Early Medieval Philosophy (480–1150): An Introduction* (London: Routledge and Kegan Paul, 1983), pp. 131–139.

38. See Maurice de Wulf, *History of Medieval Philosophy*, translated by Ernest C. Messenger (London: Longmans, Green, and Co., 1926), 1:108.

39. Julius Gross suggests the latest date for Odo's work, although without providing any evidence to support his claim. See his *Geschichte des Erbsündendogmas 3: Entwicklungsgeschichte des Erbsündendogmas im Zeitalter der Scholastik (12.–15. Jahrhundert)* (Basel and Munich: Ernst Reinhart Verlag, 1971), p. 28.

40. For the dating of Anselm's work, see *Anselm of Canterbury*, edited and translated by Jasper Hopkins (New York: Edwin Mellen Press, 1974–1976), 3:259, n.1. Most historians assume that Odo was dependent, in some sense, upon Anselm's work. But they fail to demonstrate any real relationship between the two. See Odon Lottin, *Psychologie et morale aux XIIe et XIIIe siècles* (Louvain: Abbaye du Mont César, 1954), 4:167–168.

41. For Anselm's discussion of original justice and original sin, see especially *De conceptu virginali et originali peccato* 1–2. For a good discussion, see A. Michel, "Justice

satisfaction, found in Anselm's *Cur Deus Homo*, which identifies the satisfaction of the God-man as necessary to remove the stain of original sin.[42] It is not so clear, however, that Odo and Anselm agree on the most probable philosophical solution to the problem of the transmission of original sin, especially if we accept Gilbert Crispin's apparent traducianism as Anselm's own. Odo displays a preference for the creationist solution, although not without recognizing the advantages offered by traducianism.[43]

What distinguishes Odo's work on original sin is the effort to set out and consider according to philosophical principles the two most probable options—traducianism and creationism—in order to discover the truth about them. He defends his philosophizing as a pedagogical device, confessing that he does not philosophize in order to demonstrate the truth of faith but only in order to teach that truth more effectively. The philosophical discipline assists the teacher of truth, he claims, inasmuch as many clerks in his church are trained in the liberal arts and will be convinced more quickly and easily through them.[44] At the same time, however, he recognizes a broader mandate for philosophy. Truth, he claims, is something so weighty and difficult that even the learned man has trouble discovering it. But the learned man is one who seeks the reasons (*rationes*) for things, so that the

---

originelle," *Dictionnaire de théologie catholique* 8:2020–2042. Grabman describes Odo as a member of Anselm's school of thought, at least in his teaching on original sin. See Martin Grabmann, *Die Geschichte der scholastischen Methode* (Berlin: Akademie-Verlag, 1956), 2:156. Fairweather repeats this claim in his *Scholastic Miscellany*, p. 58. For Odo's definition of original justice, see *De peccato originali* (PL 160: 1075–1076).

42. For Odo's treatment of the Incarnation and Atonement, see his *Disputatio contra Judaeum Leonem nomine de adventu Christi filii Dei* (PL 160:1101–1112).

43. See E. Amann, "Odo de Cambrai," *Dictionnaire de théologie catholique* 11:933–934. For extensive discussion of Odo's *De peccato originali*, see F. Labis, "Le bienheureux Odon, évêque de Cambrai," *Revue catholique* 8 (1856): 453–460, 519–585; and Blaise Hauréau, *Histoire de la philosophie scolastique* (Paris: Durand et Pedone-Lauriel, 1872), 1:296–309.

44. *De peccato originali* 3 (PL 160:1102C): "Philosophicas considerationes quod posuimus, ne precor, arguant fratres quasi catholicam fidem munire voluerim per philosophicam rationem. Non feci ut munirem, sed ut docerem. . . . Ideoque philosophica quaedam adhibuimus, quia novimus de clero Catholicos, liberalibus eruditos artibus, videre clausa citius per ea quae noverant."

hiddenness of truth will be disclosed and mysteries revealed.[45] With Anselm, then, Odo seems to move from faith to understanding by seeking the necessary reasons for things.[46]

ODO OF TOURNAI'S *DE PECCATO ORIGINALI*

An edition of Odo's text is found in Migne's *Patrologia Latina* (PL 160:1071–1102). This edition is based on the older *Maxima Bibliotheca Veterum Patrum*.[47] Although no critical edition of the text is available, I have compared these printed editions with one another and with a twelfth-century manuscript, Douai Bibl. mun. 201 (fol. 92–112), and find them reliable and reasonably free of corruption.

Odo's treatise is divided into three books. In the first book, he attacks the Manichaean conceptions of evil as a real nature or essence and of sin as a positive defect. Evil, he explains, is only a privation of good, while sin is the privation or absence of justice in the will of the rational soul.

The soul is created good by God. Injustice enters when the soul fails to preserve and guard the gift of original justice that God conferred upon the first human being as a natural or preternatural gift. Although we give names to various evils—injustice, impiety, darkness, blindness—these names do not signify real existents. If these privations can be ordered by the mind under genus and species, they cannot be subsumed under the most general genus, being itself. Properly speaking these evils have no essence, no species or genus. Their order and the names they bear are borrowed from real existents—injustice from justice, impiety from piety, and so on. The mind, Odo explains, can only contemplate nonexistents by borrowing forms (*formas*) from existing things. So too language can only refer to nonexistents by borrowing the names of things that really exist, "for speech follows

---

45. *De peccato originali* 3 (PL 160:1102C): "Sed veritas ponderosa est et gravis . . . quam vix eruditus invenit. Ideo sunt undequaque rationes quaerendae, ut aperiatur occulta non ut muniatur fortissima; ut detegatur clausa mysteriis, non ut roboretur immutabilis."

46. Labis describes Odo's logical exposition as "un des plus beaux spécimens de considérationes rationelles sur les dogmes catholiques que présente la théologie scolastique" (see his "Le bienheureaux Odon," p. 519).

47. *Maxima Bibliotheca Veterum Patrum*, edited by Maguerin de la Bigne, 27 vols. (Cologne, 1577), 21:227–241.

thought, so that language has not established words other than as thought orders images."[48]

Similarly, the art of the painter can only represent nonexistent or fantastic things by employing the forms of things that are. But the forms of evil then are not derived in the customary way—i.e., by a process whereby mind 'selects' and forms figures (*figurae*) of real things. Rather, they are assumed or borrowed according to their likeness to real essences. Consequently, one cannot say that evil or injustice is 'in' a subject in the same way that knowledge-of-grammar, for example, is 'in' Socrates. When we say injustice is 'in' Adam, we mean rather that the positive essence, justice, is no longer 'in' Adam.

Justice is a species under the genus, the Good. While all things are good, as Boethius taught, so far as they exist, not all are just.[49] The essence of justice is not 'in' all things, not even all good things. Moreover, justice is properly predicated only of rational agents. Thus, when one says that the human being is unjust, one expresses a privation rather than a simple negation, because justice is lacking where it ought to be. Sin is not the presence of a positive defect in human nature so much as it is the absence of the positive gift of original justice, which Adam ought to have preserved along with his nature.

Once Odo has explained that the 'nature' of sin is injustice, he moves in book 2 to consider how that shadow nature is transmitted from Adam to subsequent generations. Essential to his discussion is Paul's claim that 'in' Adam all human beings have sinned. One concern, then, is to explain in what sense all human beings are 'in' Adam and how Adam's sin can be communicated to others.

Odo acknowledges that in a genetic sense all human beings are 'in' Adam, who is a material cause.[50] Just as my body is contained in the seed of my father, his body is contained in the seed of his father, and so on, even to the first parent of the human race. All can thus be said to descend from Adam according to the flesh. This theory helps to

---

48. *De peccato originali* 1 (PL 160:1076D): "Nam sermo sequitur cogitationem, ut non aliter digerat lingua sermones quam cogitatio dictat imagines."

49. See Boethius's *Quomodo substantiae in eo quod sint bonae sint cum non sint substantialia bona*, edited by E. K. Rand in *Boethius: The Theological Tractates* (Cambridge, Mass.: Harvard University Press, 1918); reprint ed. (1962), pp. 38–50.

50. Anselm argues as well that all of us exist in Adam materially through Adam's seed, according to our nature although not according to our person. See his *De conceptu virginali* 23.

explain how certain family resemblances or physical characteristics pass from one generation to the next.[51] It would be simple enough to aver that Adam's sin passes from parent to child with the material seed during the process of procreation. But Odo rejects this claim, just as Augustine had, inasmuch as Adam's sin is located in the soul—more specifically, in the will—and not in the flesh. Merely the instrument of a sinful soul, the body is of itself capable of neither good nor evil.

Still, procreation provided a powerful model from ordinary experience in order to explain both the sense in which all are 'in' Adam and the way in which sin is transmitted from Adam to later generations. The spiritual traducianists argued by analogy that just as my body is 'in' Adam and descends from his, so too my soul is 'in' Adam and descends from his along with the seed of the flesh. There are a number of advantages to this view. Just as certain physical resemblances in later generations could be explained according to the genetic model, whereby the body of the child is produced by the separation of the seed from the body of the parent, so too certain moral or psychological dispositions could be explained by the hypothesis that the soul of each child is contained virtually or in some other way in the soul of the parent and, ultimately, in that of the first parent. Adam's sin deprived his soul of original justice. His descendants receive their souls from his concomitant with the seed that flows from him. Their souls thus display the same lack or privation that Adam contracted, as well as the same inclination toward sin, which is concupiscence.

Despite the advantage traducianism offered, Odo identifies creationism not merely as equally likely (which Augustine was often inclined to do) but as the orthodox view,[52] although he does not cite a single orthodox defender of this position. He remarks, "the orthodox say that the human soul in no wise descends from a soul, but that new ones are made daily by God for new bodies."[53] His willingness to identify creationism as the orthodox view makes it certain that Odo will not oppose this position, unless one wishes to attribute to Odo an uncharacteristic and dangerous irony.[54]

51. *De peccato originali* 3 (PL 160:1098–1099).
52. *De peccato originali* 2 (PL 160:1077B).
53. *De peccato originali* 2 (PL 160:1078B): "Dicunt ergo orthodoxi humanam animam ab animo nullo modo descendere, sed in recentibus novas a Deo corporibus fieri quotidie."
54. The claim that Odo clearly perceives the theological difficulties inherent in

Although Odo will defend creationism, he recognizes all too well that certain difficulties arise with the orthodox view. The most powerful objection arises from reason: "If I have only the body from Adam, and the soul truly is not from Adam but from God alone, and since sin is only in the soul and not in the body, then how can I say that I have sinned in Adam?"[55] Creationism, then, might lead to either one of two unacceptable conclusions: (1) We do not sin 'in' Adam, and therefore do not suffer the guilt of original sin. (2) Since God creates new souls *ex nihilo* that are defective, lacking the justice they ought to have, God is the author of their sin or evil.

Odo perceived that the first conclusion led to Pelagianism, the second to Manichaeanism. It is all the more surprising that he vigorously defends creationism. Although creationism does allow Odo to defend the notion that God is the proximate efficient cause of every soul in a way that God is not for every body, this is not the focus of his work. Rather, the effort to understand the orthodox view provides the occasion for a detailed exposition of Odo's metaphysics. This exposition will conclude that God does, in one sense, create defective or deprived souls *ex nihilo*, but it insists that Adam is responsible for the defect. It also concludes, however, that the embodied soul that God creates is modeled after that unchanging human nature or species that is 'in' Adam. The soul, then, is created anew, but also from a 'root' or antecedently existing species, even if it is not transmitted directly from this root species but through some third thing (such as semen).[56]

---

traducianism and defends creationism is widely accepted. See, for example, A. Auger, *Etude sur les mystiques des pays-bas au moyen âge*, in *Mémoires couronnés et autre mémoires publiés par L'académie royale des sciences, des lettres et des beaux-arts Belgique* 40 (1892): 70; Gross, *Entwicklungsgeschichte des Erbsündendogmas*, p. 31; Tullio Gregory, *Platonismo medievale* (Rome: Istituto storico Italiano per il Medio Evo, 1958), pp. 47–50; Amann, "Odo du Cambrai," p. 934; and Michel, "Traducianisme," p. 1355. While Odo perceived that traducianism had certain advantages, it seems that Frederick Copleston was mistaken when he insisted that "what Odo of Tournai maintained was a form of traducianism" (see his *A History of Philosophy 2: Mediaeval Philosophy from Augustine to Scotus* [New York: The Newman Press, 1971], p. 141). Copleston merely repeated here the opinion he first expressed in *Medieval Philosophy* (New York: Philosophical Library, 1952), p. 36.

55. *De peccato originali* 2 (PL 160:1078C): "Nam si solum corpus ab Adam habeo, animam vero non ab Adam, sed a solo Deo, cum peccatum in anima tantum sit, et non in corpore, quomodo dicor in Adam pecasse?"

56. *De peccato originali* 2 (PL 160:1085C–1087A).

It is not new in an absolute sense. Thus, both alternatives—creationism and traducianism—appear in Odo's discussion. It reflects traducianism because God creates our souls after an existing nature; it reflects creationism because these later souls are not created from Adam's individual soul.

If this solution is to have any merit, Odo must first explain how Adam's individual sin could possibly affect the species-nature that we all share. Only then can he absolve God of all guilt for having created souls *ex nihilo* that yet carry the defect of the privation of original justice. A large portion of his text, then, is given over to a discussion of the manner in which Adam's sin could affect the human nature itself.

It is the orthodox view, Odo contends, that the whole and entire human species was 'in' Adam at creation. Though an individual man distinguished by the addition of various accidents, Adam nevertheless constituted the entire human species. The species had only a single member.

Although it is the proper nature of the species that it is common to many, *per accidens* it may have but a single member. Odo provides other examples of species having only one member: the phoenix, the world. There is a phoenix nature, but only one phoenix. What can be said of the individual phoenix can also be said of the phoenix nature or species. Similarly, there is only one world, so that what can be said of this world can also be said of world as species-nature. Moreover, there is a phoenix nature, and a world nature, and a human nature—in the case of these single-member classes—because there is an individual; at the same time, there is an individual phoenix because there is a phoenix nature. The existing species-nature and an individual imply one another. There cannot, for Odo, be a species without any individual or particular instantiation of the species-nature. Yet even in the case of the species-nature that has a single member, species and individual are not logically identical. Each has its own peculiar properties. The species, by definition, can be predicated of many even if *per accidens* it has but one member. The individual, however, cannot.

The relationship between the individual and the species-nature in the instances mentioned above is, for Odo, rather different than it is for species having many individuals. In the cases above, apart from those logical properties that pertain to the species *per se* (e.g., that it can be predicated of many), the individual is closely identified with the universal. In other cases, the individual is merely a part of the whole nature, as a point is only a part of a line. In some cases, the individual is clearly distinct from the species, as an individual dog reveals only a 'part' of the dog nature. As a result, for a species having many members, the accidents of the individual distance it from the species-nature. In these cases, it is not true that whatever is said of a single individual can also be said of the species. Rather, only what can be said of all individual dogs—that is, what they have in common— can be predicated of the species.

While it is possible for the species to have but a single member, this is not true, Odo insists, for the genus. There can be no genus having a single species for the simple reason that the species is the genus with a substantial difference added. If there were a genus with a single species, species and genus would collapse into one another. If the genus "animal" had the single species "rational animal," then all animals would be rational. Consequently, genus and species would be both logically and ontologically indistinguishable. There is, however, a genus "animal" that subsumes the species "rational animal" and "irrational animal," and the two species differ substantially from the genus.

While the species must differ substantially from the genus, the individual does not differ substantially, but only accidentally, from its species-nature. Thus, the individual human being can be identified with the species in a way in which the single species cannot be identified with the genus.

Although philosophical considerations lead Odo to distinguish species and genus in this way, there seems also to be an underlying theological interest. For him, Adam is 'in' the species (and the species nature is 'in' Adam) in a way in which he is not 'in' the genus. Moreover, the properties of the individual are communicated to the species—as in the case of the species with only one member—in a way in which they are not communicated to the genus, which must have at least two species under it. Odo intends that Adam's loss of original justice is communicated to the species, but not to the genus. Consequently, as we shall see, it is appropriate to speak of a sin of human nature even while that sin is not attributed to the entire genus "animal."

Despite the special character of the relationship between the individual and the species in the case of the species that has *per accidens* only a single member, Odo is careful to distinguish the two. Otherwise, one might be tempted to add that whenever the individual changes, the species also changes. But one must still introduce a distinction. Species have their own properties by which they differ from individuals. For species are, in themselves, unchangeable, incomposite, and incorruptible, while individuals do change, are composite, and, ultimately, will die. The species, by its very nature, is universal and can be said of many. The individual, on the other hand, is singular and not universal,[57] and it is constituted as or in its substance by its accidents.[58] Some accidents and properties of individuals, however, can be predicated of the universal in a secondary sense, even though they are not 'in' the universal in the same way that they are 'in' individuals.[59] In particular, the species possesses those characteristics through which it differs from other universals because there is an individual that possesses them. Because there is some individual man, Peter, the human species has that property (rationality) that distinguishes it from the genus.[60]

These properties can be shared in some way through the substantial union of the individual and the species, in a manner analogous to the way in which the attributes of the soul affect the body when the soul is infused in the body or, conversely, as the passions and needs of the body affect the soul. Odo explains that the individual human being is actually a composite of many substances or forms (*multiplex substantia*). Unlike the Godhead, in whose single substance subsist three persons, the human person is a rational individual composed of several substances.[61] But 'person' is properly said only of the rational soul and not of the body alone. Although a composite of many substances, the human being is a person first and foremost through the human soul. Yet when the soul is joined to a body, the properties of the soul are communicated to the body in much the same way that the properties of the divine person are communicated to the human nature assumed

---

57. *De peccato originali* 2 (PL 160:1079B): "Individuum non nisi de uno dici potest. Species etiamsi de uno solo dicitur, universalis est; individuum vero nonnisi singulare est."
58. *De peccato originali* 2 (PL 160:1079B).
59. *De peccato originali* 2 (PL 160:1082B–C).
60. Cf. *De peccato originali* 2 (PL 160:1083B): "Id autem quo species ab universalibus differt non habet nisi in individuo, et sic habet in individuo quasi non sit aliud quam ipsum individuum, cum tamen species sit et non individuum."
61. *De peccato originali* 3 (PL 160:1088B).

in the Incarnation.⁶² In both cases there is a *communicatio idiomatum*, a sharing of properties.

In another way, as each form comes to constitute the human substance in the individual, each shares its specific nature with the whole. So, for example, one may call someone just, when properly speaking justice only belongs to his or her soul or rational nature. Similarly, one says that someone is black, when properly speaking it is only his or her body that is black. Just as seemingly incompatible attributes can be predicated of the God-man, so, too, seemingly incompatible attributes can be predicated of the human person as a result of this communication of properties. Insofar as the human person is a singular subject, it is indivisible; insofar as it is a whole and a composite, it can be divided.⁶³ Insofar as the soul is immortal, so too is the body, just as the corruptibility of the body can be communicated to the soul.⁶⁴

As with this communication of properties between body and soul or singular and composite, there is a communication of properties between individual and species or common nature. On Odo's account, this communication is never whole or entire. There will always remain certain properties that are proper to the individual or the species alone, which properties distinguish them. Otherwise the individual and the species would perfectly coincide, which is not the case even for the species having a single member. For the first human being as well, soul is joined to body to constitute a (composite) human individual. But the species or universal itself is not material, and it is by its nature incomposite.

Yet the privation of original justice can be shared by the individual person and the species-nature. In original sin, it is the soul of Adam— his human soul—that has sinned. The human species has not sinned *qua* species, however, but only in the individual, namely Adam (and Eve). What Odo will attempt to demonstrate is this: that as the species-nature (rational animal) possesses its substantial difference of rationality only because there is a rational individual, so the species-

---

62. *De peccato originali* 3 (PL 160:1087D–1088A).
63. *De peccato originali* 3 (PL 160:1088A).
64. Augustine also notes that although the soul is immortal, it is not immortal in the sense that God is immortal, for the soul is corruptible whereas God is incorruptible. Cf. *Epistle* 166.3.

nature can lose its property of original justice when there is no individual possessing this property.

PERSONAL SIN AND NATURAL SIN

When the human species was first created, Odo explains, the human soul was 'divided' in two persons, Adam and Eve, yet it remained whole and entire. The human soul *per se*, the species-nature (*specialis natura*), is distinct from the soul in Adam and the soul in Eve.[65] Yet this same human soul or substance is common to both Adam and Eve. It is a unique property of the species to be common to many. Moreover, the species or common nature existed in no other individuals than these two.

Each of the two persons fell into sin at the suggestion of the serpent. More: each fell into the same sin. Because there were no other human persons, and because they committed the same sin, in each of them the species-nature (*natura specialis*) was stained by sin. But if every individual human person has fallen into the same sin, then the whole human nature has contracted the same sin:

> Therefore in the soul of Adam and in the soul of Eve, who have sinned personally, the whole nature of the human soul is stained by sin; that substance which is common, is special for each. For beyond these two it does not yet have being. If it had been divided among others, the whole would not have been corrupted by these two alone. Because if these had sinned, perhaps some others would not have sinned, in whom the nature of the human soul would be undamaged. Now then where could a sinless human soul be which was everywhere a sinner?[66]

The actions of Adam and Eve, then, affected human nature, the *natura specialis*. Although they are two individuals, scripture often treats them as one, explains Odo, by referring to them according to

---

65. *De peccato originali* 2 (PL 160:1079D).
66. *De peccato originali* 2 (PL 160:1081D–1082A): "In peccatricibus ergo personis est infecta peccato natura specialis, quae non est alibi quam in ipsis. In anima Adae ergo in anima Evae, quae personaliter peccaverunt, infecta est peccato tota natura humanae animae; quae communis substantia est, est specialis utriusque. Extra has enim nondum est eam esse. Si enim fuisset in aliis divisa, pro ipsis solis non inficeretur tota. Quia si peccassent istae, forsitan non peccassent aliae, in quibus esset salva humanae animae natura. Nunc autem ubi poterat anima humana munda esse quae peccatrix erat ubique?"

one name, Adam. It does this in order to indicate that they are both guilty of the same sin, and that it has passed to human nature itself. Therefore, although Adam and Eve are two, they may be treated in this sense as a single individual, and what happens to the "one" happens to the whole. Their special situation is comparable to that of the phoenix, the world, or any other species having a single member. This is, for Odo, a distinctive case: "Only when a species is said of a single individual is one able to speak of the accident of the species just as much as of the individual, although principally and in the first place there are accidents only in individuals."[67]

Odo acknowledges the objections of critics, who insist that it is absurd to say that the species has sinned. "Universals always are what they are," they object, "and, however individuals may change, universals endure immutably, and although mutability may be predicated of them through individuals, still it is not in them."[68] Odo agrees that the species does not sin in itself but in its persons. Still in much the same way that the accidents of the single individual of the species are shared or communicated with the universal, and the qualities of the part can be predicated of the whole, so too the sin of all individuals together is communicated to the universal. As the property of original justice is one that belongs to the species and is communicated to the individual soul, so the loss of original justice among all human persons is communicated to the species. If original justice is no longer found in human individuals, then it cannot be said either to be shared or common to many, therefore it is no longer 'in' the universal. "Therefore," he concludes, "a person does not have sin without his species, since it has to be one and the same with it substantially, and there is in the first man a sin of nature personally, and yet not naturally. Because principally sin is in the person who has sinned, and secondarily in the species which has sinned."[69]

---

67. *De peccato originali* 2 (PL 160:1079C): "Et quando de solo species dicitur individuo, tantumdem accidens dicere et de individuo valet et de species quamvis principaliter et primo loco sint in individuis accidentia."

68. *De peccato originali* 2 (PL 160:1082B): "Sed forte dicet aliquis . . . universalia semper sunt quod sunt, et, utcumque varientur individua, consistunt immutabiliter universalia, et quamvis de ipsis vere dicatur mutabilitas individuorum, non est tamen in ipsis."

69. *De peccato originali* 2 (PL 160:1083C): "Non habet ergo persona peccatum sine sua specie, cum qua unum et idem habet esse substantiale, et est in primo homine

Because of this communication of accidents, the human soul, which is whole and entire in Adam and Eve, is guilty of sin, and other human persons, born in the natural way, cannot be created without that sin. Every person coming after Adam's personal sin, then, is naturally sinful.[70] An understanding of original sin leads Odo to assert that he has sinned as a human being, but not as Odo; as a substance, although not as a person.[71]

Again, just as something can be said of the whole on account of the part, so too some things can be predicated of the universal on account of the individual. Consequently, even though the soul is only a 'part' of the human being, Adam's sin affected not only his soul but the entire human species-nature, body and soul.[72]

This certainly constitutes a change of some sort in human nature. But for Odo it does not represent an essential change in what the human being *is* so much as a change in what the human being *has*. Humankind no longer has original justice, and therefore God cannot justly create human souls possessing original justice after the fall. It may perhaps best be described as a change of relation: the relationship between Adam (and therefore humanity as such) and God has changed insofar as Adam failed to offer God God's due. A change of "relation" does not result in a change in the substance.

While this explanation does not solve the problem of the origin of the soul—Odo will attempt to do that at some length in other chapters in his work—it does establish a separation between the individual soul of Adam and the *natura specialis*, even as it provides for the communication of change in the individual to the nature. The change remains, even after Adam is gone. Creating the individual soul according to the same "form" or "nature" in Adam, God does create "new" souls suffering from a privation of original justice, but does so under a just necessity. While new as individual persons, they are

---

personale peccatum naturae, non naturale. Quia peccatum principaliter est in persona quae peccavit quidem, secundo loco in specie quae peccavit quidem . . . "

70. *De peccato originali* 2 (PL 160:1084A). Note that Odo does not hold that Adam alone is a human person who sinned, and not Eve, when he claims that the whole soul is in Adam. He is merely following the authority of scripture: "Ut igitur secundam Scripturae loquamur auctoritatem, quae primae conditionis duas personas accipit pro una et uno nomine vocat eas, id est Adam" (*De peccato originali* 2 [PL 160:1083B]).

71. *De peccato originali* 2 (PL 160:1085B–C).

72. *De peccato originali* 3 (PL 160:1088C).

created according to the preexisting species: "Therefore, God makes a new soul which does not have a new nature. It is then new in the same nature, and not new. In the person it is new, in the species it is not new. It is new in personal property, but not new in its common property."[73] This paradoxical formulation reflects the tension throughout Odo's work between creationism and traducianism. While Odo vigorously defends creationism, the tension is never resolved. His effort to defend the orthodox theological position demands more than his philosophical skills can provide. But his detailed discussion of genus, species, individual, universal, and person in order to solve a theological difficulty reflects a renewed interest in the instruments of philosophy and identifies Odo as a significant philosophical writer of the early twelfth-century renaissance.

University of Tennessee at Chattanooga

---

73. *De peccato originali* 3 (PL 160:1091A): "Facit ergo Deus animam novam, quae naturam non habet novam. Est ergo eadem natura nova, et non nova. In persona nova est, in specie nova non est. Nova est proprietate personali, non nova proprietate communi."

Signification and Modes of Signifying in Thirteenth-Century Logic: A Preface to Aquinas on Analogy

E. J. Ashworth

In 1935 M. D. Chenu wrote, "Preoccupied as we are with such leading figures as Thomas Aquinas and Bonaventure, we all too easily lose sight of the massive dialectical learning which provided the foundation for both the teaching and the general thought-patterns of thirteenth-century masters."[1] Unfortunately, Chenu's words have not been well heeded, and one of the outstanding features of the extensive literature on Aquinas's doctrine of analogy is the complete absence of any attempt to set him in the context of contemporary logic.[2] Some attempt has been made to read him in terms of specula-

---

1. M. D. Chenu, "Grammaire et théologie aux XIIe et XIIIe siècles," *AHDLMA* 10 (1935–1936): 7: "Tout occupés que nous sommes par les grandes figures d'un Thomas d'Aquin et d'un Bonaventure, nous perdons de vue trop facilement la massive culture dialectique qui constitué la base de l'enseignement et la mentalité générale des maîtres du XIIIe siècle." Chenu's paper is still well worth reading.

2. An exception to this remark is provided by a paper which has just appeared: Alain de Libera, "Les sources gréco-arabes de la théorie médiévale de l'analogie de

tive grammar,³ but this is unhelpful so far as equivocation and analogy are concerned, since speculative grammarians did not usually take up these topics.⁴ So far as logicians are concerned, the most frequently cited figure is Cajetan, who was writing over two centuries later, and who discussed these matters from a perspective that is far removed from that of the thirteenth century, particularly with respect to general theories of signification. Yet thirteenth-century logicians did discuss equivocation and analogy, sometimes at considerable length, and it is at least worthwhile considering what they had to say.

My study of Aquinas in the context of thirteenth-century logic has two parts. In the first part, which constitutes the present essay, I shall explore the general theory of language that lies behind theories of equivocation and analogy. I shall explain such key concepts as imposition, signification, and *res significata*, and I shall pay particular attention to the notion of *modi significandi*. In the second part, to be published separately,⁵ I shall survey thirteenth-century accounts of equivocation from Peter of Spain to John Duns Scotus. I shall show how the discussion of analogy came to be subsumed under discussions of equivocation and how logicians developed a threefold classification

---

l'être," *Les études philosophiques* 3/4 (1989): 319–345. However, De Libera is more concerned with metaphysical than with logical issues.

3. See, for instance, a recent paper by Keith Buersmeyer, "Aquinas on the *Modi Significandi*," *The Modern Schoolman* 64 (1987): 73–95. The paper has an interesting discussion of the relations between *modi essendi*, *modi intelligendi*, and *modi significandi* in Aquinas, though it is marred by not using recent sources on speculative grammar, including the various text editions now available. For a very interesting use of speculative grammar to interpret Aquinas on the language of the sacraments, see Irène Rosier, "Signes et sacrements: Thomas d'Aquin et la grammaire spéculative," *Revue des sciences philosophiques et théologiques* 74 (1990): 392–436.

4. Boethius of Dacia refers the reader to his questions on the *Sophistical Refutations* for a discussion of equivocation. See his *Opera: Modi significandi sive quaestiones super Priscianum Maiorem*, edited by Jan Pinborg and Heinrich Roos, CPDMA 4.2 (Copenhagen: Gad, 1969), p. 128. John of Dacia does include a discussion of equivocation in his *Summa grammatica*, as in his *Opera*, edited by Alfred Otto, CPDMA 1.1 (Copenhagen: Gad, 1955), pp. 364–386. He seems, however, to have borrowed from an earlier commentary on the *Sophistical Refutations*: see the anonymous *Quaestiones super Sophisticos Elenchos*, edited by Sten Ebbesen, CPDMA 7 (Copenhagen: Gad, 1977), p. xxxvi (I shall refer to this work as CPDMA 7).

5. See my "Analogy and Equivocation in Thirteenth-Century Logic: A New Approach to Aquinas," forthcoming in *Mediaeval Studies*.

of analogy that has a close relation to Aquinas's own classification in his *Sentences*-commentary.

In embarking on this study, I am guided by the belief that to understand Aquinas fully we need to know how his words would have been understood by his contemporaries. We need to know which phrases had a standard technical usage and what distinctions were routinely made. I do not intend to argue that we will always find just one correct interpretation, nor do I want to claim that Aquinas was never innovative in his use of material taken from logicians. I am convinced, however, that a careful reading of the logicians will not only show us which interpretations of Aquinas's philosophy of language can be ruled out as fanciful reconstructions, but will also shed light on much that is currently obscure to the twentieth-century reader.

TERMINOLOGY AND TEXTS

So far as terminology is concerned, I shall stick to the term 'equivocation', in the nonpejorative medieval sense, since it covers both the case of homonymy ("two or more words having the same pronunciation and/or spelling") and polysemy ("one word having two or more senses").[6]

Moreover, to speak of 'equivocation' avoids the problem that proper names provided a standard example of pure equivocation, whereas one might not want to say that a proper name is polysemous. It is also important to make a preliminary observation about the word 'analogy'. In Aristotle's Greek, *analogia* was used to refer to a similarity of two proportions involving at least four terms. What came to be called *analogia* in thirteenth-century Latin covered what Aristotle called *pros hen* equivocation. The word in its new use apparently first appeared in translations of Averroes's commentaries on Aristotle, and by about 1250 it had been absorbed into the logic textbooks, within discussions of equivocation.[7] People were aware that the Greek *analogia* was the same as the Latin *proportio*, but little was made of this by logicians until the sixteenth century.

---

6. For these definitions, see Geoffrey Leech, *Semantics* (Harmondsworth: Penguin Books, 1974), p. 228. Homographs with a different pronunciation were not regarded as equivocal.

7. For details, see the paper cited in note 5.

The texts of which I shall make most use fall into two groups. First, there are logical *summulae* from the first half of the thirteenth century, especially those by Peter of Spain and William of Sherwood from the 1230s and by Lambert of Auxerre and Roger Bacon from around 1250.[8] Second, there is a series of commentaries on Aristotle's *Categories* and *Sophistical Refutations*. Those by Albert the Great are from before 1270,[9] but the rest were all written by logicians working at the University of Paris between 1270 and 1300.[10] Probably the earliest of these is Martin of Dacia's commentary on the *Categories*.[11] Next comes Giles of Rome on the *Sophistical Refutations*, together with the commentary on the *Categories* which has been ascribed to him.[12] From about 1275 we have an anonymous commentator on the *Sophistical*

8. Peter of Spain, *Tractatus Called Afterwards "Summule Logicales,"* edited by L. M. de Rijk (Assen: Van Gorcum, 1972). For William of Sherwood, see Charles H. Lohr with Peter Kunze and Bernhard Mussler, "William of Sherwood, *Introductiones in Logicam*: Critical Text," *Traditio* 39 (1983): 219–299. For an English translation of William of Sherwood, see Norman Kretzmann, *William of Sherwood's Introduction to Logic* (Minneapolis: University of Minnesota Press, 1966). For Lambert of Auxerre, *Logica (Summa Lamberti)*, edited by Franco Alessio (Florence: La Nuova Italia Editrice, 1971). For Roger Bacon, Alain de Libera, "Les *Summulae dialectices* de Roger Bacon," *AHDLMA* 53 (1986): 139–289; 54 (1987): 171–278.

9. Albert the Great, *Liber de Praedicamentis*, in *Opera omnia*, edited by Auguste Borgnet (Paris: Vivès, 1890), vol. 1; and *Liber I Elenchorum: Tractatus II*, in *Opera omnia*, vol. 2.

10. For full details of dating, see the introduction to CPDMA 7, passim, and the introduction to Simon of Faversham, *Quaestiones super libros Elenchorum*, edited by Sten Ebbesen, Thomas Izbicki, John Longeway, Francesco del Punta, Eileen Serene, and Eleonore Stump (Toronto: PIMS, 1984), *passim*. It will be noted that I am using only printed texts, nearly all of which are available in good modern editions. For references to manuscripts, see Charles H. Lohr, "Medieval Latin Aristotle Commentaries," *Traditio* 23 (1967): 313–413; 24 (1968): 149–245; 26 (1970): 135–216; 27 (1971): 251–351; 28 (1972): 281–396; 29 (1973): 93–197. For a list of *Categories* commentaries from this period, see Robert Andrews, *Peter of Auvergne's Commentary on Aristotle's "Categories": Edition, Translation, and Analysis*, 2 vols. (Dissertation, Cornell University, 1988), 1:6–7. For references to manuscripts of commentaries on the *Sophistical Refutations*, see the numerous works by Ebbesen listed in the bibliography of Sten Ebbesen, "The Way Fallacies Were Treated in Scholastic Logic," *CIMAGL* 55 (1987): 107–134.

11. Martin of Dacia, *Quaestiones super librum Praedicamentorum*, in *Opera*, edited by Heinrich Roos, CPDMA 2 (Copenhagen: Gad, 1961), pp. 153–263.

12. Since the ascription is not certain, the dating of this text cannot be certain either. I base my remarks about the uncertainty of ascription on Andrews, *Peter of Auvergne's Commentary on Aristotle's "Categories,"* 1:53, n. 36. For the two texts, I have used Renaissance editions: Giles of Rome, *Expositio supra libros Elenchorum*

Refutations, with a new series of questions dated about 1280.[13] There are two commentaries on the *Categories*, one by Peter of Auvergne[14] and one by an anonymous author, Anonymus Matritensis.[15] From about 1280 we have John of Dacia, who included some material probably drawn from earlier questions on the *Sophistical Refutations* in his *Summa Grammatica*.[16] Simon of Faversham wrote on both the *Categories* and the *Sophistical Refutations* around 1280.[17] Around 1295 we have the commentaries on the *Categories* and the *Sophistical Refutations* by the young Duns Scotus.[18] Finally I shall make some references to the commentaries on the same works by Radulphus Brito, dating from around 1300.[19]

SIGNIFICATION AND IMPOSITION

In this section I shall attempt to lay out the basic semantic theory found in the texts I have mentioned above and in Aquinas himself. The central semantic notion was *significare*, with its correlates *significatio*, *significatum*, and *res significata*.[20] The first thing to notice is that *significare* should not be translated as 'to mean' and *significatio* should not be translated as 'meaning'. As Paul Spade has emphasized,

---

(Venice, 1500); Giles of Rome, *Expositio in Artem Veterem* (Venice, 1507), reprint ed. (Frankfurt: Minerva, 1968).

13. See CPDMA 7.

14. Robert Andrews, "Petrus de Alvernia, *Quaestiones super Praedicamentis*: An Edition," *CIMAGL* 55 (1987): 3–84.

15. Robert Andrews, "Anonymus Matritensis, *Quaestiones super librum Praedicamentorum*: An Edition," *CIMAGL* 56 (1988): 117–192.

16. See note 4, above.

17. For the *Categories* commentary, see *Quaestiones super libro Praedicamentorum*, in *Magistri Simonis Anglici sive de Faverisham Opera Omnia* 1: *Opera Logica*, edited by Pasquale Mazzarella (Padua: CEDAM, 1957). For the questions on the *Sophistical Refutations*, see note 10, above.

18. John Duns Scotus, *In librum Praedicamentorum quaestiones*, in *Opera omnia* 1 (Paris: Vivès, 1891); *In libros Elenchorum quaestiones*, in *Opera omnia* 2 (Paris: Vivès, 1891).

19. Radulphus Brito, *Questiones super Arte Veteri* (no place, no date) (copy in the Bibliothèque Mazarine, Paris). For a list of published extracts from his commentary on the *Sophistical Refutations*, see Ebbesen, "The Way Fallacies Were Treated in Scholastic Logic," p. 130.

20. We also meet the phrase *ratio significandi*, which is roughly a word's capacity for signifying. See, e.g., CPDMA 7, p. 122; Martin of Dacia, *In Praed.*, p. 163; John of Dacia, p. 374. Aquinas uses the notion in his *Sentences*-commentary: see, e.g., *Scriptum super Sent.* 1.18.1.2 ad 4, 1.22.1.3 ad 2.

"signification is a psychologico-causal property of terms."[21] In the texts we shall be considering the most usual definition is that "to signify is to establish an understanding" ("significare est intellectum constituere").[22] Yet signification is also closely associated with being a sign, that is, with representing or making known something beyond itself.[23] In this context, another crucial text is from earlier in *On Interpretation*: "Spoken words are signs of concepts" (or, "Sunt ergo ea quae sunt in voce earum quae sunt in anima passionum notae," as the normal medieval translation has it.)[24] It was this phrase that led to the great debate about whether words signified concepts or things.[25] In order to understand this debate it is necessary to realize that everyone agreed on two things. First, spoken words will have signification only

21. Paul Vincent Spade, "The Semantics of Terms," in *The Cambridge History of Later Medieval Philosophy*, edited by Norman Kretzmann, Anthony Kenny, and Jan Pinborg (Cambridge: Cambridge University Press, 1982), p. 188.

22. Based on Aristotle *On Interpretation* 16b19–21, as in AL 2/1–2: *De Interpretatione vel Periermenias*, edited by Lorenzo Minio-Paluello and Gérard Verbeke (Leiden: E. J. Brill, 1965), p. 5. See also Jacqueline Hamesse, *Les Auctoritates Aristotelis: Un florilège médiéval: Etude historique et édition critique*, PM 17 (Louvain: Publications Universitaires, and Paris: Béatrice-Nauwelaerts, 1974), p. 305, no. 6. I intend to locate quotations from Aristotle in *Les Auctoritates Aristotelis* wherever possible, since this florilegium (which dates from between 22 November 1267 and the year 1325) is an extremely useful guide to the commonplace tags picked up and used by almost all logical writers. This particular tag is found, e.g., in CPDMA 7, p. 279; Simon of Faversham, *Quaestiones super libro Perihermeneias*, ed. Mazzarella, p. 154; Duns Scotus, *In Praed.*, p. 456A.

23. See, e.g., *Dialectica Monacensis*, edited in L. M. de Rijk, *Logica Modernorum* (Assen: Van Gorcum, 1962–1967) 2/2:463; Lambert of Auxerre, pp. 205–206. This passage has been translated in Norman Kretzmann and Eleonore Stump, *The Cambridge Translations of Medieval Philosophical Texts* 1: *Logic and the Philosophy of Language* (Cambridge: Cambridge University Press, 1988), pp. 104–105. This is the sense of the phrase that became most prominent in later medieval logic. See E. J. Ashworth, "Jacobus Naveros (fl. ca. 1533) on the Question: 'Do Spoken Words Signify Concepts or Things?'" in *Logos and Pragma: Essays on the Philosophy of Language in Honour of Professor Gabriel Nuchelmans*, edited by L. M. de Rijk and H. A. G. Braakhuis, Artistarium Supplementa 3 (Nijmegen: Ingenium Publishers, 1987), p. 190.

24. Aristotle *On Interpretation* 16a3–4, in AL 2/1–2:5; *Les Auctoritates Aristotelis*, p. 304, no. 1. See Aquinas, *Summa theol.* 1.13.1: "secundum Philosophum, voces sunt signa intellectuum, et intellectus sunt rerum similitudines"; Giles of Rome, *In SE*, f. 10vb: "voces sunt signa eorum conceptuum qui sunt in anima."

25. For some references and discussion, see E. J. Ashworth, "Jacobus Naveros," pp. 189–214.

if they are related to a mental word or concept, whether this relationship is described as one of signification or, as Ockham preferred, subordination. Second, spoken words, with the obvious exception of syncategorematic terms such as 'not' and of words picking out fictional or mental entities such as 'chimera' and 'concept', typically refer to things in the external world. The main question was how these relationships were to be interpreted and ordered. Was one primary? If so, which? For Aquinas, the signification of concepts was immediate and the signification of external objects mediate.[26] There is no time to pursue this debate here, but it is worth noting that it had an effect on the discussion of equivocation. In Duns Scotus, for instance, we find the question raised whether the dual signification of things and concepts counted as equivocation.[27]

An important corollary of the three-termed relationship between words, concepts, and things is that while concepts were said to have natural signification, in the sense of being the same at least for all with the same experiences, spoken words were said to have purely conventional signification, which they received through an act of imposition. The notion of imposition will be important for subsequent discussion because it was supposed to be a complete endowment of a word not only with a primary signification but also—for many thirteenth-century logicians—with a complete set of secondary significations, consignifications, and grammatical *modi significandi*. The effect of such a doctrine was to downplay the importance of use and of context and to make the approach to sentence meaning remarkably inflexible.[28] It also meant that analogy and equivocation were discussed as if they

---

26. Aquinas, *Sent. Peri hermeneias*, 1.2, in *Opera Omnia* (Rome: Commissio Leonina, and Paris, J. Vrin, 1989), T.I•/1, p. 11: "ideo necesse fuit Aristotili dicere quod uoces significant intellectus conceptiones inmediate, et eis mediantibus res." Compare Simon of Faversham, *In Periherm.* 5: " . . . queritur utrum voces significent res extra animam existentes vel passiones rerum," pp. 154–155; CPDMA 7, 811: "Consequenter quaeritur utrum possibile sit vocem rem veram significare," pp. 278–280.

27. John Duns Scotus, *In duos libros Perihermenias quaestiones*, in *Opera Omnia* 1:541B–542A. (This is the first of his two commentaries on *On Interpretation*.) He denied the point, because only one act of signifying was involved. But see Ashworth, "Jacobus Naveros," p. 199, for more discussion.

28. See Sten Ebbesen, "The Dead Man Is Alive," *Synthese* 40 (1979): 47, 51–52. This inflexibility was perhaps one of the reasons that the fourteenth century reverted to a focus on supposition theory, which was very much concerned with context.

were properties of single terms, with correspondingly adverse effects on the development of a fully satisfactory philosophy of language.[29]

Imposition crops up in two places in the texts I am considering. One has to do with denominative terms.[30] Why do logicians say that concrete accidental terms (such as 'just') come from abstract terms, whereas grammarians say the reverse? Lambert of Auxerre and Roger Bacon both suggested that grammarians were more concerned with what was seen and felt, whereas logicians were a more subtle group and gave priority to the truly simple (i.e., abstract properties) over what was composite.[31] In order to argue that the mode of understanding whereby something is placed in a category is prior (so that the logicians were in the right), Martin of Dacia appealed to the common view that abstract terms such as *albedo* could be placed in a category whereas *album* could not.[32] This is hardly an empirical approach to the question of how words achieve signification, and the reliance on metaphysical principles such as the priority of the simple is noteworthy.

The second problem of imposition related to current issues has to do with etymology. A name may be imposed or endowed with signification because of what one might be tempted to regard as some relationship between its sound and the sounds of words already associated with the thing being named. Thus Isidore of Seville's claim that a 'stone' (*lapis*) is 'what hurts the foot' ("quod laedat pedem")[33] was picked up by Peter of Spain, Lambert of Auxerre,[34] and Martin of Dacia.[35] However, Aquinas's handling of the example seems to show

---

29. See James F. Ross, *Understanding Analogy* (Cambridge: Cambridge University Press, 1981).

30. Denominative terms, or concrete accidental terms, are Aristotle's paronyms: see *Categories* 1a13–15.

31. Lambert of Auxerre, *Logica*, p. 66. Roger Bacon, *Summulae* 1, p. 191.

32. Martin of Dacia, *In Praed.*, p. 168. For the category problem (discussed in terms of genus), see the discussion and references in Robert Andrews, "Denomination in Peter of Auvergne," in *Meaning and Inference in Medieval Philosophy*, edited by Norman Kretzmann (Dordrecht, Boston, and London: Kluwer Academic Publishers, 1988), p. 94. See also Bacon *Summulae* 1, p. 185.

33. Isidore, *Etymologiarvm sive originvm libri XX*, edited by W. M. Lindsay (Oxford: Clarendon Press, 1911), vol. 2, 16.3.1.

34. Peter of Spain, *Tractatus*, p. 62; Lambert of Auxerre, *Logica*, p. 8. Lambert also used Isidore, 11.1.5: "Nam proprie homo ab humo."

35. Martin of Dacia, *Modi significandi*, in *Opera*, pp. 36–37. He said that *lapis* was

that the actual property of foot-hurting is more important than any relationship of sounds.

In his discussion of imposition, Aquinas used a traditional distinction between that in virtue of which a name was imposed ("id a quo imponitur") and that which the name was imposed to signify ("id ad quod significandum nomen imponitur").[36] In his *Sentences*-commentary, he tied this distinction to Priscian's claim that a name signifies substance with quality.[37] He explained that the definition had nothing to do with logical categories, but rather with the grammarians' *modi significandi* (see below). Quality concerns what the name is imposed from, i.e., the form which as it were produces knowledge of the thing in question. Substance concerns what the name is imposed to signify, i.e., the thing viewed as subsistent, even if it is not in fact capable of subsisting. In the case of *albedo*, that from which the name is taken and that which the name is imposed to signify are identical, but in the case of *homo* the two are distinct. Later in the *Sentences*-commentary, he used the notion of supposition and said that a name properly speaking signifies the form or quality from which it was imposed and supposits for that on which it was imposed (*cui imponitur*).[38] Similarly in the *Summa theologiae* he remarked that for a name to signify substance with quality was for it to signify a *suppositum* with a nature or determinate form in which it subsists.[39] Thus it looks as if what the name is taken from gives the *significatum*, and what a name is imposed to signify gives the *suppositum*. This account needs consider-

---

masculine because it is connected with *laedens pedem*, which is understood *per modum agentis*. *Petra* is feminine because it is connected with the passive *pede trita*.

36. *Scriptum super Sent.* 1.22.1.1 ad 3, 3.6.1.3; *Summa theol.* 1.13.8. The distinction, and the connection with Priscian, go back to the twelfth century. See Ebbesen, "Concrete Accidental Terms: Late Thirteenth-Century Debates about Problems Relating to Such Terms as *Album*," in *Meaning and Inference*, p. 142.

37. See passages cited in previous note and also *Scriptum super Sent.* 1.9.1.2. For Priscian, see *Institutionum grammaticarum libri XVIII*, in *Grammatici Latini*, edited by Heinrich Keil (Leipzig: Teubner, 1855), reprint ed. (Hildesheim and New York: Georg Olms, 1981), 2:55: "Proprium est nominis substantiam et qualitatem significare."

38. *Scriptum super Sent.* 3.6.1.3.

39. *Summa theol.* 1.13.1 ad 3.

able modification, however, in the light both of what Aquinas says about abstract and concrete nouns and of his handling of the *lapis* case and others similar to it.

In the first place, Aquinas is frequently concerned, in the *Sentences*-commentary as in later writings, to remove the element of subsistence or existence as a subject from some names. Certainly if one is thinking of a noun as opposed to a verb, it signifies a thing able to be understood as existing *per se* or as a subject;[40] but if one considers abstract nouns as opposed to concrete nouns, there is a sharp distinction. An abstract noun signifies something simple that can exist only as characterizing another thing, whereas a concrete noun signifies something composite and subsistent.[41] It is precisely because of these *modi significandi* that we have so much difficulty in naming God, who is simple and subsistent at one and the same time. If we apply abstract terms to God, the *modus significandi* of subsistence is lost and the inappropriate *modus significandi* of dependence is added. If we apply concrete terms, the *modus significandi* of simplicity is lost and the inappropriate *modus significandi* of composition is added.[42] In the *Summa theologiae* this distinction between abstract and concrete terms is further explained, not in terms of imposition, but in terms of supposition theory. A concrete term such as *homo* has *modi significandi* such that while signifying a form it supposits for a person, at least in the absence of a special context such as "homo est species." Abstract terms have a *modus significandi* such that they do not supposit for individuals. Thus *deus* and *deitas*, while referring to the same reality, function differently with respect to supposition.[43]

---

40. *Sent. Peri herm.* 1.5, p. 29.
41. This account has to be modified for adjectives, which strictly speaking signify only a form. See *Scriptum super Sent.* 3.5.3.3: "*substantiva* enim significant non tantum formam, sed etiam suppositum formae. . . . *adjectiva* autem significant tantum formam" (Mandonnet-Moos, 3:210). However, concrete accidental terms, including adjectives, do make known their subject in some way. See *Scriptum super Sent.* 1.18.1.2 ad 3: "hoc nomen 'donum' vel 'datum' . . . dat intelligere rem quamdam quae datur; quamvis forte non sicut partem significationis nominis, quia subjectum non includitur in significatione nominis significantis accidens concretive, ut dicit Commentator" (Mandonnet-Moos, 1:440).
42. *Scriptum super Sent.* 1.33.1.2; *Summa theol.* 1.13.1 ad 2.
43. *Summa theol.* 1.39.4 corpus and ad 3, 1.39.5. In fact *deus*, unlike *homo*, can supposit for an essence in the presence of an active verb such as *creat*, and, depending

In the second place, as his handling of the *lapis* example shows, Aquinas really wants to use the distinction between that from which a name is imposed and that which it is imposed to signify in order to accommodate our epistemological situation. In particular, he wants to argue that though the names of God are taken from created things, they can nevertheless signify God himself. In the *Summa theologiae* Aquinas notes once more that in some cases what a name is taken from and what it is intended to signify are the same; he once more uses *albedo* as an example, along with heat and cold. We know these directly as properties of things, and because we perceive these properties, we impose the words 'heat', 'cold', and 'whiteness' to signify them.[44] Here there is no harm done if we identify the *significatum* of a name with what it is taken from. Where substances are concerned, however, we know them, at least at first, only indirectly through their properties and effects. Thus, we first know stones through their propensity to hurt feet; but we nevertheless impose the name *lapis* to signify the true nature of stone.[45] It would be a mistake to think of foot-hurting as being essential to stones, or to suppose that the word 'stone' signified any object with the propensity to hurt feet. He suggests that we can indeed come to know the quiddity of a stone, but also that this is not essential to signification. Even though we cannot know God's quiddity, at least in this life, the pattern of imposition remains the same: we take a divine name from effects and impose it to signify the essence of the object named. In these cases, what the name is taken from is not the *significatum*, and the qualities which lead to imposition need not enter into the essence of the thing named.

Aquinas also uses the distinction in order to argue that some names are more appropriate than others in certain respects. His example, drawn from religious language, is that of two names of God: *Qui est* (He who is) and *Deus*. If one considers that from which these names are imposed, 'He who is' is the most appropriate name, since it is drawn from *esse*. If one considers that which names are imposed to signify, 'God' is the most appropriate name, since it is imposed in

---

on context, it can also supposit for just one or just two or all three persons of the Trinity. Thus *deus* differs from other members of the same word-class.

44. *Summa theol.* 1.13.8.
45. *Summa theol.* 1.13.8 corpus and ad 2, 1.13.2 ad 2, 1.59.1 ad 2. For another example, that of *vita*, see 1.18.2.

order to signify the divine nature.[46] Aquinas made considerable use of this broader distinction between what a name is imposed from and that which it is imposed to signify in his account of 'before and afterwards' in the functioning of analogous names.

SIGNIFICATUM AND RES SIGNIFICATA

The threefold relationship of word, concept, and external thing referred to in the previous section has to be kept somewhat separate from the question of the *significatum* of a word.[47] Here there are two quotations from Aristotle, both from *Metaphysics* 4, that are of particular relevance. One is a claim made in the discussion of whether an equivocal word could really have many significates: "A term which does not signify one thing signifies nothing" ("⟨terminus⟩ Qui non unum significat, nihil significat").[48] The other key text linked the *significatum* with definition: "The analysis which a term signifies is the definition" ("Ratio quam significat nomen est definitio").[49] These two tags indicated that just one object would count as a *significatum*, and that it would be an intelligible object. This was not a new idea, for in early sources we find the *significatum* identified with "the form or analysis by virtue of which ⟨a name⟩ is imposed" ("forma sive ratio a qua imponitur").[50] William of Sherwood said explicitly that signification is the presentation of some form to the intellect,[51] and in both

---

46. *Summa theol.* 1.13.11 ad 1.

47. Rosier points out that it also has to be kept distinct from the triad *modi intelligendi, modi essendi,* and *modi significandi.* See Irène Rosier, *La grammaire spéculative des Modistes* (Lille: Presses Universitaires de Lille, 1983), p. 212, n. 88. Buersmeyer, "Aquinas on the *Modi Significandi,*" p. 73, runs the triads together.

48. *Les Auctoritates Aristotelis*, p. 123, no. 100; Aristotle *Metaphysics* 4.4.1006b7. I have added the word *terminus* which appears in Martin of Dacia, *In Praed.*, p. 159. The answer to the problem was that a word had to have at least one significate, but that others were not ruled out. See Martin of Dacia, *In Praed.*, pp. 159–161; CPDMA 7, pp. 73, 80; Simon of Faversham, *In SE*, pp. 57, 59.

49. *Les Auctoritates Aristotelis*, p. 124, no. 116, with an addition by Aquinas; Aristotle *Metaphysics* 4.7.1012a24–25. The phrase is frequently cited by Aquinas: see, e.g., *Summa theol.* 1.13.1, 1.13.4, 1.13.8 ad 2.

50. Chenu, "Grammaire et théologie," p. 25. The only reference is to Albert the Great, but Chenu claims that the view is found in twelfth-century logicians.

51. William of Sherwood, p. 265: "Est igitur *significatio* praesentatio alicuius formae ad intellectum."

Aquinas and Duns Scotus we find the claim that 'man' signifies human nature.[52] The interpretation of this claim, however, depended on the attitude towards common natures.

Avicenna's notion of common natures as neither universal nor particular, neither existent nor nonexistent, had its part to play.[53] This is particularly clear in Simon of Faversham's commentary on *On Interpretation*, in which he says that words do not signify things according to the characteristic (*ratio*) whereby they exist outside the mind, or according to the characteristic whereby they exist in the mind, but rather in themselves (*absolute*). He then linked this with the second quotation from *Metaphysics* 4, saying that a definition signifies a thing in itself, apart from any accident ("diffinicio significat rem quantum ad id quod est simpliciter et absolute, circumscribendo quodlibet accidens"). As a result, words did not lose their signification when external objects perished.[54] Aquinas did not wish to give common natures any intermediate status involving quasi-existence, so for him the solution lay in the notion of the *verbum mentale* or *conceptio* which is a mental object but which is distinct from the *species intelligibilis*.[55] This inner conception is identified with the definition formed when the mind understands a simple object, or with the proposition formed when the mind compounds and divides. Thus the analysis signified by a name is the intellect's understanding of the thing signified by the name ("Ratio enim quam significat nomen, est conceptio intellectus de re significata per nomen").[56]

Whether one speaks of an Avicennian common nature or of Thomas's inner word, there is a tension here between two approaches to signification. One of them focuses on the universal nature as captured by a definition, while the other focuses on the nature in actual individuals. In the texts I am concerned with, this tension is illustrated by the relation between *significatum* and *res significata*. On some

---

52. Aquinas, *Sent. Peri herm.*, 1.2, p. 11: "significat enim hoc nomen 'homo' naturam humanam in abstractione a singularibus"; Duns Scotus, *In Praed.*, p. 16A: "homo significat naturam humanam."

53. See Sten Ebbesen, "Concrete Accidental Terms: Late Thirteenth-Century Debates about Problems Relating to Such Terms as *Album*," in *Meaning and Inference*, p. 114.

54. Simon of Faversham, *In Periherm.*, p. 155. Compare CPDMA 7, p. 279.

55. *Super Evangelium S. Ioannis Lectura* 1.1 n.25; *De veritate* 4.2; *De potentia* 8.1.

56. *Summa theol.* 1.13.4; compare 1.5.2.

views the two are identical: "The significate is the very thing signified" ("significatum est ipsa res significata").[57] Martin of Dacia is more ambiguous. He says that the external thing, the understood thing, and the signified thing are identical ("res extra, intellecta et significata sunt una et eadem res"),[58] but he also says that the significate is nothing other than the concept represented by the utterance ("significatum speciale nihil aliud est quam intellectum per vocem repraesentatum").[59]

Aquinas recognizes that there is an ambiguity. In *De veritate* he remarks that what is understood can be either the thing itself or the intellect's conception, just as what is said can be either the thing expressed by the word or the word (*verbum*).[60] If one considers the way in which he uses the term *significatum*, it looks as if the *significatum* of a name is the analysis (*ratio*) that is identified with the intellect's conception. Thus in *Summa theologiae* he speaks of the imperfect modes that are included in the *significatum* of such names as *lapis*, rendering them inapt to be used of God unless metaphorically.[61] On the other hand, *res significata* is used by him to pick out natures and properties as externally exemplified. His explanations of how it is that transcendental terms differ[62] and how it is that words used of God are not synonymous even though God's nature is absolutely simple[63] de-

---

57. CPDMA 7, p. 278, in the statement of opposing views. Compare Simon of Faversham (on the view of "some people"), *In SE*, p. 56.

58. Martin of Dacia, *Modi significandi*, p. 6.

59. Martin of Dacia, *Modi significandi*, p. 8. The *significatum speciale* is the significate of a word, as opposed to the *significatum generale*, which characterizes a class of words. See Michael A. Covington, *Syntactic Theory in the High Middle Ages* (Cambridge: Cambridge University Press, 1984), p. 26. Lambert of Auxerre said that grammarians were concerned with the latter, logicians with the former (*Logica*, p. 8).

60. *De veritate* 4.2 ad 3.

61. *Summa theol.* 1.13.3 ad 1 and ad 3. Cf. *Scriptum super Sent.* 1.22.1.2 ad 2: "possumus nomen imponere ipsi perfectioni absolute, non concernendo aliquem modum significandi in ipso significato, quod est quasi objectum intellectus." Notice that we have here a usage of *modus significandi* that suggests that it can be mixed in with the *significatum*.

62. *De veritate* 1.1. That we are not to take *ens*, *verum*, *unum*, and *bonum* as merely having the same extension in terms of actual individuals is born out by the use of *in* in such remarks as, "etsi ens, verum, unum et bonum magis uniantur in Deo quam in rebus creatis, non tamen oportet, ex quo in Deo ratione distinguuntur, quod in rebus creatis distinguantur etiam realiter" (ad 5 sc).

63. *Summa theol.* 1.13.4.

pend on a distinction between what the name signifies in the sense of *significatum* or *ratio* and what the name signifies in the sense of external object (where a nature can be regarded as externally existent in individuals). To quote a sentence already cited: "The analysis that the name signifies is the intellect's conception of the thing signified by the name" ("Ratio enim quam significat nomen, est conceptio intellectus de re significata per nomen").[64] Indeed, it is only by taking the *res significata* to be externally existent that one can make sense of Aquinas's claim that when the word 'wise' is used of God "it leaves the thing signified as incomprehended, and as exceeding the signification of the name" ("relinquit rem significatam ut incomprehensam, et excedentem nominis significationem").[65] The same passage reminds us that the thing signified is usually a perfection or nature rather than the individual having that nature,[66] though of course in the case of God no real distinction can be made between the two. Just as *significatum* and *res significata* have to be kept distinct, so *suppositum* and *res significata* have to be kept distinct. This is why the discussion of the *res significata* has to be separated from the controversy concerning whether words signify concepts or things. The latter focused on the contrast between concepts and external individuals, the things of which such predicates as 'is running' were to be verified, rather than on the distinction between concepts and externally existent natures.

CONSIGNIFICATION AND MODES OF SIGNIFYING

We must now turn to the definition of consignification and *modi significandi*. Here we are concerned with secondary signification, though 'secondary' in this context should be distinguished (a) from the kind of secondary signification that an equivocal term such

---

64. *Summa theol.* 1.13.4.
65. *Summa theol.* 1.13.5, cited in the translation by the Dominican fathers.
66. Compare *Summa theol.* 1.39.5: "Nam hoc nomen *Deus*, quia significat divinam essentiam ut in habente, ex modo suae significationis naturaliter habet quod possit supponere pro persona." However, proper names signify individuals rather than natures, as in *Summa theol.* 1.13.9: "Si vero esset aliquod nomen impositum ad significandum Deum non ex parte naturae, sed ex parte suppositi, secundum quod consideratur ut hoc aliquid, illud nomen esset omnibus modis incommunicabile: sicut forte est nomen Tetragrammaton apud Hebraeos."

as 'man' can have when it signifies a painted man secondarily, (b) from the kind of secondary signification that a denominative term such as 'white' can be said to have when it signifies the subject of whiteness secondarily, and (c) from the kind of secondary signification that a term has in signifying an external thing as opposed to a concept (when this was said to be signified primarily).[67] The terms *consignificatio* and *consignificativus* were used in three contexts, each having to do with a type of word. Purely syncategorematic terms were called consignificative because they signified only in conjunction with other terms.[68] Second, following *On Interpretation*, the verb was said to consignify time.[69] Third, and this is the sense with which I am concerned here, consignification had to do with *modi significandi*. For a term to have *consignificatio* was for it to have *consignificata* or *modi significandi*, where these two notions were used interchangeably.[70]

There is a strong temptation to associate the notion of *modi significandi* with the *Modistae*, or speculative grammarians, whose work began in the 1240s and is captured in a series of important texts written from about 1270 on.[71] The notion that words have *modi significandi* has its roots in Boethius,[72] however, and was already widely used in the twelfth century in philosophical and theological, as well as gram-

---

67. The vocabulary used was variable. The phrase *per prius et posterius* was most often used in relation to (a), but *significare ex consequenti* could be used both of (a) and of (b). See, respectively, Giles of Rome, *In SE*, f. 10rb, and Peter of Auvergne, p. 20.

68. See, e.g., *Dialectica Monacensis*, p. 605. Compare William of Sherwood, *Introductiones*, p. 224: "omnes partes indeclinabiles . . . non significant proprie, sed consignificant, id est cum alio significant." Rosier, *La grammaire spéculative*, p. 68, says that this is the primary usage of the term, i.e., to describe the opposition between noun, verb, and other parts of speech.

69. Aristotle *On Interpretation* 16b6, as in AL 2/1–2, p. 7: "Verbum autem est quod consignificat tempus."

70. See John of Dacia, pp. 370–371; Duns Scotus, *In SE*, p. 27A. Compare CPDMA 7, p. 108. For a quotation from Simon of Faversham's commentary on Peter of Spain, see L. M. de Rijk, "On the Genuine Text of Peter of Spain's *Summule logicales*, 2: Simon of Faversham (d. 1306) as a Commentator of the Tracts I–V of the *Summule*," *Vivarium* 6 (1968): 85. Simon wrote, "Nota differentiam inter *significare* et *consignificare*. Significare enim ex parte significati attenditur, consignificare ex parte modi significandi et non ex parte significati. Et ideo ut gramaticus dicit *modum significandi*, ita loycus dicit *consignificare*."

71. For excellent recent discussions of speculative grammar, see Rosier, *La grammaire spéculative*; and Covington, *Syntactic Theory*.

72. Charles Thurot, *Extraits de divers manuscrits latins pour servir à l'histoire des*

matical, writings. For our purposes it is, initially at least, the grammatical uses that are most important,[73] but we cannot overlook the relationship between grammar and ontology. As Covington writes, "In fully developed modistic theory, all modes of signifying are held to be, in one way or another, representations of the properties of real-world objects: that is, all *modi significandi* are *rationes consignificandi*. Tense 'consignifies' time; the singular and plural in grammar are representations of singularity and plurality of real objects; and the noun-verb distinction mirrors the distinction between substance and process in the real world."[74]

In order to get a better understanding of the issues involved we need to distinguish between three main groups of *modi significandi*. First, there are those, such as gender and case, which were called accidental modes.[75] The word *episcopi* will be important here, since its diversity of *modi significandi* in the sense of case is what gives rise to equivocation. In one standard example—"The bishops [*episcopi*] are priests, these asses are the bishop's [*episcopi*]; therefore these asses are priests"[76]—*episcopi* can be either genitive singular or nominative plural. In some sources, the *modi significandi* were spoken of as primarily belonging to this group.[77] Accidental modes also included time, as is shown through discussion of *laborans* as it appears in another standard paralogism: "Whoever was being cured is healthy, the sufferer [*labo-*

---

doctrines grammaticales au moyen âge (Paris, 1869), reprint ed. (Frankfurt: Minerva, 1964), cites two relevant passages from Boethius, p. 150, n. 2.

73. For a useful list of questions associated with philosophical grammar and thought to be answered by the doctrine of *modi significandi*, see Covington, p. 25.

74. Covington, p. 28. Of course, as Rosier points out (*La grammaire spéculative*, pp. 58–62), authors were aware that there was no necessary isomorphism between the *modi significandi* and the ways in which an object actually existed.

75. On accidental modes see Covington, p. 29; Rosier, *La grammaire spéculative*, pp. 96, 101–104.

76. William of Sherwood, trans. Kretzmann, p. 136. As Kretzmann points out (n. 23), only the spoken version has the intended effect in English.

77. The *Summe Metenses* said that the *modi significandi* of a word are those which order it towards construction and embrace case, gender, number, time, and person: see *Summe Metenses*, ed. De Rijk, *Logica Modernorum* 2/1:475–476. Compare Lambert of Auxerre on *consignificare*, p. 9: "Dicitur autem ⟨nomen⟩ consignificare illud quod ei accidit ultra principale significatum ut 'homo' consignificat nominativum casum et numerum singularem, et alia que sibi accidunt."

rans] was being cured; therefore the sufferer is healthy."[78] Here the consignification of time is at issue because *laborans* can signify a present sufferer or one who suffered in the past. An important distinction was often made between the two examples, however. Some accidental modes, such as time, were said to be absolute and hence unaffected by context; others, notably case, were respective or relational and could be affected by sentential context.[79]

Second, there are the so-called essential *modi significandi* such as being a noun, verb, or adjective, which were thought to have important implications for the word-thing relationship.[80] For instance, one could speak of a noun as having the mode of signifying an independent object, whereas an adjective has the mode of signifying something dependent and inherent.[81] Peter of Spain had already objected to this way of talking. He argued that *significatio* could not be described as substantive or adjectival, since *adiectivatio* and *substantivatio* were modes of the things signified and not of signification. Instead, he advocated the use of the adverbs *substantive* and *adiective*.[82]

Peter of Spain also discussed what I shall consider a third approach to *modi significandi* since it seems to be independent of word-inflection and word-class.[83] He began with the definition, "Equivocation is when different analyses of things are simply united in the same name" ("equivocatio est cum diverse rerum rationes in eodem simpliciter nomine uniuntur"). Peter held that *res* could here include the modes and relations of things, and that modes included, not just the *modus consignificandi* whereby a word signifies its own accidents (i.e., its own grammatical features), but also the *modus significandi* whereby the one

---

78. William of Sherwood, trans. Kretzmann, p. 136. The example comes from Aristotle *Sophistical Refutations* 166a1–6.

79. See Covington, pp. 29–30; Rosier, *La grammaire spéculative*, pp. 96, 102–103. Compare Peter of Spain, pp. 114–115, where he refers to case as an *accidens respectivum*, and also speaks of *accidentia absoluta*, such as time. See also CPDMA 7, pp. 322–323; Duns Scotus, *In SE*, pp. 26A–27A.

80. On essential modes, see Covington, p. 29; Rosier, *La grammaire spéculative*, pp. 94–96.

81. See, e.g., Boethius of Dacia, pp. 86–95; Anonymus Matritensis, p. 126; Simon of Faversham, *In SE*, pp. 63, 119; CPDMA 7, p. 121.

82. Peter of Spain, p. 80.

83. Peter of Spain, pp. 98–99. But compare p. 105, where he writes of the third type of equivocation that it arises "a parte consignificationis, in qua attenditur diversitas non rerum significatarum, sed modorum significandi."

health signified by 'healthy' is signified in various modes. Thus 'healthy' said of an animal signifies health as in a subject; said of urine it signifies a sign of health; said of food it signifies a cause of health; said of diet it signifies a conserver of health; and said of a potion it signifies something preparative of health. The example is of course absolutely standard,[84] but Peter's focus on things is doubly instructive. In one way it is instructive because it points us to a distinction that some later *Modistae* felt impelled to make, that between *modi significandi activi*, which are properties of the word, and *modi significandi passivi*, "which are the properties of the real-world object that the word consignifies."[85] Peter's focus on things is instructive in a second way because it helps us to get a handle on at least one claim that has been made about the proper interpretation of Aquinas's view of *modi significandi* (see below).

Aquinas tends to keep the *significatio*, *consignificatio*, and *modi significandi* of a word separate[86] and to use *consignificatio* for the signification of time. Thus verbs and participles are generally said to consignify time,[87] as do specific words such as *datum*.[88] He mentions the consignification of gender,[89] but unsurprisingly he is not normally concerned with these more purely grammatical issues. His main use of the notion of *modi significandi* falls into the second of the two groups I identified. I have already discussed his distinction between concrete and abstract names. He was also concerned with the distinction between substantive names, which signify through the mode of sub-

---

84. Normally the example is discussed in terms of *significata* and not of *modi significandi*. See, e.g., John of Dacia, 2:370. However, Boethius of Dacia provides an exception (pp. 127–128). Using the example of health, he explores the various ways in which one thing can be in another, and argues that they give rise to different *modi significandi*: "et secundum istos modos essendi in altero sunt diversi modi significandi." Equivocation arises because "plures proprietates et modi essendi designantur per unum modum significandi." Thus *sanum* looks like a simple adjective, thereby masking the diversity of modes of being involved.

85. Covington, p. 31. This distinction should not be confused with a distinction between activity and passivity as included in the *modi significandi* of different words. This sense is found in earlier *Modistae* (e.g., Boethius of Dacia, p. 5) and in Aquinas (e.g., *Scriptum super Sent.* 1.18.1.2.)

86. See *Scriptum super Sent.* 1.18.1.2; *Summa theol.* 1.13.11.

87. *Summa theol.* 1.13.1 ad 3.

88. *Scriptum super Sent.* 1.18.1.2.

89. *Summa theol.* 1.31.2 ob. 4.

stance (*per modum substantiae*), and adjectival names, which signify through the mode of accident (*per modum accidentis*), where an accident both inheres in a subject and derives its unity from it.[90] For instance, although 'God' signifies having deity ("Deus significat habentem deitatem"), the *modi significandi* of 'God' and 'having deity' are different, since 'God' signifies *substantive* and 'having deity' signifies *adiective*.[91] Note that Aquinas is using the adverbial locutions recommended earlier by Peter of Spain.

There are also places where Aquinas seems to use the notion of *modus significandi* without tying it very closely to the notion of word-class. In the *Sentences*-commentary, in his discussion of the difference between *donum* (gift) and *datum* (given),[92] he says that these words differ in *significatio*, in *consignificatio* (because *datum* as a participle consignifies time), and in *modi significandi*, because *datum* imports actual giving (*dationem in actu*) whereas *donum* imports aptitude for giving (*aptitudinem ad dandum*). It is not clear how these modes could be related to the difference between a name and a participle, even though Aquinas has taken the trouble to point out that two different word-classes are involved. In the *Summa theologiae*'s discussion of *donum*, *modi significandi* are not mentioned, though Aquinas once more interprets *donum* in terms of aptitude.[93] Also in the *Summa theologiae* he says that with one exception any name determines "some mode of the substance of a thing" ("aliquis modus substantiae rei"), the exception being the name *Qui est*, which is so universal that it does not determine any mode of being.[94] These remarks seem to be linked to *modi significandi*. Aquinas states that *Qui est* is suitable as a name for God because of its *significatio*, its *modus significandi*, and its *modus consignificandi*. Of the three points he makes in the article's corpus, the first is explicitly related to signification, and the third to consignification, which leaves the second, about universality, for *modi significandi*. Once again it is not clear whether we are dealing with word-class or

90. *Scriptum super Sent.* 1.9.1.2 corpus and ad 4; compare *Summa theol.* 1.39.3. Incidentally, in ad 2 of the latter passage, Aquinas notes that different languages have different ways of pluralizing and cites Greek and Hebrew.
91. *Summa theol.* 1.39.3 ad 1.
92. *Scriptum super Sent.* 1.18.1.2.
93. *Summa theol.* 1.38.1–2. In 1.38.1 he writes, "in nomen *doni* importatur aptitudo ad hoc quod donetur."
94. *Summa theol.* 1.13.11.

with an extended notion of *modi significandi* that is independent of word-class. The point here may simply be that any word-class less universal in its scope will have *modi significandi* that are inappropriate when used of God.

In his discussion of words that may be used both of God and creatures, Aquinas insists that a distinction has to be made between the *res significata* and the *modus significandi*.[95] He first makes a careful distinction between the *modus significandi* that is "given to be understood by the name as a consequent" ("qui datur ex consequenti intelligi per nomen")[96] and a mode of participation that may be included in the *significatum*. Some words such as 'wise' and 'good' are imposed to signify a perfection *simpliciter*, and others are imposed to signify "a perfection received according to some mode of participating." Thus 'sense' signifies "cognition through that mode by which it is received materially according to a power conjoined to an organ," and 'lion' signifies a corporeal form according to a determinate mode of participating in life. Such words can be used only metaphorically of God and hence do not pose any particular problem.[97] It is those words intended to signify an unqualified perfection that have to be considered further. Because words are imposed by us on the basis of our knowledge of creatures, any word inevitably has a creaturely mode of signifying. In *Summa contra gentiles*, Aquinas explains this by explicit reference to concrete and abstract terms: the words we apply to individuals signify them as composites with separable properties, and none of this is applicable to God.[98] In *De potentia* he says that we understand *esse* as inherent and concreated (*per modum concreationis*) so that we have to transcend the *modus significandi* when we speak of God as subsistent *esse*.[99] More often, he speaks of our having to deny the creaturely *modi significandi* when we apply words to God.[100] He links these remarks with an insistence that *modi significandi* are related to *modi essendi* not as the latter are in things but only as they are under-

---

95. *Scriptum super Sent.* 1.22.1.2; *Summa theol.* 1.13.3.
96. *Scriptum super Sent.* 1.22.1.2 ad 3.
97. *Scriptum super Sent.* 1.22.1.2 ad 4; *De veritate* 2.11; *Summa contra gentiles* 1.30; *Summa theol.* 1.13.3 ad 1 and ad 3.
98. *Summa contra gentiles* 1.30.
99. *De potentia* 7.2 ad 7.
100. *Scriptum super Sent.* 1.22.1.2 ad 1; *De potentia* 7.5 ad 2; *Summa contra gentiles* 1.30.

stood by us,[101] so that there is nothing odd about the *modi significandi* of a word being inappropriate to what is spoken of.

There are three general points to be made about *modi significandi* in relation to analogy and religious language. First, as I show in my companion paper, thirteenth-century logicians did not use the notion in their explanation of analogy as such, but only in their explanation of other types of equivocation. Second, one cannot equate all distinctions between *modi significandi* with the distinction between religious and nonreligious language. As Aquinas's discussions of *deus* in relation to *deitas, habens deitatem*, and the name *Qui est* show, *modi significandi* also enable us to make distinctions within religious language. Third, while the distinction between *res significata* and *modi significandi* is central to Aquinas's theory of religious language, it is in no way central to his theory of analogy (insofar as he has a general theory). It plays no role in his explanation of the use of such words as *sanum* and *ens*.

At this point I disagree with Ralph McInerny, who claims that "a name predicated analogically of many has the same *res significata* but different *modi significandi*."[102] He then argues that where the term 'healthy' is concerned, health is the *res significata* and 'subject of . . . ', 'cause of . . . ', and 'sign of . . . ' are different *modi significandi*. Filling in the blanks with 'health' gives us a series of *rationes* that are partly the same and partly different. McInerny bases his account on a brief passage in the *Sentences*-commentary where Aquinas says that an analogous term is divided according to different modes.[103] The modes in question are called *modi praedicandi*, and Aquinas explains that *ens* is divided among the ten categories according to ten *modi praedicandi*, each category having its own mode of predication, but that only two of these modes (substantial and relative) can be used of God. It is certainly true that Aquinas explicitly links these *modi praedicandi* with *modi significandi*, insofar as he is replying to the objection

---

101. *Summa theol.* 1.13.9 ad 2.

102. Ralph McInerny, "Can God Be Named by Us?" in *Being and Predication: Thomistic Interpretations* (Washington, D.C.: The Catholic University of America Press, 1986), pp. 274–275.

103. *Scriptum super Sent.* 1.22.1.3 ad 2. Compare 1.8.4.2 ad 1, where Aquinas says that 'substance' is predicated analogically of God and creatures because of a diverse *modus praedicandi*. He explains that the name 'substance' comes from "standing under" and that it picks out a quiddity different from an object's *esse*.

that God can have only one name (if one thinks of what is signified) or perhaps just two (if we think of the *modi significandi*), but it is not a theme he pursues elsewhere, so far as I know. Moreover, this interpretation is at odds with both Aquinas's actual discussions of the word 'healthy' and the normal interpretation of *modi significandi* in terms of such grammatical features as word-class. On the other hand, McInerny's account fits in very well with what Peter of Spain had to say about the use of the word 'healthy', so it is not alien to at least one thirteenth-century thinker.

PROBLEMS OF USE AND CONTEXT

The doctrines of a word as having, through its *significatio* and *consignificatio*, both a *significatum* and *modi significandi* and as being the subject of voluntary imposition led to a problem that is of particular importance in the context of equivocation and analogy—the relationships to use in terms of speaker intention and in terms of being a grammatical part of a sentence. There were two particular areas of concern. The first, which I shall not discuss here, involved the notion of transferred or extended sense where a word acquires what looks like a second *significatum*, as when 'foot' is said of a mountain, or an accident is called a 'being', or urine is called 'healthy'. Is there a second imposition, or is it the use that produces the new signification, or is the new signification somehow included in the old? The second area of concern had to do with restriction, or the process whereby a given significate or mode of signifying is brought into play. This problem was posed particularly sharply in the case of purely equivocal terms such as *canis*, which can signify a four-footed animal, a marine animal, or a star. If one says "The dog barks," or "The dog swims," or "The dog gives light," has one restricted 'dog' to one *significatum*? If so, how? Similarly, with words such as *amor*, which can be both noun and verb, or *episcopi*, which can have two cases, one can ask whether it is the context or something else that produces the intended *modus significandi*.

We find two quite different approaches to such problems in medieval logic. In supposition theory there is a focus on ways of verification and on context. Type of predicate, tense of verb, and syncategorematic terms all had their part to play in explaining the type and range of reference of a given word in a sentential context. The other approach tends to characterize the logicians with whom I am currently concerned. It involves the central claim that a word has not only its significates but also its *modi significandi,* before it enters a sentence. What is more, these *modi* cannot be altered by the role the word plays in a sentence. Peter of Spain was an early hard-liner in this respect. He wrote that one who imposes a word to signify such and such a thing, at the same time imposes it to signify such and such a gender and number. Peter excluded case from his remarks, however, since this is indeed given to a word so that it may be ordered in relation to other words.[104]

So far as restriction is concerned, there was general agreement that an equivocal term could actually be used and understood only in one of its senses. Albert the Great explained that a distinction must be made between intentional use and mere utterance. So far as mere utterance was concerned, an equivocal term had more than one significate (by definition), and different hearers—or one person using the term twice—could each think of a different significate. Since only one thing can be understood at a time, however, a word uttered or heard with understanding by one person at one time could signify only one thing. Peter of Auvergne, the anonymous *Auctores,* and Simon of Faversham all concurred in this view.[105] It is a pity none of them considered puns and double entendre, let alone the intention to mislead through using equivocal language, all of which seem to involve some kind of multiple understanding.

What it is that causes the hearer to focus on a single significate or *modus significandi* was the subject of much debate in the last decades of the thirteenth century. The *Auctores* and Simon of Faversham gave the same series of arguments.[106] They drew an initial distinction between mediate and immediate determination. "Canis latrabilis currit" was a case of immediate determination, since the restricting term *latrabilis* is part of the subject phrase, but both "Canis est latrabilis" and "Canis latrat" were cases of mediate determination. Mediate determination was said to have no effect in restricting reference to any particular significate. After all, both significate and *modus significandi*

---

104. Peter of Spain, *Tractatus,* p. 114. For case, see pp. 108, 114–115.
105. Albert the Great, *In SE,* p. 541A–B; Peter of Auvergne, pp. 14–15; CPDMA 7, pp. 75–76, 81–82, 286–288; Simon of Faversham, *In SE,* pp. 63–66.
106. CPDMA 7, pp. 125–129, 298–301; Simon of Faversham, *In SE,* pp. 73–75.

are essential to a term, at least once it has been imposed, and determination, which is accidental, cannot alter what is essential. If a term has three significates, those three significates cannot be removed from play through mediate determination. Nevertheless, the "usage of authors" (*usus auctorum*) shows that restriction does take place in the case of immediate determination. The problem is how to account for this. No *a priori* explanation can be given, since imposition is the result of arbitrary action. Nor is an appeal to the intention of the actual user sufficient. There must be something in the literal sense (*virtus sermonis*) of the words to explain the presence of restriction. Hence one has to say that it just is the case that purely equivocal terms are imposed to signify more than one thing when they are taken by themselves, and that they are also imposed to signify just one thing in certain sentential contexts, those involving immediate determination.

The situation with analogous terms was said to be the exact opposite. The use of authors shows that analogous terms are so imposed that taken by themselves they signify just one thing:[107] in the case of contexts involving immediate determination, they signify their secondary significate; in the case of contexts involving mediate determination, they signify one or the other significate in such a way that the senses have to be distinguished before judgments about truth-value can be made. Thus *ens* by itself will signify substance; and in the phrase 'dead man' (*homo mortuus*), *homo* will stand for its secondary significate, a corpse.[108] Aquinas seems to have agreed with these points when he remarked in *De veritate* that a term which is said of more than one thing in a prior and a posterior way can be taken for the posterior significate by reason of some adjunct. Thus the addition of 'in another' causes 'being' to stand for accident, and the addition of 'book of' to 'life' causes 'life' to stand for created life.[109] In *De veritate* he implicitly accepts that such words stand for their prior significate when taken simply, and he does so explicitly in other places.[110]

---

107. In the common phrase, they stand *pro modo famosiori*: CPDMA 7, pp. 129, 311; Duns Scotus, *In SE*, p. 23B.

108. For this treatment of *homo* as an analogical term, see Ebbesen, "The Dead Man Is Alive," pp. 43–70.

109. *De veritate* 7.5 ad 3.

110. *Sent. Peri herm.* 1.5, p. 30; *Scriptum super Sent.* 1.9.1.1 ad 2.

Duns Scotus and Radulphus Brito responded to the arguments of earlier logicians with some amazement. Scotus pointed out that if one could explain immediate restriction by appeal to the will of the imposer, then there was no reason why one could not do the same for the case of mediate restriction.[111] He also rejected the view that no further reason could be sought for restriction: one was dealing with the significates of complex phrases, and such cases were always to be explained in terms of the significates of the incomplex terms entering into the complex phrase or sentence. That being said, Scotus claimed that equivocal terms could not be restricted in their reference through immediate determination any more than they could through mediate determination. Reference can of course be restricted, but only when a true common term is involved, as in such phrases as 'some white man'. No equivocal term can be restricted by its sentential context. The context of utterance is another matter, however. The hearer knows that the speaker who uses an equivocal term must intend to refer to just one thing, and by an inferential process, working from the clues provided by the immediate determinants, the hearer can decide what that thing is. Thus the addition of 'Helias' to 'Petrus' does not make 'Petrus' have determinate signification, but it does allow the hearer to become cognizant of the intended reference. Duns Scotus did accept one of the common examples of restriction, agreeing that when *canna*, which in the feminine is a reed pipe and in the masculine the name of a river, is joined to an adjective in the masculine case, it becomes clear that the Roman river and not a reed pipe is the subject of discourse.[112] However, this is to be explained in terms of the way respective or relational *modi significandi*, such as gender, function; it has nothing to do with equivocal terms as such. It is a case of restriction *per accidens* with respect to *canna* taken as equivocal. So far as analogous terms are concerned, given Scotus's earlier arguments, they have to be treated as either purely equivocal or as univocal.[113]

---

111. Duns Scotus, *In SE*, pp. 16B–18B. Brito described the view that a term could be imposed in this way as *fuga rationum*. See his *In SE*, as in Ebbesen, "The Dead Man Is Alive," p. 60.

112. John Duns Scotus, *In SE*, pp. 16B, 18B. The example comes from Boethius, as in *Liber de divisione*, in PL 64:890. Compare CPDMA 7, pp. 126, 298; Simon of Faversham, *In SE*, p. 83.

113. Duns Scotus, *In SE*, pp. 23A–25A. For Scotus's rejection of analogous terms,

SIGNIFICATION AND MODES OF SIGNIFYING 65

Radulphus Brito also rejected the arguments found in the *Auctores* and Simon of Faversham.[114] He claimed that a properly analogical term has to be distinguished in terms of its literal sense wherever it is found, and he rejected the rule that it stands for its principal significate unless specially restricted. All it has through imposition is the ability to stand for two significates; imposition does not specify any sentential context in which restriction to one of them alone takes place. Radulphus added, however, that this fact about literal meaning (*virtus sermonis*) does not prevent someone from understanding a given significate to be intended.[115]

While the logicians I have been discussing tended not to use supposition theory to solve problems arising from the use of equivocal and analogical terms, they did consider the issue of whether diverse acceptance was itself a cause of equivocation. It seems that even apparently univocal terms can be used in different ways: "Man is a species," "Man is a noun," and "Man is running" all use 'man' in different ways. If 'man' here is a covertly equivocal term, then what happens to the theory of supposition, whereby a term has to have a settled signification before it enters a sentence and can be attributed different kinds of supposition?[116] But if 'man' here is a genuine univocal term, one with a single, settled signification, and if the mark of a univocal term is its role in contradiction, as Simplicius had said, do we not run the risk of such contradictories as "Man is a noun" and "Man is not a noun" both being acceptable?[117] A few of the authors I have considered did in-

---

see Ashworth, "Analogy and Equivocation in Thirteenth-Century Logic: A New Approach to Aquinas."

114. Brito, *In SE*, as in Ebbesen, "The Dead Man Is Alive," pp. 60–61. Brito rejects the *homo mortuus* case as not properly one of analogy.

115. Brito, as in Ebbesen, p. 61: "dico quod de bonitate intelligentis ex quadam assuefactione potest esse quod terminus analogus secundum se sumptus stat pro primario eius significato, quia primo apprehendimus per terminum analogum suum primum significatum, illud enim est quod primo ibi occurrit intellectui."

116. Rosier points out that the relationship between supposition theory and univocal terms produced a view of univocity different from that current today. In her introduction to *L'ambiguïté: Cinq études historiques* (Lille: Presses Universitaires de Lille, 1988), p. 13, she wrote that *univoca* became "le concept clé de la théorie de la supposition, recouvrant un ensemble de phénomènes référentiels, ce qui le rend fort différent de ce que nous entendons aujourd'hui sous le terme *univoque*."

117. Simplicius, *Commentaire sur les Catégories d'Aristote, traduction de Guillaume de Moerbeke*, ed. Adrien Pattin (Louvain: Publications Universitaires de Louvain, and

clude different suppositions as a kind of equivocation;[118] but the main view seemed to be that acceptance or supposition could be classed under "diverse causes of truth" and should be distinguished from the case of "diverse significates." The reason given for the distinction was that difference in acceptance did arise from sentential context, whereas neither signification nor consignification could be altered in that way.[119] Aquinas himself said plainly that diversity of supposition did not cause equivocation.[120] Duns Scotus, on the other hand, adopted a more nuanced position. True equivocation is not involved because a word neither signifies nor consignifies different acceptances; but simple univocation is not involved either, since there is no single analysis of 'man' whereby the term can be truly predicated both of a species and of Socrates.[121] The question was one that was to be more

---

Paris: Béatrice-Nauwelaerts, 1971), 1:45: "Univocum autem non suscipit contradictionem." See also Duns Scotus's mature theory, discussed by Steven P. Marrone, "The Notion of Univocity in Duns Scotus's Early Works," *Franciscan Studies* 43 (1983): 350. Marrone does not note the possible historical antecedents of what he describes as Duns Scotus's "famous and more flexible definition" of univocity in terms of contradiction. So far as the example is concerned, Boethius (using the example *homo ambulat/homo non ambulat*) counted this type of case as preventing the formation of a true contradiction. See his *In librum de Interpretatione editio secunda*, in *Commentarii in librum Aristotelis "Peri Hermeneias,"* edited by Charles Meiser (Leipzig: Teubner, 1880), reprint ed. (New York and London: Garland, 1987), 2:133. See Rosier, "Evolution des notions d'*equivocatio* et *univocatio* au XIIe siècle," in *L'ambiguïté*, p. 118, especially n. 23; and Sten Ebbesen, *Commentators and Commentaries on Aristotle's Sophistici Elenchi: A Study of Post-Aristotelian Ancient and Medieval Writings on Fallacies* (Leiden: E. J. Brill, 1981), 1:197–199. For more about fallacies of univocation in general, see De Rijk, *Logica Modernorum*, vol. 1, *passim*.

118. *Dialectica Monacensis*, p. 561, included material supposition; Bacon, *Summulae* 3:241–242, referred to supposition in general and gave simple as against personal supposition as an example. Rosier, "Evolution des notions d'*equivocatio* et *univocatio* au XIIe siècle," notes that in the first commentaries on the *Sophistical Refutations* there was hesitation about where to class paralogisms involving a shift from one kind of acceptance to another, and that they were eventually moved from equivocation to figure of speech or accident (see pp. 155–156 and *passim*).

119. CPDMA 7, pp. 106–107; John of Dacia, p. 371. See also Sten Ebbesen, "Can Equivocation Be Eliminated?" *Studia Mediewistyczne* 18 (1977): 107; and Alain de Libera, "The Oxford and Paris Traditions in Logic," in *The Cambridge History of Later Medieval Philosophy*, p. 184.

120. "Diversitas suppositionis non facit aequivocationem; sed diversitas significationis." *Scriptum super Sent.* 3.6.1.3 ad 1.

121. Duns Scotus, *In Praed.*, p. 452A–B.

important in the fourteenth century, especially in the theories of Ockham and Buridan.[122]

CONCLUSION

What I have examined in this paper is a theory of language that tends to take words as units, endowed both with their signification and their *modi significandi* before they enter sentences and independently of speaker intention on any given occasion.[123] This attitude was reinforced by Priscian's claim that the noun has priority over other parts of speech, which led logicians to argue that the noun received its imposition first.[124] One might think that equivocal and analogical terms are precisely those whose functioning is best explained through context and use, but although Roger Bacon at least did recognize that any term could be used equivocally,[125] there was a tendency to speak as if equivocal and analogical terms formed special classes that could be identified in advance of use. To the extent that Aquinas's doctrine of analogy is embedded in such a general theory, one may fear that it will share the theory's defects.[126]

University of Waterloo

---

122. See E. J. Ashworth, "Equivocation and Analogy in Fourteenth-Century Logic: Ockham, Burley, and Buridan," in *Historia Philosophiae Medii Aevi: Studien zur Geschichte der Philosophie des Mittelalters*, ed. Burkhard Mojsisch and Olaf Pluta (Amsterdam: John Benjamin, 1991).

123. For some references to authors who paid more attention to speaker intention, see Rosier, "Signes et sacraments."

124. Priscian, 2:115–121. Priscian's remarks were used to show that an equivocal noun could not have a conjunctive signification, since syncategorematic terms were posterior to nouns. See CPDMA 7, p. 291. Compare Simon of Faversham, *In SE*, p. 68; Duns Scotus, *In SE*, p. 13A.

125. Karin Margareta Fredborg, Lauge Nielsen, and Jan Pinborg, "An Unedited Part of Roger Bacon's *Opus maius: De signis*," *Traditio* 34 (1978): 109–110.

126. I would like to thank Norman Kretzmann, for teaching me to read Aquinas, and the Canada Council, for the Killam Research Fellowship that has given me the time to write this essay.

Beauty in the Middle Ages: A Forgotten Transcendental?

Jan A. Aertsen

"Habent sua fata libelli" (Books have their own fates). This saying is especially applicable to the scholarly work of Umberto Eco. In the fifties he published in Italian studies of Thomas Aquinas's aesthetics and of beauty in the Middle Ages that shared the lot of so many scholarly publications: they attracted attention only in a restricted circle. But after the success of Eco's novel, *The Name of the Rose*, his earlier studies too have gained a large audience among publishers and the public. In 1986, *Art and Beauty in the Middle Ages* appeared, followed in 1988 by the English translation of Eco's dissertation, *The Aesthetics of Thomas Aquinas*.[1]

There is no reason to be unhappy about this development. Eco's studies are among the best that have appeared in this field. They distinguish themselves from many other studies by their concern for

---

This paper was presented as the Cardinal Mercier lecture at the Catholic University of Louvain on 22 February 1990.

1. Umberto Eco, "Sviluppo dell'estetica medievale," in *Momenti e problemi di storia dell'estetica* 1: *Dall'antichità classica al barocco* (Milan: Marzorati, 1959), pp. 115–230, translated as *Art and Beauty in the Middle Ages* (New Haven and London: Yale Univ. Press, 1986); Eco, *Il problema estetico in san Tommaso*, 2d ed. (Milan: Valentino Bompiani, 1970; 1st ed. 1956), translated as *The Aesthetics of Thomas Aquinas* (Cambridge, Mass.: Harvard Univ. Press, 1988).

the historical context of the medieval doctrine of beauty and for the links between medieval aesthetics and the realities of the age. In both books Eco pays much attention to a question he calls "one of the main problems of Scholastic aesthetics," namely, "the problem of integrating, on the metaphysical level, beauty with other forms of value." It was not by accident that in this period, in contrast to the tendency in our times, the problem of integration was philosophically prominent. An integrated sensibility was characteristic of the aesthetic experience of the medievals. Life appeared to them as something wholly integrated, in the sense of a culture whose value systems are related to one another.[2]

The strategy that scholastic philosophy developed for the integration of values involved the doctrine of the *transcendentia*. Transcendentals are concomitant conditions of being. They thus transcend the particular modes of being, which Aristotle called the "categories." Transcendentals, such as one, true, and good, are properties of being as such. Medieval philosophy aspired to establish that the values of unity, truth, and goodness are not actualized sporadically and accidentally but adhere rather to being as coextensive metaphysical properties. Every being is one, true, and good. Transcendentals are convertible with being and with one another. Yet this doctrine stresses at the same time that transcendentals are not identical with one another. They differ conceptually (*ratione*). The notion of being is different from that of unity, truth, or goodness. Transcendentals refer to the same reality but do so in different ways. Each transcendental is conceptually distinctive.[3] So Eco observes that the doctrine of transcendentals tried to allow both for the autonomy of values and for their place within a unitary vision of the transcendental aspects of being.[4]

The basic question now is whether there is a distinct place for beauty in the doctrine of transcendentals.[5] If the beautiful is con-

---

2. Eco, *Art and Beauty*, pp. 15–16.
3. For a general discussion of the doctrine of transcendentals, see Jan A. Aertsen, "Die Transzendentalienlehre bei Thomas von Aquin in ihren historischen Hintergründen und philosophischen Motiven," in *Thomas von Aquin: Sein Leben, sein Werk und seine Zeit in der neuesten Forschung*, edited by A. Zimmermann, Miscellanea Mediaevalia 19 (Berlin and New York: De Gruyter, 1988), pp. 82–102.
4. Eco, *Art and Beauty*, pp. 16, 19.
5. Eco deals with this question in *Art and Beauty*, pp. 17–27; and in *Aesthetics*, pp. 20–48.

sidered to be a transcendental, the fundamental consequence is that "it acquires a metaphysical worth, an unchanging objectivity, and an extension which is universal."[6] The beauty of the universe would be founded on a metaphysical certainty and not on mere poetic sentiment. But for the medievals *is* beauty a transcendental property of being? I want to examine this question by focusing on Thomas Aquinas's thought, which also occupies a prominent place in Eco's studies.

THOMAS ON BEAUTY

A fact that has often been noted but still needs to be mentioned again and again is that one cannot speak properly of "the aesthetics of Thomas Aquinas." Nowhere in his writings does he present a systematic treatise on this theme or engage in an extensive discussion of the beautiful. We find in his work only scattered remarks about the subject. These remarks concern especially the proper *ratio* of the beautiful. Thomas even provides a definition of his own: "Those things are called beautiful which please when they are seen" ("quae visa placent").[7] Two things are expressed in this definition. The beautiful is that which pleases and delights; it is that in which the appetite comes to rest. The beautiful is ordered to appetite and is thereby set in close relation to the good, for Thomas counts the good as the proper object of the appetite. Yet at the same time the definition relates the beautiful to seeing, by which is not exclusively meant knowing by sense. Beauty is the object of contemplation.

Eco advances an objection to Thomas's definition. "The phrase . . . *visa placent* . . . is a disturbing intrusion into the whole question." It introduces a subjective condition for beauty ("when they are seen"), and thus points "to a denial of its transcendental status."[8] But is this conclusion correct? To answer this question we must notice the peculiar character of Thomas's definition. This character may be elucidated through a comparison with the definition of the good provided by Aristotle at the beginning of the *Nicomachean Ethics* and adopted by Thomas : "The good is that which all things desire" ("quod omnia appetunt"). Thomas points out in his commentary that this phrase does not indicate the essence of the good. It is rather a definition *per*

---

6. Eco, *Aesthetics*, p. 22.
7. *Summa theol.* 1.5.4 ad 1.
8. Eco, *Aesthetics*, p. 39.

posteriora: the good is determined through its proper effect.⁹ The definition accordingly does not mean that something is good because it is desired but rather the reverse: that something is desired because it is good. The cause, the essence of the good itself, is manifested by the effect. The relation to the appetitive power does not constitute the good, but rather follows upon the essence of the good. Now something similar is the case in Thomas's definition of beauty. Indeed, I think it likely that Thomas framed this definition on analogy to that of the good. "Something is not beautiful because we love it; rather, it is loved by us because it is beautiful and good."¹⁰ The phrase *quae visa placent* is a definition *a posteriori*. It does not introduce a subjective condition of the beautiful so much as it defines the beautiful from its proper effect. "That which pleases when it is seen" does not say what the beautiful itself is.

What then is the essence of the beautiful? In a classic passage in the *Summa theologiae* (1.39.8), Thomas states that three things are required for beauty: *integritas*, or *perfectio*, that is, "integrity," or "completeness"; *debita proportio*, or *consonantia*, that is, "due proportion," or "harmony"; and *claritas*, that is, "clarity," "brightness," or "splendor." Thomas provides no explanation of this notion but only an example ("whence things are called beautiful which have a bright color"). However, this triad does not seem to have an absolute force or canonical meaning. In other places he mentions only two conditions: "clarity" and "due proportion," so he says, go together in the *ratio* of beauty.¹¹ In all texts Thomas is satisfied just to enumerate the conditions of beauty. He puts them side by side but does not indicate their mutual relationship in such a way that the *a posteriori* definition of the beautiful becomes clear from it.

If the beautiful is a transcendental, then it must participate in the two features of transcendentals: because of their universal extension they are really identical, but they differ from one another conceptually. Thomas's work contains passages, as we have seen, about the proper *ratio* of the beautiful. But with respect to the other

9. *Super Ethic.* 1.1.9.
10. *Super De div. nomin.* 4.10 (no. 439): "Non enim ideo aliquid est pulchrum quia nos illud amamus, sed quia est pulchrum et bonum ideo amatur a nobis."
11. *Summa theol.* 2–2.145.2: "Ad rationem pulchri, sive decori, concurrit et claritas et debita proportio." Compare 2–2.180.2 ad 3.

feature of transcendentals, their convertibility with being, the situation is different. No texts affirm that the beautiful is a universal property of being or express explicitly the transcendentality of beauty. Yet most modern scholars hold that the beautiful in Thomas does have a transcendental status.

A strong impulse to this trend in research stemmed from Maritain's *Art and Scholasticism*. He argued that the beautiful belongs to the order of transcendentals. "It is in fact the splendour of all the transcendentals together."[12] Umberto Eco too is of the opinion that the beautiful is a transcendental, albeit implicitly so. He admits that "Aquinas's text is filled with uncertainties and hesitations."[13] Such reserve and caution are absent in three German monographs devoted to beauty in Thomas. Francis J. Kovach arrives at the conclusion that the beautiful is "the richest, the most noble, and the most comprehensive of all transcendentals"; it is "the only transcendental that includes all the other transcendentals."[14] In the judgment of Winfried Czapiewski, the beautiful is the original unity of the true and the good.[15] Günther Pöltner, finally, regards beauty as "the origin of thought in Thomas Aquinas"; the beautiful is the unity of the transcendental determinations of being.[16]

The outcome of the studies in question confronts us with a striking paradox. The discussion of the beautiful occupies a marginal place in Thomas's work. Nowhere does he himself say that beauty is a transcendental property. Gilson has spoken in this regard of a "forgotten transcendental."[17] But in the Thomas research of the last decades,

12. Jacques Maritain, *Art and Scholasticism* (London: Sheed and Ward, 1939), p. 172, n. 63b. An elaboration of Maritain's view can be found in G. B. Phelan, "The Concept of Beauty in St. Thomas Aquinas," in *Selected Papers* (Toronto: Pontifical Institute of Mediaeval Studies, 1967), pp. 155–180.

13. Eco, *Aesthetics*, pp. 46–47.

14. Francis J. Kovach, *Die Ästhetik des Thomas von Aquin* (Berlin and New York: De Gruyter, 1961), p. 214; Kovach, "The Transcendentality of Beauty in Thomas Aquinas," in *Die Metaphysik im Mittelalter*, edited by P. Wilpert, Miscellanea Mediaevalia 2 (Berlin: De Gruyter, 1963), p. 392.

15. Winfried Czapiewski, *Das Schöne bei Thomas von Aquin* (Freiburg: Herder, 1964).

16. Günther Pöltner, *Schönheit: Eine Untersuchung zum Ursprung des Denkens bei Thomas von Aquin* (Vienna: Herder, 1978), p. 76.

17. E. Gilson, "The Forgotten Transcendental: *Pulchrum*," in *Elements of Christian Philosophy* (New York: Doubleday, 1960), pp. 159–163.

more attention has been devoted to the beautiful than to any other transcendental. No other of them has such an extensive literature.[18] Moreover, it is suggested that the beautiful has a central role in Thomas's thought, since it would be the synthesis and unity of all transcendentals.

Now that the English version of Eco's studies has drawn attention once again to the aesthetics of Thomas Aquinas, there is every reason, I believe, to review the thesis of the transcendentality of the beautiful and to take stock of the discussion about it. From what follows it will become clear that in my view the arguments that have been advanced for the status of the beautiful as a distinct transcendental are unsound for philosophical and historical reasons.

THE POSSIBLE SYSTEMATIC PLACE OF THE BEAUTIFUL

The only writing in which Thomas presents a systematic exposition of the transcendentals is *De veritate*. He does so here even twice, namely, in q. 1 (concerning truth) and in q. 21 (concerning goodness). Although there are differences between the two texts, these need not engage us now. As the point of departure for my analysis, I take *De veritate* 1.1, because it is the more complete account.

There are in Thomas's exposition three points having significance for the discussion of the beautiful. The first point may seem self-evident, but its import will become clear in the sections to come. It concerns the ontological perspective within which Thomas places the doctrine of transcendentals. In the first article of *De veritate* he posits that our concepts must be reduced to "first," immediate insights. This first, the inception of thought, is being. "That which the intellect first conceives, as best known, and into which it resolves [*resolvit*] all its concepts, is being [*ens*]." Thomas presents no argument for this priority. He does do so in *Summa theologiae* 1.5.2, where he raises the question "Whether the good is prior in concept [*secundum rationem*] to

---

18. See, in addition to the studies mentioned above, A. A. Maurer, *About Beauty: A Thomistic Interpretation* (Houston: Center for Thomistic Studies, Univ. of St. Thomas, 1983); Mark D. Jordan, "The Evidence of the Transcendentals and the Place of Beauty in Thomas Aquinas," *International Philosophical Quarterly* 29 (1989): 393–407.

being." There he says again that the first thing conceived by the intellect is being, but he also gives a reason: "For everything is knowable only insofar as it is in act." Hence being is the first intelligible and is prior in concept to the good. The priority of being is based on its actuality.

If being is the first known, then it follows that all other concepts arise by addition to being. How is this possible? Nothing can be added to being that is not itself a being; outside of being there is nothing. Other concepts can therefore only add something to being in the sense that they express a mode of being that the term "being" itself does not yet express. The *transcendentia* are terms that make explicit, not some special, categorial mode of being, but a general mode consequent on every being ("modus generalis consequens omne ens").[19] From this the ontological import of the doctrine of transcendentals becomes clear. Each of them expresses a general mode of being. If the beautiful is a transcendental, it must present a further explication of being as being.

A second point deserving of attention is connected with a constantly recurring theme in Eco's studies. In his view, Thomas's definition of the beautiful introduces a subjective element ("a reference to a knowing subject") that is hardly compatible with the transcendentality of the beautiful.[20] Now we have already noticed the peculiar character of this definition. But from *De veritate* 1.1 it also appears that the opposition suggested by Eco is alien to Thomas. For Thomas's exposition makes clear that transcendentals can be *relational* without thereby being subjective.

He divides the transcendentals into two groups, since the general mode of being expressed by them pertains to every being either in itself (*in se*) or in relation to another (*in ordine ad aliud*). To the first group of transcendentals belong "thing" (*res*) and "one." With respect to the relational transcendentals Thomas presents a further division. The relation of one being to another can be considered in the first place according to their division. This is expressed by the name "something" (*aliquid*), which according to Thomas says literally "some other thing" (*aliud quid*). But there is besides that a more positive relational mode of being, namely, the "conformity" (*convenientia*) of

---

19. This term is not used in *De veritate* 1.1, but it does occur in 21.3.
20. Eco, *Aesthetics*, pp. 118–119.

one being to another. The condition for such a relation is something whose nature it is to accord with every being. Such is the soul which, as Aristotle said (*On the Soul* 3.8.431b21), "is in a certain sense all things." In the soul there are a cognitive power and an appetitive power. The conformity of being to the appetite is expressed by the name "good," for the good is defined as "that which all things desire." The conformity to the intellect is expressed by the name "true."[21] In Thomas's determination of the true and the good, the special place of the spiritual being amidst the other beings is recognized. The *anima* is the being that can accord with every being. Humankind is marked, so one might say, by a transcendental openness. Thomas's reflection on the transcendentals reveals an anthropocentrism.

The third point of importance is a simple observation. In *De veritate* 1.1, Thomas presents six transcendentals: *ens, res, unum, aliquid, verum,* and *bonum.* In 21.1, he names four; *res* and *aliquid* are not mentioned. In neither of the two texts, however, does he affirm that the beautiful is a transcendental.[22] This observation gives rise to two questions. If the beautiful is a transcendental for Thomas, as modern scholars suggest, why is it not named? And if the beautiful is a transcendental, what might be its systematic place in the list of transcendentals?

Eco takes hardly any notice of these two questions, but the other writers mentioned do. For Maritain neither question constitutes a serious problem. The "classic table" in *De veritate* 1.1, so he says, "does not exhaust all transcendental values." The reason that the beautiful is not included is "that it can be reduced to one of them," namely, to the good.[23] This argument is not very convincing. If the beautiful is really a transcendental, then it must make explicit a gen-

---

21. *De verit.* 1.1: "In anima autem est vis cognitiva et appetitiva; convenientiam ergo entis ad appetitum exprimit hoc nomen 'bonum', unde in principio Ethicorum dicitur quod 'bonum est quod omnia appetunt,' convenientiam vero entis ad intellectum exprimit hoc nomen 'verum'."

22. The only place in *De veritate* where the beautiful comes up for discussion is 22.1 ad 12. There it is subsumed under the notion of good: "Ex hoc enim ipso quod aliquid appetit bonum, appetit simul pulchrum et pacem: pulchrum quidem, in quantum est in seipso modificatum et specificatum, quod in ratione boni includitur. . . . Unde quicumque appetit bonum, appetit hoc ipso pulchrum."

23. Maritain, *Art and Scholasticism*, p. 172, n. 63b.

eral mode of being and add a value to being conceptually that cannot be reduced to another transcendental.

Kovach recognizes that Thomas in *De veritate* 1.1 has elaborated a "complete system." The reason for the absence of the beautiful in the list must be that Thomas arrived at insight into the transcendentality of the beautiful only after *De veritate*. Hence Kovach's thesis is that Thomas's thought exhibits an "immanent development" on this point.[24] A decisive role in this development was played by Thomas's commentary on the *De divinis nominibus* of pseudo-Dionysius the Areopagite. In this commentary, which can be dated to 1265–1267, about ten years after *De veritate*, Thomas comes to see that the beautiful is a transcendental. We shall postpone discussion of Kovach's thesis to the following section, in which we analyze Thomas's commentary.

As to the systematic place of the beautiful, Kovach holds that it belongs at the end of the list of transcendentals. The beautiful is the final integration of the transcendentals; it has a synthetic function. For the uniqueness of the beautiful is that it is the relation of being to the two faculties of the soul, the cognitive and the appetitive, these faculties taken not separately but *jointly*.[25] Yet it is doubtful whether this synthetic view of the beautiful fits into the doctrine of transcendentals. Transcendentals do not stand apart from each other, but are marked by a progressive explication of being. There is an *ordo* of the transcendentals: being is the first, next comes the one, then the true, and finally the good. In this order what is later includes conceptually what is earlier: the good presupposes the true, i.e., the intelligibility of that which is ("bonum praesupponit verum").[26] The determination good includes that of being, one, and true.[27] From a systematic point of view there is no room in Thomas's doctrine for a unique transcendental, the beautiful, that would synthesize the other transcendentals. Transcendentals have as such a real unity, which is founded in the

---

24. Kovach, *Ästhetik*, pp. 75–76, 183.

25. Kovach, *Ästhetik*, pp. 212–214; "The Transcendentality of Beauty," pp. 391–392.

26. *De verit.* 21.3: "Et ita plura includit in se ratio boni quam ratio veri, et se habet quodammodo per additionem ad illa; et sic bonum praesupponit verum. . . . Unde istorum nominum transcendentium talis est ordo, si secundum se considerentur, quod post ens est unum, deinde verum, deinde post verum bonum."

27. *De verit.* 21.6 ad 2.

first, being, and a conceptual order, which is completed in the ultimate, the good.

Kovach is not alone in setting out to determine the place of the beautiful on the basis of Thomas's definition of it, which relates to both the cognitive and the appetitive. That is apparent in Czapiewski's approach. To him the beautiful is not the transcendental that is the last in the list but the one that precedes the true and the good. The beautiful must be taken to be the *one* relation of being to the *two* spiritual faculties of the soul, the intellect and the will. The beautiful is the original unity from which the true *and* the good unfold. Yet this unity of the true and the good remains hidden; it cannot be adequately conceived. It can only be approached from the different points of view of the true and the good. For the finite spirit realizes itself, precisely because of its finiteness, through the duality of intellect and will, to which the duality of the true and the good corresponds. That is why the beautiful cannot be given a place in the list of transcendentals.[28]

Czapiewski's solution is Kovach's in reverse. The beautiful is not the final synthesis of the transcendentals but the original unity of truth and goodness. Yet this solution gives rise to an objection similar to the one evoked by Kovach's. The idea that the unity of the true and the good is based on an earlier transcendental—Czapiewski speaks of an "Urmodus"[29]—is inconsistent with the order of transcendentals stated by Thomas. In this order the later includes the earlier conceptually, and not the earlier the later.

The essence of Czapiewski's interpretation is in fact that he thinks that Thomas's exposition in *De veritate* concerning the positive relational transcendentals needs completion. The triad soul–intellect–will posited by Thomas would require a corresponding triad of beautiful–true–good. As the duality of intellect and will, which is characteristic of the finite spirit, is rooted in the unity of the spirit, so likewise the true and the good unfold from a unity, and this unity is the beautiful. But Thomas's train of thought is an essentially different one and, so I would add, a more satisfactory one from a transcendental point of view. He posits a relationship of correspondence between being–true–good on the one hand and soul–intellect–will on the

---

28. Czapiewski, *Das Schöne bei Thomas*, pp. 121–131.
29. Czapiewski, p. 140.

other hand. He justifies this correspondence from what we called earlier the "transcendental openness" of the spirit. The soul is the being that can accord with every being—the soul is "in a certain sense all things," has an infiniteness.[30] Now there is in every spiritual nature, not only in the finite spirit, an intellect and a will.[31] The acts of both faculties manifest the infiniteness of the spirit, for their formal objects are the true and the good, respectively, which are convertible with being.[32] The emphasis in Thomas's exposition is not on the finiteness of the spirit but on its intentional infiniteness. There is in his doctrine no need whatsoever for a hidden transcendental that would be the unitary center of the true and the good. The attempts of various writers to find a distinct place for beauty as a transcendental must be regarded as having failed.

THE BEAUTIFUL IN *DE DIVINIS NOMINIBUS* OF PSEUDO-DIONYSIUS

The most important authority for Thomas's concept of beauty is pseudo-Dionysius the Areopagite. Now Kovach suggested, as we have seen, that Thomas's thought on beauty shows development. Not until his commentary on pseudo-Dionysius's *De divinis nominibus* would he have arrived at insight into the transcendentality of the beautiful.[33] But what clues does Dionysius's text offer for the transcendental status of the beautiful? Is there evidence in Thomas's commentary to support Kovach's view?

Dionysius's intention in this treatise is to elucidate the names attributed in Scripture to God that manifest God's causality

---

30. Compare *Super Sent.* 3.27.1.4: "Res immateriales infinitatem habent quodammodo, quia sunt quodammodo omnia."

31. Compare *Summa theol.* 1.19.1: "Dicendum in Deo voluntatem esse, sicut et in eo est intellectus: voluntas enim intellectum consequitur."

32. *Summa theol.* 1.54.2: "Secunda autem actio [that is, an immanent action] de sui ratione habet infinitatem vel simpliciter, vel secundum quid. Simpliciter quidem, sicut intelligere, cujus objectum est verum; et velle, cujus objectum est bonum; quorum utrumque convertitur cum ente; et ita intelligere et velle, quantum est de se, habent se ad omnia."

33. See also Francis J. Kovach, "Der Einfluss der Schrift des Pseudo-Dionysius 'De divinis nominibus' auf die Schönheitsphilosophie des Thomas von Aquin," *Archiv für Geschichte der Philosophie* 63 (1981): 150–166.

with respect to creatures. The primary of these divine names for Dionysius is the Good, that is, the name ascribed in Neoplatonism to the first principle. "The sacred writers have preeminently set apart from all other names for the supradivine God the name 'Good.'"[34] Good is the first, prior even to Being, because this name manifests most fully the processions of the creatures from God.

The consequence of Dionysius's intention is that his emphasis lies on the transcendence of the Good and the other names. The (Neo)platonic way of thought is eminently suited to this transcendence, and Dionysius's treatment of the divine names is accordingly strongly inspired by it. His way of speaking about God is Platonic, as Thomas in his Commentary observes: the divine good is "beyond" all that exists, is "the good itself," "the *per se* good," the supergood.[35] Dionysius's perspective is therefore different from that of Thomas's doctrine of the *transcendentia*. The good is for Dionysius the first, while from the transcendental point of view being is the first and the good the ultimate. Dionysius's concern is the transcendence of the divine, not the transcendentality of the most general determinations of being.[36]

One of the most remarkable aspects of Thomas's commentary on *De divinis nominibus* is that he makes an attempt to connect the different approaches. In the prologue Thomas wants to justify Dionysius's Platonic way of speaking of God. He describes the Platonists as wanting to reduce all that is composed to simple and abstract (*abstracta*) principles. Thus they posit the existence of separate Forms of things ("Human being *per se*," "Animal *per se*"). They apply this abstract approach not only to the species of natural things but also to that which is most common (*maxime communia*), namely, good, one, and being. They hold that there is a first, which is the essence of goodness, of unity, and of being, a principle that we, Thomas says, call "God." The other

---

34. *De divinis nominibus* 4 (PG 3:693B). Thomas explains Dionysius's intention in *Super De div. nomin.* 3.1 (no. 227): "Intendit enim in hoc libro agere de divinis nominibus manifestantibus processiones creaturarum a Deo, secundum quod est causa rerum. Id autem quod habet rationem causae, primo et universaliter est bonum."

35. *Super De div. nomin.* prooemium.

36. See my essay "Good as Transcendental and the Transcendence of the Good," in *Being and Goodness: The Concept of the Good in Metaphysics and Philosophical Theology*, edited by Scott MacDonald (Ithaca, N.Y.: Cornell University Press, 1991), pp. 79–102.

things are called "good," "one," and "being" because of their derivation from the first principle.

In the continuation of the prologue Thomas rejects the first application of the Platonic method, subscribing to Aristotle's criticism: there are no separate, subsisting Forms of natural things. But with regard to the first principle of things, Thomas recognizes the legitimacy of the Platonic approach.[37] He advances no argument for the validity of the Platonic method, but this can lie in nothing else than in its application to that which is most common. For Thomas, the Platonic reduction to abstract principles is only justified at the level of the *maxime communia*, that is, at the transcendental level. In this way he establishes a connection between the transcendental approach and the transcendent approach of the Platonists. This connection is possible because there is a causal relation between the first "separated" principle and the transcendentals. The *maxime communia* have to be reduced to God as the most universal cause. What belongs to these *maxime communia* Thomas enumerates: good, one, and being. He does not, however, name the beautiful, although that cannot of course serve as a decisive argument against the transcendentality of the beautiful.

Dionysius deals with the divine name the Beautiful in *De divinis nominibus* 4. The context of this exposition is not without importance for its interpretation. Chapter 4, the most extensive one in the whole work, treats successively the Good, Light, Beauty, Love, Ecstasy, and Zeal, to close with a treatise on evil. Thomas would not be Thomas if he did not endeavor to discover a connection in this diversity of names and themes. In his first *lectio* of chapter 4, he indicates what this connection is: all these subjects are directly connected with the Good, the primary name. Evil is dealt with because evil is the opposite of the good, and opposites belong to the same consideration. Love and the related notions are dealt with because the act is known through the object, and the good is the proper object of love. Thomas explains the reason that chapter 4 also deals with

37. *Super De div. nomin.* prooemium: "Haec igitur Platonicorum ratio fidei non consonat nec veritati, quantum ad hoc quod continet de speciebus naturalibus separatis, sed quantum ad id quod dicebant de primo rerum principio, verissima est eorum opinio."

beauty: "Because the good is that which all things desire, there belongs to the *ratio* of the good everything that possesses of itself the *ratio* of desirability. Of that nature are light and the beautiful."³⁸

Thomas's structuring of chapter 4 brings out the close connection between the good and the beautiful. In this way he expresses aptly the idea dominating Dionysius's exposition of the beautiful. For Dionysius concludes, as we shall see, that the good and the beautiful are identical. The Areopagite is in this respect a typical representative of Greek thought, for in it the beautiful and the good are brought together in a single notion, the *kalokagathia*.³⁹

The identity Dionysius posits between the good and the beautiful is something that must always be kept in mind in the interpretation of his statements about the beautiful. When he says, for example, "There is no being that does not participate in the good and the beautiful,"⁴⁰ this seems to suggest that the beautiful is a transcendental. Every being is in some way beautiful. Kovach takes Dionysius's statement, which Thomas in his commentary cites verbatim, in this sense. But this interpretation overlooks a decisive point. Dionysius does not mean to say that the beautiful is a property next to and distinct from the good. And this is precisely the point at issue with respect to the transcendentality of the beautiful.

Dionysius's discussion of the beautiful is focused, in keeping with the general intention of *De divinis nominibus*, on the question of how the names Beauty and Beautiful are attributed to God. Two elements in his account deserve attention.

First, Dionysius expresses what he understands by beauty. God is called Beauty because, so he says, God confers beauty on all things, is the cause of the consonance and clarity in all things. Dionysius's conception of beauty combines the two streams of Greek aesthetics:

---

38. *Super De div. nomin.* 4.1 (no. 266): "Cum bonum sit quod omnia appetunt, quaecumque de se important appetibilis rationem, ad rationem boni pertinere videntur; huiusmodi autem sunt lumen et pulchrum."

39. See, for this notion, *Historisches Wörterbuch der Philosophie* 4 (Darmstadt: Wissenschaftliche Buchgesellschaft, 1976), pp. 681–684. Thomas himself points to the relationship between the Greek names for "the good" (*kalos*) and "the beautiful" (*kallos*) in *Super Sent.* 1.31.2.1 ob. 4.

40. *De divinis nominibus* 4 (PG 3:704B). Compare *Super De div. nomin.* 4.5 (no. 355).

the older Pythagorean, Platonic one with the Neoplatonic one. According to the older Greek thinkers beauty is based on a relationship of parts and harmony. But Plotinus had argued that beauty also occurs in simple things: the sun and the evening star are beautiful not because of their proportion but because of their brilliance. Light, therefore, is no less a determining factor of beauty than harmony is.[41] Thomas observes in his commentary that the *ratio* of beauty consists in these two characteristics.[42] We saw above that Thomas sometimes names three conditions of beauty—*perfectio, proportio* or *consonantia*, and *claritas*—but sometimes only the last two. Now it becomes clear that the dual formula goes back to the authority of Dionysius. Thomas always refers to this text when he restricts the features of the beautiful to *consonantia* and *claritas*.[43]

What deserves attention in the second place is Dionysius's description of God as "the most beautiful."[44] Here again it becomes apparent how strongly the Areopagite is inspired by Platonism. For he employs verbatim in this passage the formulations that are used in Plato's *Symposium* (211A–B) to describe the Idea of the Beautiful. God is enduringly and uniformly beautiful, while the beauty of earthly things is mutable and corruptible. The divine beauty does not wax and wane. God is not beautiful in one respect and ugly in another. Beauty is not God's in a limited way. God is beautiful through and in Godself. Plato's description is eminently suited to show the uniqueness and transcendence of the divine beauty. It is in this that Dionysius is interested. It is therefore somewhat surprising that Czapiewski considers Thomas's commentary on this passage, in which Aquinas adds nothing essential to Dionysius's words, to be the (only) text that undeniably implies the transcendentality of the beautiful.[45]

In the *Symposium* it is said that Eros is love for the beautiful, which is at once love for the good, since the good is also

---

41. W. Tatarkiewicz, *History of Aesthetics 2: Medieval Aesthetics* (The Hague and Paris: Mouton, 1970), pp. 30, 15–16.
42. *Super De div. nomin.* 4.5 (no. 339).
43. See, for instance, *Summa theol.* 2–2.145.2: "Sicut accipi potest ex verbis Dionysii, 4 cap. De divinis nominibus, ad rationem pulchri . . . concurrit et claritas et debita proportio."
44. *Super De div. nomin.* 4.5 (nos. 345–347).
45. Czapiewski, *Das Schöne bei Thomas*, pp. 29–31.

beautiful (201C). Dionysius concurs with this idea. He concludes that the good and the beautiful are identical. His arguments are that all things desire the beautiful and the good as a cause in every one of its ways (thus the Beautiful-and-Good is the efficient, exemplary, and final cause of all things) and, further, that there is "nothing that does not participate in the beautiful and the good." But Thomas modifies Dionysius's conclusion and adds an observation of his own, which is worth citing in its entirety:

> Although the beautiful and the good are the same in reality [idem subiecto]—because both clarity and consonance are contained in the notion of the good—nevertheless, they differ in concept. For the beautiful adds to the good an ordering to the power that is able to know that a thing is of such a kind.[46]

In this passage Thomas clearly goes beyond Dionysius. He introduces a new element, although he does not elaborate it. He asserts that there is a conceptual difference between the beautiful and the good. The beautiful adds to the good a relation to the cognitive power. By the same token it is striking that Thomas formulates the identity of, and the difference between, the beautiful and the good in terms that he usually employs in connection with transcendentals. Eco stresses this point: "These two features—being identical in the subject, but differing *ratione*—are features appropriate to transcendental attributes; this, for example, is the case with the good and the true."[47] Does not Thomas therefore suggest in this passage that the beautiful is a transcendental?

Yet there is a fundamental objection to be raised against the interpretation that Thomas at this place in his commentary teaches the transcendentality of the beautiful. The outcome of our analysis of Thomas's exposition in De veritate 1.1 was that his doctrine of transcendentals is set in an ontological perspective. Transcendentals express a general mode of being, they add something conceptually to being. So true adds to being a relation to the intellect; good adds the notion of the appetible or desirable.[48] Here Thomas does not say, however, that the beautiful expresses a general mode of being, nor does he speak of an addition to being. The beautiful adds something to

---

46. *Super De div. nomin.* 4.5 (no. 356).
47. Eco, *Aesthetics*, p. 31.
48. *Summa theol.* 1.16.3: "Sicut bonum addit rationem appetibilis super ens, ita et verum comparationem ad intellectum."

the good; it expresses a mode of the good. This idea is strengthened further by the fact that in the passage cited clarity and consonance—of which Thomas had said earlier in his commentary that they form the proper *ratio* of the beautiful—are contained in the notion of the good ("sub ratione boni"). Eco too must acknowledge that "this explanation seems rather to assimilate the beautiful into the good than to identify both of them with being."[49]

Our conclusion must be that Thomas in his commentary does not teach that the beautiful expresses a general mode of being, on the basis of which it would have to be incorporated in the list as a new transcendental. He does distance himself from Dionysius by claiming that the beautiful adds a relation to the cognitive power, a new element that will still have to engage our attention. But what the beautiful adds is an addition to the good, not to being. For it is the true that adds to being the relation to knowledge. Thomas follows Dionysius in seeing the beautiful in connection with the good.

The identity of the good and the beautiful is affirmed repeatedly in the continuation of chapter 4. It may suffice to refer to two characteristic passages. When, after his treatment of the Beautiful, Dionysius proceeds to the discussion of Love, he begins his exposition with the statement: "The beautiful and the good are for all things desirable and lovable" (*amabile*).[50] Both the beautiful and the good are the object of love. It is this statement that Thomas cites at many places in his work. The second passage occurs at the end of chapter 4. There Dionysius endeavors to determine the various types of evil from their opposite, the good. Thomas summarizes the line of argument as follows: Dionysius first establishes the *ratio* of the good in general, and then what follows upon the general *ratio* of the good. Beauty belongs to the latter, for "the beautiful is convertible with the good" ("pulchrum convertitur cum bono").[51] The beautiful is a property of the good as good.

TWO TEXTS IN THE *SUMMA THEOLOGIAE*

The outcome of the analysis of Thomas's commentary on Dionysius is confirmed by the fact that there is no breakthrough to the

---

49. Eco, *Aesthetics*, p. 31.
50. *De divinis nominibus* 4 (PG 3:708A). Compare *Super De div. nomin.* 4.9 (no. 400).
51. *Super De div. nomin.* 4.22 (nos. 589–590).

beautiful as transcendental in Thomas's writings after this commentary. In his *Summa theologiae*, Thomas deals with the good (1.5–6), the one (1.11), and the true (1.16), but he devotes no separate *quaestio* to the beautiful. When we gather together Thomas's statements in the *Summa* about the status of the beautiful, the entire file turns out to consist of just two texts. It is striking that in both texts the beautiful comes up only in objections, not in the *corpus* of the article, and that the context of the discussion is always the good.

The first relevant text is *Summa* 1.5.4, where Thomas raises the question "Whether the good has the character of a final cause." The first objection refers to the opening sentence of Dionysius's exposition on beauty in *De divinis nominibus*: "The Good is praised as beautiful." Now the beautiful has the character of a formal cause. Therefore the good must have the same character. In his reply to this objection, Thomas first emphasizes the real identity of the beautiful and the good. They are the same in subject because they are based on the same reality, namely, the form. Yet they differ conceptually (*ratione*). Proper to the good is that it relates to the appetite, for the good is what all things desire; thus the good has the character of an end. The beautiful, on the other hand, relates to the cognitive power ("respicit vim cognoscitivam"). Thomas then presents his definition of the beautiful, which we have already discussed: "For those things are called beautiful which please when they are seen." Now because cognition is effected through assimilation, and likeness (*similitudo*) concerns the form, the beautiful properly pertains to the notion of a formal cause.

The second text is *Summa* 1–2.27.1, "Whether the good is the only cause of love." In the third objection, Thomas cites Dionysius's statement in chapter 4 of *De divinis nominibus* that the beautiful as well as the good is lovable for all things. The good is thus not the only cause of love. In his reply to this objection, Thomas once again elaborates the conceptual difference between the good and the beautiful. The *ratio* of the good is "that in which the appetite comes to rest." It pertains to the notion of the beautiful that the appetite comes to rest in the sight or knowledge of it ("in ejus aspectu seu cognitione"). Thus it appears that the beautiful adds to the good an ordering to the cognitive power. Good refers to that which simply pleases the appetite ("simpliciter complacet appetitui"). Beautiful refers to that the apprehension of which pleases ("id cujus ipsa apprehensio placet").

The two texts in fact present a further elaboration of Thomas's observation in his commentary on Dionysius that the beautiful adds to the good a relation to cognitive power. The novelty of medieval, as compared to Greek, thought about beauty is this emphasis on the relation of the beautiful to knowledge (*cognitio, visio, aspectus, apprehensio*). The beautiful is *quae visa placent*. But in both texts the transcendental status of the beautiful remains unclear.

Eco is of the opinion that "these two passages seem definitive, though only implicitly so. They are definitive because . . . they establish that beauty is a constant property of all being. . . . That is, beauty is identified with being simply as being."[52] But this "definitive" conclusion can certainly not be inferred from the two texts. The beautiful is not identified with being but with the good. Thomas's formulations suggest rather that the beautiful is a specification of the good: the good is that which *simply* pleases; the beautiful is that of which *the apprehension* pleases. It is on the basis of these phrases that Cajetan in his commentary on *Summa theol.* 1–2.27.1 ad 3 concludes that the beautiful is "quaedam boni species."[53]

Thomas's texts offer no definite answer about the transcendentality of the beautiful. But its status can be clarified by placing both texts in a broader context and considering them in connection with other thirteenth-century expositions on the beautiful.

HISTORICAL BACKGROUND

Eco devotes much attention to the thirteenth-century discussion of the beautiful. He relies on the documentation assembled by Pouillon in an influential study.[54] The historical background is indeed illuminating for the understanding of Thomas's texts, but, as it turns out, in rather a different way than Eco intends.

The doctrine of transcendentals was formed in the thirteenth century. Generally, the *Summa de bono* of Philip the Chancellor, written about 1230, is regarded as the first treatise on transcendentals. In the prologue Philip establishes that being, one, true, and good are the most

---

52. Eco, *Aesthetics*, p. 36.
53. Cajetan's commentary can be found in *S. Thomae Aquinatis Opera Omnia* (ed. Leonina), vol. 6 (Rome, 1891), p. 192.
54. H. Pouillon, "La beauté, propriété transcendantale chez les scolastiques (1220–1270)," *AHDLMA* 21 (1946): 263–329.

general things (*communissima*).⁵⁵ He does not, however, name the beautiful. Neither is the beautiful mentioned among the transcendentals in the *De bono* of Albert the Great (1243), which depends heavily on Philip, nor in Albert's commentary on the *Sentences* (1245). It is in the *Summa fratris Alexandri*, attributed to Alexander of Hales but in fact the work of a number of Franciscan authors, that for the first time room is made for the beautiful. The first part contains an extensive treatise on transcendental properties, written by John of La Rochelle (d. 1245).⁵⁶ In discussing the good, he includes an article on the relation between the good and the beautiful. It is this exposition that deserves special attention, because it became the model for later writers.

The question is raised "Whether the good and the beautiful are the same in concept" (*secundum intentionem*).⁵⁷ In the arguments *pro*, Dionysius is the authority, of course. A number of his statements identifying the beautiful with the good are cited. In the arguments *contra*, it is claimed that the beautiful and the good differ conceptually, because the beautiful has the character of a formal or exemplary cause, the good, on the other hand, the character of a final cause.

In his reply to the question, John of La Rochelle departs from ideas derived from Augustine. Augustine had distinguished between two kinds of good: the befitting, or virtuous (*honestum*), which is sought for its own sake; and the useful, which is referred to something else. Moreover, Augustine had identified *honestum* with intelligible beauty.⁵⁸ Through this identification Augustine in fact reestablished the close tie between the moral good and the beautiful, a connection implied in the Greek term *kalos* but that had been lost in the Latin by Cicero's translation *honestum*.

---

55. *Summa de bono* prol., ed. N. Wicki (Bern: A. Francke, 1985) 2:4. Compare H. Pouillon, "Le premier traité des propriétés transcendentales: La 'Summa de bono' du Chancellier Philippe," *Revue néoscolastique de philosophie* 42 (1939): 40–77.

56. Alexander of Hales, *Summa theologica* 1.1.3 (ed. Collegii S. Bonaventurae [Quaracchi: 1924], nos. 72–110).

57. *Summa theologica* 1.1.3.3.2 (ed. Quaracchi no. 103, 1:162–163). Eco, *Art and Beauty*, p. 24, interprets *secundum intentionem* as "with respect to the intentionality of the percipient": "In the *Summa* of Alexander, the difference *ratione* is a difference *intentione*—that is, in intentionality. Beauty is thus defined in relation to the knowing subject." But this interpretation is incorrect. *Intentio* has in this context the same meaning as *ratio*; a difference *intentione* means a difference in concept.

58. The *Summa* refers to Augustine's *De diversis quaest.* 83 30 (PL 40:19).

On the basis of Augustine's ideas, John of La Rochelle concludes that the good, taken as *honestum*, is the same as the beautiful. But they differ, so he adds, conceptually. "For the beautiful is a disposition of the good insofar as it pleases the apprehension ["secundum quod est placitum apprehensioni"], whereas the good relates to the disposition insofar as it delights the affection." So they differ with respect to the notion of final cause. He goes on to add that they also differ with respect to the notions of the other causes, the efficient cause and the exemplary cause. He expounds these further differences, but the details need not concern us here. Of importance is John's reply to the objection that the beautiful has to do with the formal or exemplary cause, and the good with the final cause. He stresses that the form sometimes receives the character of end, and the end the character of form. In a similar way the beautiful assumes the character of the good, and the good that of the beautiful, although John of La Rochelle recognizes that "the primary notion of the beautiful is derived from the exemplary cause, and the primary notion of the good from the final cause."[59]

When we compare the exposition in the *Summa fratris Alexandri* with the texts of Thomas mentioned above, we find that there are striking similarities. Thomas uses similar formulations to indicate the conceptual difference between the good and the beautiful (the beautiful is "that of which the apprehension pleases"). One also finds in him that the beautiful relates to the formal cause, the good to the final cause. Finally, we can establish that Thomas later in the *Summa* (2–2.145.2), with an appeal to Augustine, also identifies the beautiful with the *honestum*.[60] It is true that there are differences. Thus Thomas does not connect the *forma* with the exemplary cause; neither does he mention additional differences between the good and the beautiful related to the notions of the efficient cause and the exemplary cause. But it is beyond doubt that the core of his line of argument goes back to the *Summa* attributed to Alexander of Hales.

Yet the main problem remains. What conclusion can be drawn concerning the transcendentality of the beautiful from the exposition

---

59. *Summa theologica* 1.1.3.3.2 ad 1 (ed. Quaracchi 1:163).

60. Thomas Aquinas, *Summa theol.* 2–2.145.2: "Et ideo honestum est idem spirituali decori. Unde Augustinus dicit, in libro 83 Quaest.: 'Honestatem voco intelligibilem pulchritudinem, quam spiritualem nos proprie dicimus.'"

of John of La Rochelle? Eco agrees with Pouillon that the *Summa* of Alexander of Hales brought about an important philosophical innovation on this point. "It decisively solved the problem of the transcendental character of beauty, and its distinction from other values."[61] But is this observation correct?

John of La Rochelle commences his treatise on transcendentals by establishing that besides being there are three common determinations, namely, the one, the true, and the good.[62] He discusses these one after the other, and it is within the framework of the good that he raises the question of beauty. Yet he does not add beauty to the list of transcendentals. Eco acknowledges this fact but advances in explanation "the caution and prudence with which the medievals engaged in innovation." There was, after all, a traditional number of transcendentals, and it was no small thing to alter it. "The boldness of the innovation required caution in its implementation."[63] These arguments are not very convincing. In Albert the Great, for example, there is a clear awareness that in the doctrine of transcendentals the medievals have gone beyond the Philosopher, Aristotle.[64] Moreover Thomas Aquinas in *De veritate* 1.1 presents six transcendentals.

The picture that emerges from the exposition of John of La Rochelle is rather that the beautiful is not a new, separate transcendental, but something to be discussed within the framework of the good. This is in fact the general picture of thirteenth-century thought about the beautiful. The *Summa* of Alexander of Hales has determined the place of the beautiful, both in the *Summa theologiae* of Thomas Aquinas and in that of Albert the Great (begun after 1270).[65]

There is one exception to this *communis opinio*. The only writer in the thirteenth century who explicitly says that the beautiful is a distinct transcendental is the author of the manuscript Assisi, Biblioteca

---

61. Eco, *Art and Beauty*, p. 23.
62. *Summa theologica* 1.1.3.1 (ed. Quaracchi no. 73, 1:114): "Ens est primum intelligibile; primae autem entis determinationes sunt 'unum' et 'verum' et 'bonum'."
63. Eco, *Aesthetics*, p. 44. Compare *Art and Beauty*, p. 24.
64. Albert the Great, *In Sent.* 1.46.N.14 (ed. Borgnet 26:450): "Dicendum, quod secundum Philosophum, ante omnia sunt ens et unum. Philosophus enim non ponit, quod verum et bonum sint dispositiones generaliter concomitantes ens."
65. Albert the Great, *Summa theologiae* 1.6.26.2.3 (*Opera Omnia*, ed. Cologne 34/1:177–179): "Utrum bonum et pulchrum secundum communem intentionem sint idem vel diversa."

Comunale 186. The authorship of this manuscript is contested; it is sometimes attributed to Bonaventure.⁶⁶ It concerns an excerpt from the *Summa* of Alexander of Hales to which the anonymous author, probably a student, sometimes attaches his own conclusions. At the beginning of the text it is said that there are four general *conditiones entis*, namely, "the one, the true, the good, and the beautiful." All four add something conceptually to being: the one relates to the efficient cause; the true, to the formal cause; the good, to the final cause. The beautiful encompasses all these causes and is common to them.⁶⁷ This synthetic function of the beautiful is, however, not further elaborated in the treatise. If Bonaventure was the author of the manuscript, then it is striking that in his later works he nowhere makes mention of the beautiful as transcendental and constantly restricts himself to the triad the one, the true, and the good.⁶⁸ In doing so he follows the current opinion in the thirteenth century. That the beautiful is not a separate transcendental is the rule in this period. The title of Pouillon's study suggests more than it can substantiate.

THE PLACE OF BEAUTY

In the second section we came to the conclusion that the efforts of modern scholars to find a distinct place for the beautiful as a transcendental in Thomas's doctrine must be regarded as having failed. The previous section has now shown that the common opinion of the thirteenth century was that the beautiful is not a separate transcendental. What, then, was its place? Thomas offers no direct answer to this question. But we have found in his writings a number of statements that can serve as a basis for a reflection on his view. We

---

66. The text is edited by D. Halcour, "*Tractatus de transcendentalibus entis conditionibus* (Assisi, Biblioteca Comunale, Codex 186)," *Franziskanische Studien* 41 (1959): 41–106. The title that Halcour has given to the treatise is anachronistic. The term *transcendentalis* is unknown in the Middle Ages.

67. *Tractatus de transcendentalibus* 1.1 (ed. Halcour, p. 65): "Dicendum, quod istae conditiones fundantur supra ens, addunt enim aliquam rationem. . . . Sed pulcrum circuit omnem causam et est commune ad ista."

68. Bonaventure, *Breviloquium* 1.6.2 (*Opera Omnia* 5:215): "conditiones entis nobilissimae et generalissimae . . . hae autem sunt unum, verum, bonum." Compare Karl Peter, *Die Lehre von der Schönheit nach Bonaventura* (Werl: Dietrich-Coelde-Verlag, 1964), p. 135, n. 15.

recall his definition of the beautiful and the three essential characteristics of the beautiful that he enumerates (*integritas* or *perfectio*, *debita proportio* or *consonantia*, and *claritas* [section 1]); his observation in the commentary on Dionysius that the good and the beautiful are really identical, but conceptually different, in the sense that the beautiful adds to the good a relation to the cognitive power (section 3); and the elaboration of this conceptual difference in the two texts from the *Summa theologiae* (section 4). On the basis of this material, I shall attempt to determine the place of the beautiful systematically.

"The beautiful is convertible with the good." For Thomas, following Greek thought, the place of the beautiful is the good. The mark of the good is that it is desirable. Something is desirable insofar as it is perfect. Proper to the good as good is that it is *perfectum*;[69] it has the character of something "complete." Perfect is what attains to its end, to its proper nature. The same is denoted in a negative way by the term *integrum*, which expresses the removal of diminution (*remotionem diminutionis*).[70] Now Thomas in *Summa theol.* 1.39.8 names as the first condition of the beautiful "integrity," or "perfection," for, so he explains, "those things which are impaired [*diminuta*] are by that very fact ugly." Earlier we saw that Thomas sometimes restricts the *ratio* of the beautiful to two characteristics. There is a historical reason for this, namely, the authority of pseudo-Dionysius, who mentions only proportion and clarity. But we can now also adduce a philosophical reason for the changing number. The first condition of the beautiful, *perfectio*, is of another kind than the other two. It is a generic condition that binds the beautiful to the good as good. The beautiful pleases because it is perfect.

Summa 1.5 treats "of the good in general." The first three articles of this question concern the convertibility of being and the good, the last three what is proper to the good. In article 5 Thomas states the *ratio* of the good as good, in article 6 the division of the good. Both articles are important for the beautiful.

---

69. *Summa theol.* 1.5.5: "Unumquodque dicitur bonum, inquantum est perfectum: sic est enim appetibile."

70. *Super De div. nomin.* 2.2 (no. 115): "Integrum autem et perfectum idem videntur esse; differunt tamen ratione: nam perfectum videtur dici aliquid in attingendo ad propriam naturam, integrum autem per remotionem diminutionis."

The good is divided into the befitting (*honestum*), which is desired for its own sake; the useful (*utile*), which is desired as a means to something else; and the pleasing (*delectabile*), in which the appetite comes to rest. Thomas observes that this division properly concerns the human good. But if one considers the notion of goodness "from a higher and more universal point of view," one will find that this division properly belongs to the good so far as it is good.[71] The extension of this division to the good as such is important for the beautiful because Thomas, following Alexander of Hales, identifies the beautiful with the primary good, the *bonum honestum*. The beautiful pleases, not because it has an instrumental function, but because it is in itself good.

In article 5 Thomas teaches that the *ratio* of the good as good consists in three essential features, *modus* (measure), *species*, and *ordo*. In his account of this Augustinian triad, the notion of "form" is central. Everything is called "good" insofar as it is perfect. The perfection of a thing comes to be realized through its form. The form itself is signified by the *species*, for everything is placed in its species by its form. Now the form presupposes certain things, and from the form certain things necessarily follow. The form presupposes commensuration of its principles, and this is signified by the *modus*. Following on form is an inclination toward the end, and this relation to something else belongs to the *ordo*.

If the beautiful is identical with the good, because it is perfect, then the beautiful must follow the *ratio* of the good as good. Indeed, some medieval writers, as in the *Summa fratris Alexandri*, simply identify the essence of the beautiful with Augustine's triad of the good. In Thomas too we find statements tending in that direction. "A thing is beautiful so far as it is proportioned [*modificatum*] and specified [*specificatum*] in itself, features that are included in the *ratio* of the good."[72] His general approach is to maintain Dionysius's conception of beauty, but he does connect the three essential constituents of the goodness of things with the characteristics belonging to the *ratio* of the beautiful, *proportio* or *consonantia* and *claritas*.

---

71. *Summa theol.* 1.5.6: "Haec divisio videtur esse proprie boni humani. Si tamen altius et communius consideremus rationem boni, invenitur haec divisio proprie competere bono, secundum quod bonum est."

72. *De verit.* 22.1 ad 12.

Beauty as harmony can be conceived as an internal relation in a thing or as a relation of one thing to another. Thomas's standard example of the former is that a man is called beautiful by reason of the due *proportio,* or "commensuration," of his members.[73] Thomas uses the same term "commensuration" to describe the *modus,* the first feature of the good, and the same example to illustrate this condition.[74] He relates *consonantia* to the *ordo* to something else and claims that *claritas* refers to the form.[75] Clarity therefore corresponds to *species,* a term which itself has an aesthetic connotation (*species sive pulchritudo*) under the influence of a tradition that goes back to Augustine, as Thomas points out.[76]

The notion of *claritas* specifies wherein the aesthetic aspect of the *species* consists. For clarity is identified by Thomas with truth and the knowability of things. It is described as light.[77] The mark of light, both physical and spiritual, is that it makes things visible. It has the property of *manifestatio.* "Therefore all that is manifest is called *clarum.*"[78] Hence *claritas* is the property on the basis of which a thing is able to manifest and show itself. From this it follows that *claritas* is the feature of the beautiful that expresses what the beautiful adds to the

---

73. *Super De div. nomin.* 4.5 (no. 339); *Super Sent.* 1.31.2.1. Thomas frequently uses *commensuratio* as a synonym of *proportio.* See, for instance, *Super De div. nomin.* 4.21 (no. 554).

74. Compare *Super De div. nomin.* 4.22 (no. 589): "Primo accipienda est ratio boni in communi, ad quam tria pertinent: scilicet commensuratio aliquorum ex quibus aliquid componitur, ut . . . pulchritudo (est) commensuratio membrorum."

75. *Super De div. nomin.* 4.6 (no. 367): "Forma autem a qua dependet propria ratio rei, pertinet ad claritatem; ordo autem ad finem, ad consonantiam." Thomas, in his commentary, describes *consonantia* in terms of *ordo.* See 4.5 (no. 340): "Est autem duplex consonantia in rebus: prima quidem, secundum ordinem creaturarum ad Deum; . . . secunda autem consonantia est in rebus secundum ordinationem earum ad invicem."

76. *Super Sent.* 1.31.2.1: "Species, id est pulchritudo." *Summa theol.* 1.39.8: "Species sive pulchritudo." Thomas refers to Augustine in *Resp. ad Ioann. Vercell. de art.* 108, 57 (no. 884): "speciem interpretatur pulchritudinem."

77. *Super Job* 40: "Deus enim non habet circumdatum decorem quasi superadditum eius essentiae sed ipsa essentia eius est decor per quem intelligitur ipsa *claritas sive veritas.*" *Super Sent.* 4.49.2.3 ad 7: "Claritas dei dicitur veritas suae essentiae per quam cognoscibilis est sicut sol per suam claritatem." *Super Ioann.* 1.11 (no. 212): "Claritas Dei non est aliud quam eius substantia: non enim est lucens per participationem luminis, sed per seipsam."

78. *Super Sent.* 2.13.1.2.

good: the relation to the cognitive power. This relation specifies the place of the beautiful.

The relation to knowledge which is implied in the beautiful is not something that is foreign to the good, not something extrinsic to its concept. The order of the transcendentals is that the good presupposes the true. Appetite cannot be directed towards the good unless it is known.[79] The object that moves appetite is the *bonum apprehensum*. From this Thomas draws in *Summa* 1–2.27.2—after having shown in the preceding article that the good is the proper cause of love—the conclusion that love requires some knowledge of the good. "For this reason the contemplation of spiritual beauty or goodness is the principle of spiritual love."[80]

Yet the beautiful is something more than the true presupposed by the good—more than the *bonum apprehensum*. It is characteristic of the beautiful that its *apprehensio* is taken as "appropriate and good" ("conveniens et bonum").[81] This knowledge of the beautiful must be a special type of knowledge. For the intellect apprehends things under the aspect of the true ("sub ratione veri").[82] Nevertheless, Thomas does not hold that the beautiful is the object of a distinct spiritual power. Nowhere does he distinguish, in addition to the cognitive and the appetitive, still a third power, a kind of aesthetic experience or intuition. How then is the knowledge of the beautiful to be interpreted?

Now there is a brief text in Thomas's commentary on the *Sentences* in which he posits a connection between knowledge and the good. There he distinguishes two grades in knowledge. In the first, intellective knowledge is directed toward the true; in the second, knowledge takes the true as *conveniens* and *bonum*. From such knowledge follow

---

79. Compare *Summa theol.* 1–2.19.3 ad 1.

80. *Summa theol.* 1–2.27.2: "Bonum autem non est objectum appetitus, nisi prout est apprehensum. Et ideo amor requirit aliquam apprehensionem boni quod amatur. Et propter hoc . . . contemplatio spiritualis pulchritudinis vel bonitatis, est principium spiritualis amoris."

81. *Summa theol.* 2–2.145.2 ad 1: "Objectum movens appetitum est bonum apprehensum. Quod autem in ipsa apprehensione apparet decorum, accipitur ut conveniens et bonum."

82. *Summa theol.* 1.82.4 ad 1: "sub ratione entis et veri, quam apprehendit intellectus."

love and delight.⁸³ With respect to this second grade of knowledge, which we could call "affective," it is stated in another text in the same commentary that in it "the true is extended to the good" ("verum extenditur in bonum").⁸⁴ Because Thomas describes the apprehension of the beautiful in the same terms that he applies to the second grade of knowledge, this extension of the true to the good must be the place of the beautiful. The beautiful is the true taken as good. It pleases through its clarity and proportion.

We can find support for this interpretation in *De pulchro et bono*, which was long attributed to Thomas. It is in reality, however, a copy by Thomas of the lectures that his teacher Albert the Great had given in Cologne on pseudo-Dionysius's exposition of the beautiful. In question 1, article 1, Albert reflects on the order of the names Light, Beauty, and Love in chapter 4 of *De divinis nominibus*. This order must be understood according to the order of the processes in the mind. The first mental process is the apprehension of the true; next, the true incandesces (*excandescit*) and takes the character of good; this, finally, sets desire in motion, for desire is not moved unless directed by a prior apprehension. With these processes there corresponds, according to Albert, Dionysius's order of the names. With the apprehension of the true there corresponds light; with the apprehension of the true insofar as it has the character of the good ("apprehensioni autem veri secundum quod habet rationem boni") there corresponds the beautiful; with the movement of desire there corresponds love.⁸⁵ In Albert's treatise one finds systematically elaborated what we discovered in Thomas only through a reconstructive interpretation of scattered texts. The place of the beautiful is the true taken as good.

Thomas's aesthetics is special in that he maintains the connection between the beautiful and the good even while he relates

83. *Super Sent.* 1.15.4.1 ad 3: "Videmus autem in cognitione duos gradus. Primum, secundum quod cognitio intellectiva tendit in unum [corrige: verum. Compare the text in the next note]. Secundum, prout verum accipit ut conveniens et bonum, et nisi sit aliqua resistentia ex tali cognitione, sequitur amor et delectatio." Compare *Comp. theol.* 1.165: "Ex apprehensione convenientis, delectatio generatur, sicut visus delectatur in pulchris coloribus."
84. *Super Sent.* 1.27.2.1: "Et quia potest esse duplex intuitus, vel veri simpliciter, vel ulterius secundum quod verum extenditur in bonum et conveniens."
85. The text of Albert's *De pulchro et bono* can be found in R. Busa, ed., *S. Thomae Aquinatis Opera Omnia* (Stuttgart: 1980), 7:43–47 (p. 43).

the beautiful to knowledge, to the true. The beautiful is the object of contemplation. This relation to knowing comes to expression terminologically in many European languages. The German term for "beautiful," for example, *schön,* is cognate with the verb *schauen,* "to contemplate."

The beautiful is therefore related to the true and to the good. Its relatedness can be approached in two ways. Viewed from the Greek tradition and the perspective of pseudo-Dionysius, the beautiful is identical with the good; it adds to it conceptually a relation to knowledge. Regarded from Thomas's order of the transcendentals, the beautiful is to be taken as the extension of the true to the good. We can clarify this place of the beautiful further from the special relationship that exists between the true and the good.

These transcendentals occupy a distinct position in Thomas's exposition in *De veritate* 1.1. The true and the good are relational transcendentals: they express the conformity of being with the two powers of the spiritual being, the cognitive and the appetitive. These powers extend to all that is. The formal objects of intellect and will, the true and the good respectively, manifest the infiniteness of the spirit. This must mean that the one formal object includes the other object in its infinite horizon. The true and the good include one another.

Thomas adduces this idea when he deals with the relation between theoretical and practical reason. They seem to be two distinct powers of the soul, since they have different formal objects. The object of the theoretical intellect is the true, and of the practical intellect, the good. The consequence of this must be that the theoretical intellect and the practical intellect are distinct powers, for the different *ratio* of the object differentiates the power.[86]

Still Thomas rejects this conclusion. The theoretical intellect and the practical intellect are not two distinct powers. The theoretical intellect itself becomes practical "by extension" (*per extensionem*).[87] That is possible because the objects of the theoretical intellect and of the practical intellect are related to each other in such a way that they confirm the unity of the two powers. "The true and the good include one another" ("se invicem includunt"). For the true is something that is good, else it would not be appetible; the good is something that is

---

86. *Summa theol.* 1.79.11 ob. 2.
87. *Summa theol.* 1.79.11 sc.

true, else it would not be intelligible. The object of the appetite may be the true, then, so far as it has the *ratio* of the good. That is the case, for example, when someone desires to know the truth. Conversely, the good can be the object of the intellect *sub ratione veri*. The practical intellect considers the good as practical, that is, as directed to a work. "The practical intellect knows truth, just as the theoretical intellect, but it directs the known truth to something that has to be done." The theoretical intellect becomes practical by extending the true to the good.[88]

The extension of the true to the good is also the place of the beautiful. Yet the beautiful is not the object of practical reason, for beauty is in the medieval view not a good that is to be made. Beauty does not belong to the domain of art but is primarily a property of things themselves. Yet there are clear analogies between the beautiful and the object of practical reason: the beautiful, too, is not the object of a distinct cognitive power, and the beautiful must be understood as the extension of the true to the good, an extension that is possible because the true and the good include one another.

From this determination of the beautiful it is possible, finally, to deduce why it does not acquire a separate place in the list of transcendentals. The beautiful is not for Thomas, as modern scholars suggest, a forgotten transcendental effecting a synthesis of the true and the good. The real situation is rather the reverse: the beautiful must be understood from the inclusion of the true in the good. The aesthetic is not in the Middle Ages an autonomous domain alongside the true and the good. The integration of the beautiful with other values did not need to be based on a distinct transcendental: it was implied in the transcendental order of truth and goodness.

Vrije Universiteit, Amsterdam

---

88. *Summa theol.* 1.79.11 ad 2. Compare *De verit.* 3.3 ad 9.

Aquinas on Aristotle on Happiness

Don Adams

The first nine books of Aristotle's *Nicomachean Ethics* (EN) seem to present a complex theory of happiness. In them, it seems that happiness is a good that is composed of several goods, e.g., friends, wealth, political and social honors, and so on. There seems now to be a consensus that this is indeed Aristotle's considered view of happiness.[1] I agree with this consensus.

Given that the first nine books of the EN seem so clearly to suggest this active view of happiness, it seems odd that in his commentary on

---

1. See the following: J. Cooper, *Reason and Human Good in Aristotle* (Cambridge, Mass.: Harvard University Press, 1975), p. 99; D. Keyt, "Intellectualism in Aristotle," *Paideia*, Special Aristotle Issue (1978): 138–157; J. Whiting, "Human Nature and Intellectualism in Aristotle," *Archiv für Geschichte der Philosophie* 68 (1986): 70–95; J. L. Ackrill, "Aristotle on *Eudaimonia*," in *Essays on Aristotle's Ethics*, edited by A. Rorty (Berkeley: University of California Press, 1980), pp. 15–33; T. H. Irwin, *Aristotle, Nicomachean Ethics* (Indianapolis: Hackett, 1985); Irwin, "Permanent Happiness: Aristotle and Solon," in *Oxford Studies in Ancient Philosophy 3*, edited by J. Annas (Oxford: Oxford University Press, 1985), pp. 89–124; Irwin, "Stoic and Aristotelian Conceptions of Happiness," in *The Norms of Nature*, edited by M. Schofield and G. Striker (Cambridge: Cambridge University Press, 1986), pp. 205–244; A. W. Price, "Aristotle's Ethical Holism," *Mind* 89 (1980): 341; M. Nussbaum, "Aristotle," in *Ancient Writers* 1, edited by T. James Luce (New York: Scribner, 1982), p. 403; D. Devereux, "Aristotle on the Essence of Happiness," in *Studies in*

the EN,[2] St. Thomas Aquinas attributes to Aristotle a view quite similar to his own contemplative view of happiness. In this essay I intend to show that while Aquinas's interpretation of Aristotle[3] is incorrect, it is philosophically interesting, textually well motivated, and guilty of no interpretative crimes.

I begin by pointing out two early symptoms of the difference between Aristotle's views and the views that Aquinas attributes to Aristotle. Next, I clarify the character of the two different conceptions of happiness and raise a serious problem for Aquinas's attempt to attribute to Aristotle a view of happiness so similar to his own. Finally, I show the textual root of the difference between Aristotle's views and Aquinas's interpretation of Aristotle's views and show that given the text Aquinas had, and given the burden of interpreting Aristotle sympathetically, Aquinas's interpretation is guilty of no interpretative crimes.

TWO SYMPTOMS OF DIFFERENCE

Aquinas follows Aristotle in arguing that happiness is a complete (*teleia, perfectus*) and self-sufficient (*autarkes, per se sufficiens*) good (EN 1.7.1097a25–b15, EA 1.9 no.107).[4]

COMPLETENESS

At the end of EN 1.10 Aristotle admits that the happiness which can be attained in this life is subject to chance. Even

---

Aristotle, edited by D. J. O'Meara (Washington: The Catholic University of America Press, 1981), p. 249f. Two recent dissenters from this consensus are Robert Heinaman, "Eudaimonia and Self-Sufficiency in the *Nicomachean Ethics*," *Phronesis* 33 (1987): 31–53; and Richard Kraut, *Aristotle on the Human Good* (Princeton: Princeton University Press, 1989). Heinaman's reasons for dissenting bear little relation to Aquinas's interpretation of Aristotle, so I shall not respond to Heinaman here. I shall, however, respond briefly to Kraut in note 31, below.

2. I shall use "EA" to refer to Aquinas's commentary on the *Ethics* of Aristotle. For ease of citation, I will use both the medieval textual divisions and the section numbers originally assigned by Cathala, as reproduced in *In decem libros Ethicorum Aristotelis ad Nicomachum expositio*, 3d ed., edited by Raymundus M. Spiazzi (Turin: Marietti, 1964). All translations of Aristotle and Aquinas are mine.

3. I do not intend to look carefully at the first five questions of *Summa theologiae* (hereafter ST) 1–2, which could also be considered to be a type of commentary on EN.

4. Aquinas takes b16–20 to be a further explanation of self-sufficiency and not to

someone as prosperous as Priam can be denied happiness because of serious misfortune. (Although misfortune cannot make one unhappy, it can deprive one of some external goods required for complete happiness.)[5] This does not commit Aristotle to the view that happiness is a radically unstable or ephemeral thing, since it takes serious misfortune to take one's happiness away. Aquinas does recognize that Aristotle does not think "a person is happy in the way of a chameleon" (1.15 no. 186) and sees that this does not by itself entail that happiness is radically unstable. Nevertheless Aquinas does think that Aristotle accepts that once we admit that the happiness to be obtained in this life can be taken away by misfortune, we must accept that it cannot be truly complete. Aquinas says, "but because these things do not seem always to measure up to the conditions for happiness laid down above," i.e., completeness and self-sufficiency, as in EA 1.9 nos. 104–117, "he adds that the sort of people we call happy as human beings, who in this life are subject to change, cannot have complete happiness" (EA 1.16 no. 202). It is the mutability of this life that, according to Aquinas, rules out even the possibility of its being complete in the relevant sense. (Aquinas takes two different lines in different places about what the relevant sort of mutability is. I will return to this point below.)

This is an odd comment for Aquinas to make for two reasons: first, nowhere in the passage he is commenting upon does Aristotle explicitly deny human beings the ability to attain complete happiness in this life; but, second, the point of Aristotle's argument seems to be exactly the opposite.[6] Aristotle asks rhetorically:

> What, therefore, prevents us from calling happy the one who acts according to complete virtue and is thoroughly and sufficiently supplied with external goods not for a short time but in a complete life? . . . we lay it down that happiness is the end and is always complete in every way. But if

---

be a third feature of happiness. Taking it this way is at least strongly recommended by b20–21.

5. For one explanation of how this can be so, see Irwin, "Permanent Happiness," pp. 89–124.

6. If in book 10 Aristotle clearly claims that the active life can never be as complete as the contemplative life, there would be good reason to try to interpret this passage in the way Aquinas does. I shall return below to Aristotle's discussion of the contemplative life in book 10.

it is so, we will call blessed a living human being to whom belongs and will belong the things we have said, but happy as a human being.[7]

The point here seems clearly to be that while complete happiness is difficult to attain in this life, it is possible—however difficult it might be to attain complete virtue and sufficient external goods or to avoid misfortunes.

In defending his interpretation, Aquinas may point out that Aristotle does say that when one is happy in the way he is discussing, one is happy "as a human being." Surely in saying this he is acknowledging at least that there may be another way of being happy (compare EA 1.16 no. 202; 1.9 no. 113). But to justify his interpretation, Aquinas must show that according to Aristotle (1) there is another way of being happy which (2) has a better claim on being called complete and which (3) we can, at least theoretically, achieve.[8] Aristotle accepts claim 1 since he believes that the happiness of the gods is different from human happiness (compare EN 7.14.1154b26–31; and *Metaphysics* 12.7.1072b14–20). We will see that Aquinas also attributes claims 2 and 3 to Aristotle.

SELF-SUFFICIENCY

Aquinas follows Aristotle in holding that a good is self-sufficient if and only if it provides everything that is by itself necessary and sufficient for making a life "choiceworthy, lacking in nothing"

---

7. In this section (EN 1.10.1100b33–1101a21), Aristotle seems to be using "happy" (*eudaimôn*) and "blessed" (*makarios*) interchangeably (compare especially 1100b33–34 with 1101a6–8). Aquinas appears to follow him, using *felix* and *beatus* interchangeably (see especially EA 1.15 no. 185). Compare also 1099b9–18 and 1098a19. In his comment on this last passage (EA 1.10 no. 129) Aquinas explicitly mentions that "in praesenti vita non potest esse perfecta felicitas" but nowhere uses *beatus* or any of its cognates, which he should do if it were important for him to distinguish the *beatus* from the *felix*.

8. By condition 3, I mean two things: (3a) it is logically possible for some person to be happy in that other way, and (3b) it is logically possible for such a person to be numerically identical to someone who is a human being. Perhaps conditions 1 and 2 by themselves could help show that some nonhuman person is not completely happy, but without conditions 3a and 3b, they cannot show that the happiness of some human being is not complete. Even if neither Aquinas nor Aristotle assumes that complete happiness is logically possible, conditions 1 and 2 without 3a and 3b will not count as evidence that a human being leading the active life on earth is not completely happy.

(EA 1.9 no. 114; compare EN 1.7.1097b14–15). This is ambiguous, depending upon how we construe the subsequent few lines. I follow Irwin[9] in thinking that Aristotle takes it in the following way:

> [Happiness] is the most choiceworthy of all, not being merely one good among many—if it were merely one good among many, then clearly it would be made more choiceworthy by the addition of the least of goods, [but since it is the most choiceworthy, the addition of the least of goods will not make it more choiceworthy, so happiness is not merely one good among many].

This is the inclusive sense of self-sufficiency: if G_1 by itself makes a life choiceworthy, but a life with G_1 is made more choiceworthy by the addition of G_2, then G_3 (let $G_3 = G_1 + G_2$) is more self-sufficient than either G_1 or G_2.[10]

According to Aquinas, there are two different ways in which something can be said to be self-sufficient. The first way is the inclusive way just mentioned. "In one way, a complete [*perfectum*] good is said to be self-sufficient if it cannot receive an augmentation of good through the addition of any good thing" (EA 1.9 no. 115). In this sense, the self-sufficient good G is the one that already includes all token goods which, if added to G, would augment the goodness of G. Aquinas thinks that the only being in the universe that is self-sufficient in this way is God (EA 1.9 no. 115).

The second way in which a good can be said to be self-sufficient, according to Aquinas, is exclusive.

> By itself, nothing else included, [a self-sufficient good] is sufficient insofar as it contains everything that a human being needs of necessity . . . nevertheless, if it is included together with anything else even minimally good, clearly it will be more choiceworthy. This is because through addition there is a superabundance or augmentation of good. So the more good a thing is, the more choiceworthy it is. (EA 1.9 nos. 115–116)

This is an exclusive sense of self-sufficiency. Suppose G_1 is a self-sufficient good and suppose that the addition of G_2 makes G_1 more

---

9. Irwin, "Permanent Happiness," p. 93.
10. What Aristotle says at 10.2.1172b28–34 appears to, but need not really, support the inclusive interpretation. In this passage Aristotle may be saying only that the good cannot be made better by the addition of a new type of good thing. This does not commit him to the view that the good cannot be made better by the addition of a new token good thing, the view to which I take the inclusive interpretation to commit him.

choiceworthy. We now have two self-sufficient goods, G_1 and G_3 (where $G_3 = G_1 + G_2$). Both G_1 and G_3, therefore, provide all the "necessities of life," but G_1 is more self-sufficient than G_3, according to Aquinas, because it does not require G_2. G_3 depends upon having G_2 in addition to G_1, whereas G_1 is not dependent on the extra G_2.

The idea here, presumably, is something like this. Select a person, S, whom Aristotle would be willing to call happy. S has everything necessary for happiness, so S's life is self-sufficient and choiceworthy. Suppose now that in fact S has one million dollars, which S uses for admirable public works, benefitting friends, and so on. It seems clear that it would be an additional good for S to possess an additional million dollars, for S could then sponsor more or greater public works, more greatly benefit more friends, and so on. However, by hypothesis, this additional million is not necessary for S to be happy. So S's life with the extra million is better, and hence more choiceworthy, than S's life without the extra million. But since we said that S's life without the extra million was a happy life, it turns out that some state is more choiceworthy than the state of being happy.

Given such a story, the inclusive view seems wildly implausible. On the inclusive view we must either accept that the additional million does augment the goodness of S's life, but deny that S was happy without the additional million; or accept that S was happy without the extra million, and deny that the extra million augments the goodness of S's life. Both options seem implausible. I would like next to try to make the inclusive view seem less implausible.

THE INCLUSIVE VIEW

A clean and well-made pair of shoes is a good thing. In modern city life, one needs several such good things in order to lead a happy life. If I had no shoes, it would make my life better were a decent pair of shoes to be added to my life. A second decent pair of shoes also might make my life better. From this, however, it does not follow that it is always the case that another decent pair of shoes will make my life that much better. It is not always true that if n good things improve one's life by n degrees, then $n + 1$ good things improve one's life by $n + 1$ degrees. There comes a point, at least with respect to shoes, when enough is enough. This must be true because there is such a thing as having too many shoes. There is a number of pairs of shoes n such that having n pairs of shoes actually makes one's life a bit worse than if one were to have significantly fewer than n shoes. But here I must make an important exception.

If I had nothing at least as important to do as clean and organize my shoe collection, then perhaps I would always count an extra pair of shoes as an improvement of my life. However, if I do happen to have other things to do which are at least as important as maintaining my shoe collection, then there comes a point where maintaining that collection takes time away from other worthwhile projects, making my life worse. Or, if I fail to maintain the collection, the clutter makes it difficult to get anything done in my apartment, thus making my life worse. It is possible to have too much of a good thing. Well and good for shoes, but how about for a million dollars?

Perhaps it never hurts to have a little more money. However, the fact that x never hurts does not entail that x always helps. By hypothesis, S was happy without the extra million. Now we give S an extra million, and clearly we have not hurt S or made S's life worse. But have we really improved S's life? Before getting the extra million, S had more to do with her time than simply spend money on friends and noble public works. Where will S find the time to spend the extra million? But perhaps time is not the problem. Perhaps S will take exactly the same amount of time spending money, but during that time S will plan larger, more expensive public works, give more to the same friends, and so on. In this case, isn't more necessarily better? Clearly not.

It is quite true that the virtuous person will work for her friends and her country, and will sacrifice her money and be willing even to sacrifice her life for them (EN 9.8.1169a20). However, she will also be willing to sacrifice *actions* to her friends or her country, allowing others to perform noble deeds themselves (EN 9.8.1169a33). Perhaps it never hurts a magnificent person to receive more money, but the magnificent person may never use some of the extra money. The magnificent person knows when and how much not to spend as well as when and how much to spend (EN 4.2.1123a20–27). But we need not think of such extreme circumstances.

There is a second reason why it is not true that the greater the public work is, the better the magnificent act is. A magnificent act must be "fitting," but what is "fitting" is determined relative to the giver (EN 4.2.1122a25 and b25). Surely a magnificent person gives readily and easily, without counting every penny (1122b7), but she also does not overreach her budget. She spends what is "fitting." But so does the magnificent person with twice as much money as S. They are both doing what is fine and "fitting" on a grand scale—Aristotle does not tell us just how grand the scale must be in order to count as a magnificent work—and so they are both doing perfectly magnificent things. Consequently, if S has one million, and P has two million, P's public works may be on a grander scale than S's, but that does not entail that P is more magnificent than S, and so it does not entail that P's life is any better than S's.

Now the inclusive view may not seem so implausible. Suppose that S is happy, and that S's net worth is one million dollars. Since she is happy, she must be exercising all the virtues. She is engaging in large, noble public works, she helps out her friends and family, she takes care of her own business, goes to parties and other social gatherings, and she takes time off to relax, enjoy the company of her friends, and to study. Now we give S a second million dollars. I assume we have not made her life worse. Have we really improved it? Before she was exercising her virtues to the fullest, benefitting her friends and the community in large and small ways. Afterwards she continues to exercise the virtues to the fullest, benefitting her friends and the community in large and small ways. It looks as if the change in her life is superficial and does not make it any better. Of course there is room for intuitions to differ here, but I hope this at least makes the inclusive view seem less implausible than it did at first.

If this does help the theory of happiness that Aristotle lays out in book 1 of the *Ethics*, we might nevertheless wonder how to square it with Aristotle's claims in book 10 about what he thinks can actually instantiate the concept of happiness.[11] In book 10 Aristotle appears to accept the exclusive interpretation of self-sufficiency when it comes to describing the actual sort of life which would instantiate happiness. He seems to say that the contemplative life is preferable to the active life because it is more self-sufficient, in spite of the fact that in the

---

11. We can distinguish between the concept of self-sufficiency and what, in fact, Aristotle thinks instantiates the concept of self-sufficiency. In fact, however, I think that Irwin is right about how to translate EN 1097b14–15, and so I think that even in book 1, Aristotle does not sit on the fence about self-sufficiency, but states the inclusive view.

contemplative life, one must give up many choiceworthy things.[12] I will turn to this issue soon, but there is another to be taken up first. I have already explained what a completely happy life might look like on the inclusive view of self-sufficiency. What might it look like on an exclusive view?

TYPES OF HAPPINESS

A good is complete if and only if it is always chosen for its own sake and never for the sake of something else (EN 1.7.1097a30–34; EA 1.9 nos. 109–111). In this sense, according to Aquinas, someone who has attained her complete good has attained the "ultimate terminus of the natural motion of desire," and so she must not be merely potential in any relevant way, but must have all of her potentialities fully actualized (1.9 no. 107). While it is not obvious that Aristotle understands completeness in just this way, he does believe that a happy person must be completely actual in this sense because he believes that happiness consists in fulfilling one's nature. But here we must draw a few distinctions.

ACTUALITY AND POTENTIALITY

Consider someone who knows nothing of French or Mandarin. If she is of normal intelligence, then she has the capacity to learn both languages. Call this capacity a "first potentiality."[13] Now suppose she learns both French and Mandarin. She has exercised her first potentiality and has a developed capacity that explains why, for example, she knows what the Mandarin word for "chair" is. Call this actualized first potentiality her "first actuality." This first actuality, however, is also a potentiality, since in virtue of knowing French and Mandarin, she has the capacity to speak either language at will. So the first actuality is the "second potentiality." Finally, when she is actually

---

12. Specifically at EN 10.7.1177a15 and 1178a2 Aristotle appears to make such claims. Aquinas takes advantage of these passages in EA 10.10 nos. 2080–2086 and 2107–2110 to attribute the exclusive view to Aristotle. I argue below that this is a reasonable interpretation of Aristotle, provided that we can attribute to Aristotle the view that someone numerically identical to me could be completely fulfilled without living the active life.

13. For these distinctions, see Aristotle's *On the Soul* 2.1, 2.5; *Metaphysics* 4.3, 4.5, 4.7–8, 5.12, 5.20; and Aquinas's ST 1–2.49.

speaking French or Mandarin, she is actualizing her second potentiality; call this the "second actuality."

Since there are two kinds of actuality, there are two ways of being perfectly actual: (1) being actualized in all of one's first potentialities but not all of one's second potentialities (call this "perfectly 1-actual"), and (2) being actualized in all of one's second potentialities (call this "perfectly 2-actual").[14] Cutting across this distinction is a threefold temporal distinction: is one perfectly actual only over a period of time, or is one perfectly actual all at once though impermanently, or is one perfectly actual at a time and permanently? In the previous example it is clear that no one can be perfectly 2-actual at a time, permanently or impermanently. It is impossible to be speaking both French and Mandarin at the same time (for any length of time, let alone permanently). One can, however, be perfectly 2-actual over time: one can first speak French, and then Mandarin. One can be perfectly 1-actual both at a time and over time: I can have a fully developed character with all the relevant first potentialities developed, or I might lose certain character traits while developing others, so that I have developed each first potentiality at some time, though there has never been a time when all of them were actualized simultaneously.

Since Aquinas and Aristotle accept that happiness requires perfect actualization, we must ask which of the four kinds of perfect actualization they require. It is clear that both think being perfectly 1-actual is not enough, for one can be perfectly 1-actual and spend most of one's life asleep or in a coma, in which case one surely would not be happy (EN 1102a32–b12; EA nos. 231–235).[15] So both think that happiness requires being perfectly 2-actual. Which type of being perfectly 2-actual does Aquinas think happiness requires?

We saw earlier that Aquinas attributes to Aristotle the belief that mutability rules out even the possibility of a life's being complete. In different places Aquinas understands this mutability differently. In his

---

14. This definition of "perfectly 2-actual" is ambiguous. One satisfies this definition by actualizing all of one's second potentialities even if one has not actualized all of one's first potentialities. When I use "perfectly 2-actual," I will mean one who has actualized all of her or his first potentialities.

15. See also EN 1.8.1098b30–1099a7; EA 1.10 nos. 119 and 123–130, 1.12 nos. 152–153, 10.9 no. 2066.

commentary on the EN, Aquinas is fairly clear that the relevant sort of mutability is the possibility that one will change from being happy to being not happy (EA 1.16 nos. 201–202; 1.10 129). Because human happiness requires external goods, and because it is always possible that severe misfortune will take those goods away, it is always possible (in this life) to change from being happy to being unhappy. Aquinas also mentions that continuity is necessary for happiness (EA 1.10 no. 129). Because this life will end, we cannot have perfect continuity in this life, hence we cannot have perfect happiness.

Aquinas employs different notions of mutability and continuity in the ST. At ST 1–2.3.2 ad 4, Aquinas cites EN 1.10 (the passage he expounds in EA 1.16 nos. 201–202) to support his claim that much stronger sorts of mutability and continuity rule out the possibility of our being perfectly happy in this life.

> In human beings, as regards the condition of this present life, the final perfection accords with an activity by which a human is joined to God; but this activity cannot be continuous. Consequently, neither is it unique, because an activity is multiplied by being discontinued, and on account of this, in the condition of this present life, perfect happiness cannot be possessed by a human being. . . . Consequently the active life, which is occupied with many things, fits the definition of happiness less than the contemplative life which is occupied with one thing.

Here it is clear that the discontinuity is, for example, the fact that we have to leave off exercising one virtue in order to exercise another (or to sleep, for which see ST 1–2.3.2 ad 6 which Aquinas claims to have answered in ad 4). This is significantly different from the view taken in the EA. We might express this difference in the terminology introduced above by saying that in the ST, the fact that we cannot attain perfect 2-actuality at a time permanently or impermanently (but at best only perfect 2-actuality over time)[16] by itself rules out the possibility of our being perfectly happy.[17] While the EA never suggests any such criterion, it does not explicitly rule it out either. Before we go

---

16. I cannot exercise all of my developed capacities at the same time (perfect 2-actuality at a time) but only over time. I cannot exercise all the virtues at once; rather, I must exercise first one, then cease exercising that one and then exercise another and so on (perfect 2-actuality over time).

17. This seems to be what underlies Pegis's interpretation of Aquinas's commentary on Aristotle. See Anton Pegis, "St. Thomas and the *Nicomachean Ethics*: Some Reflections on *Summa contra gentiles* III, 44, 5," *Mediaeval Studies* 25 (1963): 1–25.

any further, we should examine what reason someone might have for preferring perfect 2-actuality at some time, permanently or impermanently, over perfect 2-actuality only over time.

HAPPINESS AND DESIRE

Alan Donagan sketches one motivation for preferring perfect 2-actuality at a time and permanently over perfect 2-actuality only over time.[18] He writes that "nobody who believes the Christian revelation can seriously imagine that those who see God face to face can have anything more to want . . . the only thing that will put an end to the restless striving of human beings is the vision of God" (p. 33). He then claims that we can make sense of this on the basis of something Bertrand Russell once argued.[19] In one section of the passage Donagan refers to, Russell says this: "The primitive non-cognitive element in desire seems to be a push. . . . Certain sensations and other mental occurrences have a property which we call discomfort; these cause such bodily movements as are likely to lead to their cessation" (p. 38). The cessation, however, is only temporary, and so the striving for satisfaction must continue. Perfect 2-actuality only over time does not solve this problem (if it is a problem), because one achieves perfect 2-actuality over time as a result (if Russell is right) of recurrent pain that drives one on to the next satisfaction. Perfect 2-actuality over time does not provide a way to avoid the pain of continual desire: while I satisfy one desire, the other desires ache to be satisfied. On the contrary, if one is perfectly 2-actual at a time, then at that time, one has none of those pushes and so (if Russell is right) none of the discomfort mentioned. This would be a clear reason to prefer the latter over the former if such continual striving is a problem that we should want to solve. To decide this we must decide which is better: continual striving, or the state that results from successfully curing the striving.

In the same place Russell describes the cured state in this way: "When the discomfort ceases, or even when it appreciably diminishes,

---

18. Alan Donagan, *Human Ends and Human Actions: An Exploration in St. Thomas's Treatment* (Milwaukee: Marquette University Press, 1985). Page references are given parenthetically in the body.

19. Donagan refers to Bertrand Russell, *The Analysis of Mind* (London: George Allen and Unwin, Ltd., 1921). Page references are given parenthetically in the body.

we have sensations possessing a property which we call *pleasure*." If this is all there is to recommend perfect 2-actuality at some time, and Aquinas chooses it for this reason, then Aquinas turns out to be a hedonist. He would have to accept that our ultimate end is simply to be in the state of having satisfied all the desires one happens to have. But Aquinas clearly rejects this hedonism,[20] so Donagan does well not to attribute this part of Russell to Aquinas.

Donagan does point out part of Aquinas's motivation:[21] as long as we are still desiring things, there are still things that we take to be goods and which we lack—at least we lack them when we desire them.[22] To avoid the hedonism he rejects, Aquinas must avoid making the connection Russell makes between desire-satisfaction and pleasure. On the plain desire-satisfaction view of happiness, what there is to recommend happiness to us is that it is the state in which all our desires have been brought to rest. Rest comes, not, as Schopenhauer would have it, by ceasing to have desires (without satisfying them), but by fulfilling all one's desires. On this view of happiness, perfect 2-actuality at some time (permanently or impermanently) is to be preferred to perfect 2-actuality only over time because in the latter, one never achieves the state of having all of one's desires simultaneously at rest.

This view is open to an Aristotelian objection. We are social animals by nature, and so our happiness must consist in the laborious process of exercising our potentialities over time in community with others here in our animal bodies. Aristotle might admit that Aquinas has shown that (1) there is another type of happiness, and that (2) this other type of happiness has a better claim on being called "complete," but Aristotle would deny that we can, even theoretically, be happy in that way. Perhaps there is some being whose happiness would not be complete if it were living a life like mine, but that does not tell me that my happiness is not complete.

---

20. See EN 1.5.1095b14–22, 10.6.1176b9–1177a11; and EA 1.5 nos. 56–61, 10.9 nos. 2071–2079.

21. Compare ST 1–2.5.8 where Aquinas says that "to desire happiness is nothing else than to desire that one's will be satisfied." See also 1–2.4.5 ad 5, and 1–2.3.8, where he says that "man is not perfectly happy, so long as something remains for him to desire and seek."

22. If we achieved what we desired, then we would no longer be desiring it, we would be enjoying it; cf. ST 1–2.11.3.

THE ROOT OF THE DIFFERENCE

Aquinas deals with this at ST 1–2.188.8 ad 5 by arguing that we don't have to remain sociable by nature.

> A human being can live a solitary life in two different ways. First, as being unable to tolerate human society . . . and this is brutish. Secondly, because he is immersed in divine things, and this is something superhuman. Hence Aristotle says, "He who does not associate with others is either a beast or a god," that is, a godly man.

Here we begin to get to the root of the difference between Aquinas and Aristotle, for in the Aristotelian passage Aquinas quotes here, Aristotle commits himself to the view that no human being can become a god in the relevant sense. At EN 1166a20–22 he says: "No one chooses [*hairetai*] to have all [good things] becoming another (for as it is, the god has the good), but [one chooses good things for oneself] being what one is" (EN 9.4 1166a20–22).[23] The Greek for the last phrase is "all' ôn ho ti pot' estin." The only word I have not translated is *pote*. There is an ambiguity in the force of this word. It can be just a throwaway word, not worth translating,[24] or it can add a temporal notion to a sentence.[25] Depending upon what we take to be the subject of the phrase "all' ôn ho ti pot' estin," the *pot'* may or may not have temporal force. As I have translated the passage above, the *all' ôn* phrase refers to the subject of *hairetai* at the beginning of the quotation, and if we take it this way, there would be no sense to a temporal force in the *pot'*.[26]

If, however, one thought that the subject of the *all' ôn* phrase were

---

23. Aristotle has at least good *prima facie* evidence for this view. If a human being lost the capacity of sociability, then she would lose the capacity to care about the common good for its own sake (cf. 8.1.1155a22–28), and since every virtue aims at the common good (because it aims at the fine, 5.1.1129b11–19; 3.7.1115b11–13), she would lose the capacity for having *any* human virtue. Such a person could not count as a human being. Because Aquinas has a different view of the common good, he need not deny concern for the common good to a person who is no longer a social animal by nature.

24. Compare EN 8.7.1159a10 where, quite reasonably, the Latin translator simply does not translate the *pot'*.

25. For example, "Athênaios tis erôtêsê pote ton Periclea" ("an Athenian once asked Pericles").

26. Bywater takes the passage this way and so encloses in parentheses the clause "for as it is, the god has the good" to make it clear that it is semantically and syntactically separate from the *all' ôn* phrase.

"god" in the phrase "the god has the good," there might be some temporal force to the *pot'*. The Latin translation Aquinas uses takes the *pot'* this way and so translates it as *aliquando*, "at any time": "No one chooses to have all [good things] becoming another. (For as things are, God has the good, but he always is what he is at any time.)" While this is a possible reading of the text, it is not a likely one, given that Aristotle in this passage is pointing out that a virtuous person wishes goods to himself, and conceives of himself properly—he sees that he is "most of all" his intellect (9.4.1166a23). There is some motivation for taking the subject of *all' ōn* to be the subject of *hairetai*, and none for taking its subject to be *theos*. Aquinas, however, quite reasonably follows the translation in front of him, and so makes two mistakes. In EA 9.4 no. 1807, he infers that Aristotle's point is this:

> One wills oneself to be in the sense that that which is oneself is preserved [*conservatur*]. But that which is most of all kept [*conservatur*] the same in its being is God, who of course does not will any good for himself that he does not now have, but now has in himself perfect good, and he always is what he is at any time, because he is immutable. Now we are most like God as regards intellect, which is incorruptible and immutable, and so the being of any person is considered most of all in connection with intellect, and so the virtuous man who lives entirely according to intellect and reason most of all wills that he himself be and live. He also wills that he be and live as regards what is lasting in him, but anyone who wills that he be and live primarily as regards the body, which is subject to change, does not truly will that he be and live.

This reading yields two mistakes: (1) it gives Aquinas some positive reason for thinking that Aristotle believed perfect human happiness could consist solely in the contemplative life; (2) it prevents Aquinas from seeing that in this passage Aristotle is ruling out the possibility that a human being could become a god (or a separate intellect).

The second place at which Aristotle commits himself to the view that no human being can become a god is at EN 8.7.1159a3–12. Aristotle asks if one wishes the greatest good to one's friend, namely, that the friend be a god. He answers negatively. To wish good to one's friend, one's friend must remain who he is (1159a10). One's (human) friend cannot be a god, so one cannot wish the greatest good for one's friend.

Since Aquinas thinks that one's friend could become a god,[27] how can he interpret Aristotle's claim that one wishes good to one's (human) friend only insofar as he is human? First he points out that if one's friend becomes a god, then one's friend would no longer have friends, since gods have no friends (EN 8.7.1159a7–8; EA 8.7 no. 1636). But if one's friend changed and ceased to have friends, one would lose his friendship and so would lose a friend. But since one loves oneself most of all, one will not wish the greatest good for one's friend at the cost of the loss of a lesser good to oneself (EA 8.7 no. 1638).

This interpretation makes Aristotle sound uncharacteristically self-centered, especially in view of his claim at 9.8 (1169a18–20) that a virtuous person would be willing to die for friends and country if need be. Aquinas is well aware of the ways in which Aristotle thinks a virtuous person will be self-sacrificing,[28] but he points out in his comment on the passage that the sacrifice is still for the sake of a greater good for oneself (EA 9.9 no. 1878). This sort of self-sacrificing is theoretically consistent, therefore, with Aquinas's interpretation of EN 8.7, since both assume that the goods one wishes others are limited by what is in one's own self-interest. They are not in perfect harmony, however. If there are some circumstances in which you will give your life for a friend, why might you not wish your friend to become a god even if that would deprive you of friendship with the other? This difficulty by itself does not rule out Aquinas's interpretation of EN 8.7, since he can take it as a description of how friendships

---

27. The first hint we have that something has gone wrong in Aquinas is that while the greatest good according to Aristotle (both in the Greek and the Latin translation) is to be [a] god (1159a7), Aquinas says the greatest good is to be [a] god, or [a] king, or most virtuous. Perhaps Aquinas makes these additions on the grounds that the pagans ascribe some sort of immortality or divinity to great individuals. For a summary of how Aquinas deals with Aristotle's skeptical remarks in the EN about immortality, see Harry V. Jaffa, *Thomism and Aristotelianism* (Chicago: Chicago University Press, 1952), pp. 146–148.

28. It is interesting to notice that where Aristotle says that under certain circumstances a virtuous person would be willing to die for his friends and country (*tês patridos*), the Latin translation Aquinas uses (at least most of the time) replaces *tês patridos* with *pati*, "suffer," making the claim that "one will do and suffer many things for one's friends." In his comment, however, Aquinas is faithful to Aristotle, saying that "one would do many things for friends and country [*patriae*]."

normally do operate. Normally one covets a valued friend and is sorrowed to some degree at the thought of losing the friend, even if that means the friend would be better off.

What we must notice about Aquinas's interpretation of EN 8.7 is that by assuming that being a god and being most virtuous are relevantly similar for his purposes, Aquinas gains further evidence that Aristotle took seriously the idea that a human being could become a separate intellect. Thus he fails again to learn that Aristotle did not take this seriously. So according to Aquinas's Aristotle, we are significantly far from being completely happy if we are leading an active life in accordance with the virtues of magnificence, magnanimity, generosity, and so on. If we become "gods" and lead a secluded contemplative life, however, we lead a life which is very nearly completely happy.[29]

Perhaps the most obvious objection to raise against this view is that while contemplation of the truth might count as complete happiness for a purely intellectual being, it cannot count as complete happiness for a rational animal with a compound nature, especially if happiness is the fulfillment of one's specifying capacities. Aquinas himself raises this objection (EA 10.11 nos. 2105–2106). He quotes Aristotle as claiming that "it would be absurd if one were to choose to live not in accordance with a life proper to oneself but in accord with a life [proper] to something else" (no. 2109). Indeed, it would be even stranger if one's happiness consisted in the fulfillment of a life not proper to oneself.

But these words are part of Aquinas's defense. Intellect is that which is most fundamental (*principalissimum*) in human beings (EA 10.11 no. 2110; 10.12 no. 2116; 10.13 nos. 2135–2136), and so the life most appropriate for a human being is the life of intellectual activity (10.11 nos. 2105–2110).[30] This answer will not work, how-

---

29. Aquinas does claim that Aristotle accepts the view that no recognizably human life can be truly happy at EA 1.9 no. 113; 1.10 no. 129; 10.11 nos. 2102–2116.

30. Aquinas does not advocate the secluded, contemplative life except in peculiar circumstances (see ST 2-2.188.8), for he does not even think that in this life we can attain true contemplative happiness. Thinking we could was a mistake of Averroes's that Aquinas is eager to defeat; for Aquinas, true happiness can be attained only in the beatific vision after death. For Averroes's position, see *Commentarium magnum in Aristotelis De anima libros* 3.36 (edited by F. S. Crawford [Cambridge, Mass.: The

ever, if the intellect that we are fundamentally is our practical intellect, the rational faculty that guides our active life. Aquinas notices that Aristotle sometimes seems to be suggesting that it is our speculative intellect which we are fundamentally (EN 10.7.1177a15, 1178a2; compare EA 10.10 nos. 2080–2086; 10.11 nos. 2107–2110). What Aquinas does not take to heart is that Aristotle shows, after all the praise he has heaped upon the speculative intellect, that it is still our practical intellect that we are fundamentally.[31]

Aquinas will be justified in not taking this passage to heart in this way if he can find some passage where Aristotle makes clear that someone who is a human being at some time may also legitimately be considered to be not only a compound but also an intellect capable of independent existence. In fact, he thinks he can find just such a passage.

> It is clear that prudence and moral virtue are equally related to [circa] the composite [of body and soul]. The virtues of the composite, properly speaking, are human in so far as a human being [homo] is composed of soul and body. So life, [which is lived] . . . according to prudence and moral virtue, is human, and this is called the active life. Consequently happiness which consists in this life [i.e., in the active life] is human. But the speculative life and speculative happiness, which are proper to the intellect, are separate and divine.

Mediaeval Academy of America, 1953], pp. 479–502). For Aquinas's argument against Averroes, see *Contra gentiles* 3.41–45; and Pegis, "St. Thomas and the *Nicomachean Ethics*."

31. EN 10.8.1178b5. See also EN 9.8.1168b25–1169b2, where Aristotle points out that the admirable self-lover, the one who loves what he is most fundamentally, loves his practical intellect. Kraut argues that in 10.7 Aristotle does accept that we are, fundamentally, our speculative intellect (see Kraut, *Aristotle on the Human Good*, pp. 4 n.5, 129, 183, 184, 352 n.34). This interpretation is undercut by three things. (1) At 1178a7, Aristotle hedges his claims about the merits of the speculative life by adding the condition "if a human being is most of all his [speculative] intellect." If we are most of all that which is "controlling" in us, that which represents the interests of the whole soul, then he denies the antecedent of this conditional. (2) At 1177b26 he points out that the speculative life is not a human life. In what follows, Aristotle argues that we should not let this stop us from pursuing speculation. Of course this does not entail that he thinks the purely speculative life is the best life for a human being. (3) In 10.8 Aristotle shows that he has not lost sight of the fact that we are human beings and hence are to be identified most of all with our practical intellects (see especially 1178b5).

For present purposes it is sufficient to say just this much, for a fuller explanation would be more than is directly relevant to the issue. This matter is treated in the third book of the *On the Soul* [3.4.430a22] where it is shown that intellect is separate. So it is clear that speculative happiness is better than, or preferable to [*potior*], active happiness by as much as something separate and divine is better than, or preferable to [*potior*], that which is composite and human. (EA 10.12 nos. 2115–2116)

What we must see first here is that whatever Aristotle may mean in the relevant passage of the *On the Soul*, in the passage of the EN that Aquinas is explicating here, Aristotle nowhere claims that intellect is separate from the compound of soul and body. What Aristotle does claim is that "the virtue of intellect is separate [from the compound]" ("hê de tou nou kechôrismenê," 1178a22; "Quae autem intellectus, separata"). Of course one way that the virtues of the intellect could be separate, i.e., capable of existence independent of the compound, would be if they resided in a part of us that was separate from the compound. Of course, that is not the only way in which they could be separate. They could be separate simply in virtue of the fact that some beings do possess them, but that those beings (gods), do not possess bodies as we do. This latter claim does not entail that our intellects are separate from the compound of soul and body unless one also accepts that we can become "gods."[32] The text does not rule out Aquinas's interpretation, and since he needs it to defend Aristotle against an important objection, it is reasonable for him to take it the way he does. Even so, all things considered, the interpretation seems incorrect.

Given his interpretation of the passage, Aquinas can claim that Aristotle does not find it absurd to say that our true happiness consists in living a life that is not proper to something composed of body and soul. It is not absurd because most fundamentally what we are is an intellect that is separate from the compound of body and soul. A life proper to the intellect can be a life proper to us even though it is not a life proper to something composed of body and soul.

CONCLUSION

On Aquinas's account, the happiness we can achieve in this life is neither complete nor self-sufficient. Our happiness can

---

32. For this same reason one cannot show that our intellects are separate simply by

come closer to being complete and self-sufficient if we live the contemplative life. Thus Aquinas distinguishes three types of happiness:

H1: Happiness of the active life, the happiness of the life lived according to the moral virtues

H2: Earthly, superhuman happiness, the contemplative life of an embodied soul that requires some external goods

H3: Superhuman happiness to the fullest extent, the beatitude involving one's speculative intellect and one's resurrected body[33]

The most perfect happiness to be attained in this life, therefore, would be H2, a life that is as much like H3 as is possible in this life.[34]

The contemplative life is more self-sufficient than the active life, on the grounds that the contemplative life requires fewer external goods (EA 10.10 nos. 2093–2096; 10.12 nos. 2117–2120). The contemplative life requires only the bare necessities, such as food and drink (nos. 2093, 2117). The active life requires more. To be just, for example, one must have other people to whom to be just, and others with whom to cooperate in doing just acts (no. 2094). The contemplative life, therefore, is more self-sufficient if we take self-sufficiency in the exclusive sense.

The contemplative life is more complete than the active life on the grounds that contemplation of the truth is its own reward. It is not desired for the sake of anything else, while someone always acquires something extra from external actions (EA 10.10 no. 2097; 10.11 nos. 2101–2104). Virtuous action usually brings honor or favor (no. 2097). Aquinas is not saying that virtuous actions are done for the sake of these other goods, but only that part of their attractiveness for us is that they are the sorts of actions that yield these good results. More importantly, all of the moral virtues are directed to the common good which is desired because it affords the opportunity of contemplating the truth (no. 2101–2102). Hence the immediate goals of the

---

showing that intellect can exist independently from a compound of soul and body, unless one also accepts that we can become "gods" in the relevant way.

33. Compare ST 1–2.69.3. Actually there are two types of H3, one without the resurrected body and one with it (cf. ST 1–2.4.5 corp and ad 5).

34. See O. Brown, "Saint Thomas, the Philosophers, and Felicity," *Laval théologique et philosophique* 37 (1981): 69–82, especially p. 71.

active life are themselves desired for the sake of the contemplation of the truth, and so the active life is not complete, and so not happy (no. 2102).

Nothing Aquinas did in developing his interpretation is philosophically suspect. Aquinas has independent reasons for thinking that it is impossible for us to attain our ultimate end in this life. As a sympathetic interpreter of Aristotle, he will not attribute what he takes to be a false view to Aristotle if he can find some textual grounds for attributing to him what he takes to be the true view. In the interpretations we have just seen, as well as passages about the contemplative life in EN 10, Aquinas's interpretation is certainly motivated. In fact, in his interpretation of EN 9.4 (1166a20–22), we saw that he had the best translation of the text in front of him, but unfortunately the Latin translator made an important mistake. Aquinas does have to do quite a bit of work to make his interpretation cohere with everything Aristotle says, but we have not seen him make any illegitimate moves in defending his interpretation, and, given the state of the text, any good interpretation will encounter many textual difficulties.[35]

California State University, San Bernardino

---

35. For more on the question of whether Aquinas's commentary is philosophically suspect, see Joseph Owens, "Aquinas as Aristotelian Commentator," in *St. Thomas Aquinas, 1274–1974: Commemorative Studies* (Toronto: PIMS, 1974), pp. 213–238. We have also seen enough to argue against Gilson that if Aquinas's commentaries on Aristotle are merely expositions of Aristotle's doctrines, that is not incompatible with their also being expositions of his own philosophy. See Etienne Gilson, *History of Christian Philosophy in the Middle Ages* (New York: Random House, 1955), p. 367. I am deeply indebted to Normann Kretzmann and to Terence Irwin for helpful comments on earlier drafts of this paper.

Aquinas's Parasitic Cosmological Argument

Scott MacDonald

In *Summa theologiae* (*ST*) 1.2.3 Aquinas says that his first way of proving the existence of God is clearer (*manifestior*), seemingly meaning that it is the clearest of the five ways he will offer. Most philosophers who have considered the matter, however, have disagreed. The proof from motion has been almost entirely abandoned, and philosophers from Clarke and Leibniz to Rowe and Swinburne have preferred versions of the cosmological argument nearer to Aquinas's second or third ways.[1] One reason for the neglect of the first way is that it has been generally supposed to be subject to several obvious, devastating criticisms, among them that it crucially depends on archaic physical theory, ancient astrology, and one or more elementary fallacies. In this paper I argue that the proof from motion can be freed from the trappings of ancient science and astrology and defended against the most common of the strictly philosophical criticisms of it. Having defended the argument against some well-known criticisms, I argue that it nevertheless fails as an independent proof for God's existence because it depends for its validity on another of Aquinas's

---

1. See William L. Rowe, *The Cosmological Argument* (Princeton: Princeton University Press, 1975); and Richard Swinburne, *The Existence of God* (Oxford: Clarendon Press, 1979), chapter 7.

proofs for God's existence. Commentators have not adequately appreciated the significance of the parasitical nature of the proof from motion, though Aquinas himself did, as I argue in the final section of this essay.

I will draw on both of Aquinas's statements of the proof, the "first way" found in *ST* 1.2.3 and the first of the two "Aristotelian" proofs found in *Summa contra gentiles* (*SCG*) 1.13. The *SCG* and *ST* statements of the proof differ in two significant respects. First, in the more detailed discussion in *SCG* 1.13 Aquinas offers several subarguments and often gives more than one argument for each point that he thinks needs justification. By contrast, the *ST* discussion preserves only some of those subarguments and incorporates them into the body of the proof. I discuss only those subarguments that seem to me to be strongest and most useful for making my case. Whether or not the subarguments I do not discuss are good arguments seems to me to make no difference to the points I argue in this paper. All I need to do is to trace a single defensible strand running through the proof from motion. The second respect in which the two presentations of the proof from motion differ is in the statement of the conclusion. The *SCG* version of the proof concludes: "Therefore it is necessary to suppose that there is some primary unmovable mover" (*primum movens immobile*), while the conclusion of the proof from *ST* is apparently weaker: "Therefore it is necessary to arrive at some primary mover that is not moved by anything" (*primum movens quod a nullo movetur*). I think this second difference is important and I discuss it in the seventh section, below.

Following the presentation in *SCG* 1.13, the argument can be represented as follows:[2]

1. Everything that is moved is moved by something else.

---

2. The passage reads: "Everything that is moved [*movetur*] is moved by something else. But it is clear from the senses that something—for example, the sun—is moved [*moveri*]. Therefore it is moved [*movetur*] by something else that moves [*movente*]. Therefore that mover [*movens*] either is moved [*movetur*] or not. If it is not moved [*movetur*], then we have what we set out to prove, [viz.,] that it is necessary to suppose that there is some unmovable mover [*movens immobile*], and we call this God. But if it is moved [*movetur*], then it is moved by something else that moves [*movente*]. Therefore we either proceed to infinity or arrive at some unmovable mover [*movens immobile*]. But we cannot proceed to infinity. Therefore it is necessary to suppose that there is some primary unmovable mover [*primum movens immobile*]." I have supplied the

∴   2. Something—call it A—is moved.
∴   3. A is moved by something else—call it B—that moves. [1, 2]
    4. That mover, B, either (a) is moved or (b) is not moved.
    5. If 4b is the case, then there is some unmovable mover, viz., B.
    6. If 4a is the case, then B is moved by something else—call it C—that moves.
    7. If 4a is the case, then one either (a) proceeds to infinity or (b) reaches some unmovable mover.
    8. One cannot proceed to infinity.
∴   9. If 4a is the case, then one must reach some unmovable mover. [6, 7, 8]
∴ 10. There must be some primary unmovable mover. [4, 5, 9]

Aquinas himself sees that two of the premises of the proof—premises 1 and 8—need to be argued for, and critics have generally thought that either one or both of these are demonstrably false. In the second through fifth sections I discuss these premises and some recent, influential criticisms of them. In the sixth section I examine Aquinas's apparently unwarranted assumption (in premise 5, for example) that an unmoved mover is unmovable. This apparent assumption in fact masks a deep difficulty that exposes the parasitic nature of the proof. Before turning to the difficulties raised by these three premises, however, we need to look closely at the proof's observational starting point, premise 2.

        Premise 1 might be thought of as the theoretical premise that, together with 2—the observation premise—gets the proof off the ground. Premise 2 draws our attention to certain phenomena in the world, and 1, a universal proposition that takes as its instances phenomena of that sort, starts us on a search for causes or explanations. The remainder of the proof is intended to establish that the

---

Latin corresponding to the various forms of the verb "to move" because I think, as will emerge, that something of philosophical importance turns on the grammar. I use the Leonine edition of Thomas Aquinas, *Opera omnia* (Rome, 1882–) except for *In libros Physicorum*, where I use the version in Roberto Busa's edition of the *Opera* (Stuttgart and Bad Canstatt, 1980).

search can stop only at some unmovable mover. What sort of phenomena does Aquinas think provide the basis for this cosmological argument? He says that it is an argument from motion (*motus*) and that it is evident to the senses that something is moved (*moveri*). What does he understand by "motion" and "being moved"?

Following Aristotle, Aquinas takes *motus* to be a genus having three species: local motion, alteration, and increase and decrease (change in place, quality, and quantity, respectively).[3] So *motus* includes, but is not limited to, what we would normally call "motion," namely, local motion. In the presentation of the argument in ST he considers a case of alteration (a log on the fire growing hotter), while in SCG he cites a case of local motion (the sun's moving across the sky). The proof from *motus*, then, appears to begin from commonly observable physical motions and changes.

But we have to be careful not to construe *motus* too broadly. In the first place, it does not cover everything we might be willing to call "change," even though it covers some cases (alteration, for example) that we would prefer to call "change" rather than "motion." The coming to be or passing away of substances and so-called mere Cambridge changes—George Bush's changing from not being thought of by me to being thought of by me—are not instances of *motus* for Aquinas.[4]

In the second place, the way in which the argument proceeds makes it clear that certain cases of what we would be willing to call motions or movements have to be excluded from the scope of the observation premise. We would ordinarily say that anything that moves is in motion, but it is crucial to the validity of the proof that there are moving (active) things that are not moved (passive) things; that is, cases of moving that are not also cases of *motus*. A case of motion (*motus*) is a case of a thing of which we can say that it is moved or is being moved (*movetur*)—premise 2—and all such things are moved by something else—premise 1. But Aquinas denies that a primary mover is either moved by something else or self-moved, so he

---

3. *In libros Physicorum* 5.2. Aquinas points out, however, that sometimes "motion" is taken more broadly to include coming to be and passing away (see 3.2). In its broad sense *motus* is equivalent with *mutatio*; in its narrower sense it designates a species of *mutatio*.

4. Reasons for ruling out cases of these sorts emerge later in this section.

cannot suppose that a primary mover is moved (*movetur*) or that its moving is an instance of motion (*motus*).[5] The proof, then, depends on a distinction between moving and being moved, and not all instances of moving can be instances of *motus*.

Given that the proof depends on some sort of distinction between movers and moved things, it is natural to suppose that Aquinas uses the passive and active voices of the verb to mark the distinction. One might suppose, for instance, that when Aquinas claims (in the observation premise) that something is moved (*moveri*), he means the passive voice of the verb to be taken quite literally: something is being moved (by something that is acting on it). In other words, there is something that is the passive recipient of motion (from something that is its active mover).[6] Thus, the distinction between moving and being moved, movers and moved things, on which the argument depends might be the distinction between active movers (agents that possess and exercise active causal powers) and passive recipients of motion (things possessing capacities for being affected by agents exercising active causal powers). When a man pushes a stone by means of a stick, for example, the stick and the stone are passive recipients of motion from the man, who is an active mover. On the basis of a distinction of this sort Aquinas could exempt certain movers—movers that only give motion without receiving it—from the general principle expressed in premise 1.

---

5. In the division of the text at the beginning of *ST* 1.3, Aquinas explicitly denies that motion (*motus*) characterizes God, the primary mover.

6. Kenny, however, suggests that Latin uses the passive voice of the verb "to move" to express either the genuine passive or the intransitive sense of the verb. Thus, "the sun moves" or "the sun is moving" (intransitive sense) and "the sun is being moved" (passive sense) would be rendered in Latin by the same form of the verb—*movetur*. The passive form of the verb in the observation premise, then, might indicate only the intransitive sense of "to move." See Anthony Kenny, *The Five Ways: St. Thomas Aquinas's Proofs of God's Existence* (London: Routledge and Kegan Paul, 1969), reprint ed. (Notre Dame: University of Notre Dame Press, 1980), pp. 8–9. But the fact that Aquinas cannot allow the observation premise to cover all cases of intransitive moving shows, I think, that the passive form of the verb there cannot be taken as expressing the intransitive sense. For similar reasons I reject Blair's suggestion that the principle expressed in premise 1 be rendered "whatever moves is moved by another." See George A. Blair, "Another Look at St. Thomas' 'First Way,'" *International Philosophical Quarterly* 16 (1976): 301–314. Aquinas's conclusion presupposes the falsity of the principle Blair suggests.

Of course, taking the passive voice of the verb as marking the passive side of this distinction between agents and patients will affect how we understand the proof's opening moves. First, the observation premise must be read not as the unassailable commonplace that there are instances of motion broadly speaking, but as the claim that there are passive recipients of motion. This latter claim is certainly stronger than the former, but perhaps it too is unobjectionable. The stick and the stone seem to be straightforwardly passive recipients of motion.

Second, when the passive voice of the verb is taken in the way I have suggested, the general principle expressed in premise 1 must be read as the claim that everything that is a passive recipient of motion is moved by something else. Now it might be objected that this way of reading the general principle trivializes it, since on this reading, "is moved" appears to be analytically equivalent to "is moved by something else."[7] But this objection is mistaken. Taking things that exemplify *motus* as passive recipients of motion analytically entails only that they are moved by something, but not that they are moved by something *else*. In fact Aquinas's arguments in support of premise 1 are intended to rule out the possibility that things exemplifying *motus* might be *self*-moved rather than moved by something else. So the general principle, taken as I have suggested Aquinas intends it, is not trivial.

The analysis of motion to which Aquinas appeals in support of premise 1 shows more clearly what he takes to be the significant features of these instances of *motus*.

> But everything that is moved [*movetur*] is moved by something else, for something is moved [*movetur*] only insofar as it is in potentiality with respect to that toward which it is moved. But something moves [*movet*] insofar as it is in actuality, for to move [*movere*] is nothing other than to bring something from potentiality to actuality. But something can be brought from potentiality to actuality only by some being that is in actuality [*aliquod ens in actu*]. . . . But it is not possible for one and the same thing to be in potentiality and actuality in the same respect at the same time. . . . Therefore it is impossible that something be a mover [*movens*] and a moved thing [*motus*], or that it move [*moveat*] itself, in one and the same respect. (ST 1.2.3)[8]

---

7. Blair makes this claim in "Another Look," p. 301.
8. For the version of this argument in SCG 1.13, see note 18, below.

I will take up the details of this argument in the next section, but first I want to focus narrowly on Aquinas's characterization of motion in terms of potentiality and actuality. He says that something is moved (*movetur*) only insofar as it is in potentiality, and that something moves (*movet*) only insofar as it is in actuality. The active and passive forms of the verb apparently mark a distinction that Aquinas explains in terms of actuality and potentiality.

Aquinas is following Aristotle's characterization of motion (*motus*), which he explicates in his commentary on the *Physics*:

> Therefore, one should notice that a thing [can] be entirely in actuality, entirely in potentiality, or intermediate between potentiality and actuality. Therefore, what is entirely in potentiality is not moved yet [*nondum movetur*]; what is already in complete actuality, however, is not being moved [*non movetur*] but has already been moved [*iam motum est*]; therefore, that thing is being moved [*movetur*] which is intermediate between pure potentiality and pure actuality, which is indeed partly in potentiality and partly in actuality.
>
> This is clear in the case of alteration, for when water is hot only in potentiality it is not yet moved; when it has already been heated the heating motion has been completed; but when it shares in heat to some degree, but incompletely, it is being moved [*movetur*] toward heat, for what becomes hot shares in heat gradually by degrees. Therefore, the incomplete actuality of heat existing in the heatable thing is itself motion [*motus*], not, indeed, insofar as it is in actuality alone, but insofar as what already exists in actuality is ordered toward further actuality. For if one were to take away its being ordered toward further actuality, the actuality itself (however imperfect) would be the terminus of motion [*motus*] and not motion [*motus*], as happens when something heats partially. . . .
>
> Therefore, incomplete actuality has the character [*ratio*] of motion [*motus*], insofar as it is related both as potentiality to a further actuality and as actuality to something less complete. (*In libros Physicorum* 3.2)[9]

This passage highlights three essential features of motion.

First, motion characterizes things that are specifiable in terms of their being in states of potentiality and actuality. Moreover, to specify

---

9. In discussing Aristotle's proof from *motus* in *Physics* 8, Aquinas refers to this discussion of *motus* in book 3 of the *Physics*; see *In libros Physicorum* 8.10. (The English translation of Aquinas's commentary on the *Physics* seems inadvertently to have omitted the text I have translated as the last paragraph of this quotation. See *Commentary on Aristotle's Physics*, translated by Blackwell, Spath, and Thirlkel [London: Routledge and Kegan Paul, 1963], pp. 136–137.)

a thing as being in potentiality or actuality is to specify it as being in potentiality or actuality with respect to something. When Aquinas says that a thing can be entirely in actuality, entirely in potentiality, or intermediate between potentiality and actuality, he means that it can be entirely in potentiality with respect to some state S, entirely in actuality with respect to some state S, and so forth. Thus, a kettle of cold water is entirely in potentiality with respect to being hot; a kettle of boiling water is entirely in actuality with respect to being hot, but entirely in potentiality with respect to being cold. Aquinas often leaves unstated the qualification giving the respect in which a thing is in potentiality or actuality, but there must be some such respect for any case of motion.

Second, Aquinas explains *motus* in terms of states of incomplete or intermediate actuality. These states are characterized as incomplete or intermediate in virtue of their relations to preceding and succeeding states of the thing being moved: a thing is in a state of incomplete actuality when it is in actuality relative to some preceding state of potentiality but still in potentiality relative to some succeeding state of (further) actuality. Aquinas says that a thing is being moved when it is in incomplete actuality with respect to some end-state; that is, when it is partly in actuality with respect to it but also still ordered toward it as toward a further actuality. As he says, if one were to take away a thing's being in the process of attaining further actuality, one could no longer say that it is being moved (*movetur*), but only that it has reached the terminus of the motion.[10] Presumably, for similar reasons, if one were to take away the fact that the thing has already actualized some potentiality (to some extent), one could no longer say that it is being moved, but only that it is in the state from which motion begins.[11] Hence, to say that at some time a thing is being moved

---

10. Of course the actual terminus of the motion might not be the expected or intended terminus. If I put a kettle of water on the burner intending to bring the water to a boil, I intend the end-state of this motion (the heating of the water) to be the state in which the water is boiling. But if my wife, unaware of my intentions, turns the burner off before the water boils, the actual end-state of the motion in question will be the water's state at the time she interrupts the heating process.

11. On this analysis, the two termini of a given instance of motion will not be instants at which the thing can be said to be in motion; they will be extrinsic limits of the motion. Hence, the state from which motion begins will be the state it is in at the last instant of rest (there will be no first instant of motion). For discussion of medieval

involves covert reference to the thing's states at both earlier and later times. Being moved, then, involves process. Though we might be able to identify at specific times things that are being moved, their being moved consists in their being in the process of actualizing potentiality over an interval of time.

It follows from this second feature of *motus* that anything that is being moved thereby has two aspects or can be considered in two ways. In virtue of being moved a thing is in incomplete actuality with respect to some end-state, and is thereby in actuality in one respect and in potentiality in another. It is intermediate between an initial state (the state of being entirely in potentiality with respect to the final state) and the final state (the state of being entirely in actuality with respect to that state). It can be considered relative to either terminus—as being in actuality (though still incompletely actual in the relevant respect) or as being in potentiality (though no longer completely in potentiality in the relevant respect).

Third, when Aquinas says that what is being moved is in potentiality to further actuality he means not just that it *could* go on from its present state to a state of further actuality, but that it actually *is* going on to a further actuality. The kettle can be taken off the fire when the water is at 50 degrees, in which case the water at 50 degrees is not in motion, is not being moved. The state of being 50 degrees is the end-state of this particular case of motion, the final actuality, and so the water in this state cannot be said to be in incomplete actuality (with respect to this end-state).[12]

These points suggest that we can say of some thing M at some time t that it is being moved (*movetur*) if and only if:

a. at t, M is in actuality with respect to some state S_i (an intermediate state), and
b. in any interval of time (no matter how short) immediately prior to t, there is an instant at which M was in actuality with respect

---

analyses of motion and change, see Norman Kretzmann, "Incipit/Desinit," in *Motion and Time, Space and Matter*, edited by Peter K. Machamer and Robert G. Turnbull (Columbus: Ohio State University Press, 1976), pp. 101–136.

12. This raises a problem about how we could be certain at any given instant whether or not a thing is being moved, since often we cannot be certain that a thing's present state is an intermediate state in some process rather than the process's final state, at which point it would be correct to say that the process had ceased.

to state S_{pr} (a prior state not identical with S_i), and in virtue of being in actuality with respect to S_{pr} M was in potentiality with respect to S_i, and

c. in any interval of time (no matter how short) immediately after t there is an instant at which M will be in actuality with respect to some state S_{po} (a posterior state not identical with S_i), and in virtue of being in S_i (and S_{pr}) M is (was) in potentiality with respect to S_{po}.[13]

When conditions a–c are met, M can be said to be in incomplete actuality at t because, in virtue of being in S_i, M is in actuality relative to S_{pr}, but still in potentiality with respect to the further actuality S_{po}. Of course S_{pr} need not be the state from which a given instance of motion starts, and S_{po} need not be the given motion's end-state, but at any time at which M can be said to be moved there will be states of this sort. If we let S_e be the end-state of a given instance of motion and S_b be its beginning-state, then we can say that, with respect to this instance of motion, when M is in S_b it is in complete potentiality with respect to S_e, and when it is in S_e it is in complete actuality with respect to S_e (though of course, on this analysis, M is being moved at neither S_b nor S_e).[14]

Aquinas's observation premise will be true, then, just so long as there are things that satisfy these conditions, and his other claims about motion and moved things will be true just so long as they are true of these things.

With this characterization of *motus*, of what it means to say that something is moved (*movetur*), we are now in a position to

13. When S_{pr}, S_i, and S_{po} are states involving qualities, the motion will be a case of alteration. When they involve quantities, it will be a case of increase or decrease. When they involve spatial location, it will be a case of local motion. Moreover, given this analysis we can see why coming to be and passing away fail to be cases of motion strictly speaking: cases of a thing's coming into, or going out of, existence are not cases in which that thing is in successive states.

14. This analysis exemplifies what Kretzmann has called the strong definition of motion in his "An Alleged Asymmetry between Rest and Motion: A Reply to Richard Sorabji's 'Aristotle on the Instant of Change,'" part of an unpublished exchange between Kretzmann and Sorabji in 1976. One could obtain the corresponding weak definition by disjoining rather than conjoining conditions b and c. Aquinas seems clearly committed to the strong definition.

take up premise 1 of the proof—the claim that everything that is moved (in the sense specified) is moved by something else. Three common sorts of objections have been raised against premise 1. First, it has been claimed that some cases of motion are cases in which what is moved is moved not by something else, but by itself. Cases of this sort (animal and plant motion, for instance) constitute counterexamples to the general principle; animals and plants are *self*-movers.[15] Second, it has been objected that Aquinas has not established even the weaker claim that everything that is moved is moved by *something*. Why can it not be the case that some things are simply in motion without being (or having been) moved by anything? Third, if the general principle is read as the claim that whatever is moved is *now* being moved by something else (as it seems it should, for reasons that will emerge), then cases of projectile motion—a croquet ball rolling through a hoop, for example—appear to be cases in which what is moved continues in motion *after* the causal activity of its mover.

Aquinas defends the general principle expressed in premise 1 in the passage from *ST* 1.2.3 that I quoted in the previous section, and that argument will provide replies to the first two sorts of objection. The third objection requires separate treatment; I take it up in the fourth section. The argument from *ST* 1.2.3 can be elaborated in light of Aquinas's analysis of motion and represented as follows:

  i. Whatever is being moved toward some state S is potentially in S.
  ii. Something can be brought from being potentially in S to being actually in S only by what is in actuality with respect to S.[16]
∴ iii. Whatever is being moved toward S is being brought to being actually in S by some being in actuality with respect to S. [i, ii]
  iv. To move (*movere*) is just to bring something from being potentially in some state to being actually in that state.
∴ v. Whatever moves (*movet*) something toward some state is in actuality with respect to that state. [ii, iv]

---

15. Kenny, *Five Ways*, pp. 13, 16, 17.
16. I intend "being in actuality with respect to S" to be broader than "being actually in S" in important ways that I will explain in section 3, below.

∴ vi. Whatever is being moved toward S is being moved by something that moves (*movet*) it toward S.] [iii, v]¹⁷

vii. No one thing can be in potentiality and in actuality in the same respect at the same time.

∴ viii. Whatever is being moved (*movetur*) toward S cannot be identical with what moves (*movet*) it toward S. [i, v, vii]

∴ ix. Whatever is being moved toward S is being moved by something else. [iii, vi, viii]¹⁸

Aside from the logical truth expressed in premise vii, the argument has only three premises. Two of them—i and iv—encapsulate elements of Aquinas's analysis of motion; the third—premise ii—might be thought of as a sort of principle of sufficient reason for cases of motion. Though Aquinas's analysis of motion does not by itself entail that moved things are passive recipients of motion, that analysis together with the principle of sufficient reason endorsed in this argument does entail it. Things that are being moved are in potentiality in some respect and in the process of having that potentiality actualized; but potentialities are actualized only *by something* actual in the relevant respect.¹⁹ Similarly, a thing is properly said to move (*movere*) when it brings something from potentiality in some respect to actuality in that respect, and only what is in actuality in the relevant respect can do this.²⁰ So moved things, in virtue of being in poten-

---

17. Kenny has noted that Aquinas's proof from motion diverges from Aristotle's at this point. The claim expressed in premise vi is Aristotle's conclusion in the *Physics*, but Aquinas goes on to argue that everything that is moved must be moved by something *else*. See Kenny, *Five Ways*, pp. 14–15; and *Physics* 8.4.254b25.

18. In SCG the argument is given as a supporting argument separate from the main proof: "No one thing is in potentiality and in actuality in the same respect at the same time. But everything that is moved [*movetur*], insofar as it is of this sort, is in potentiality, because motion [*motus*] is the actuality of a thing existing in potentiality, insofar as it is of this sort. But everything that moves [*movet*], insofar as it is of this sort, is in actuality, because a thing acts only insofar as it is in actuality. Therefore, nothing is a mover [*movens*] and a moved thing [*motum*] with respect to the same motion [*motus*]. And so nothing moves [*movet*] itself" (SCG 1.13). See also *In libros Physicorum* 8.10.

19. See *In libros Physicorum* 8.10: "It was established in book 3 that what is moved [*movetur*] is movable [*mobile*], i.e., is something existing in potentiality. . . . But that which moves [*movet*] is already in actuality, for what is in potentiality is brought to actuality only by what is in actuality—and this is a mover [*movens*]."

20. This claim also shows that as Aquinas uses the active voice of the verb in these contexts it has its transitive sense. That which moves, moves *something*.

tiality in the relevant respect, are passive recipients of motion from movers that are active in virtue of being in actuality in the relevant respect.

Hence, the analysis of motion that lies behind premises i and iv, together with the principle of sufficient reason expressed in ii, entails that whatever is being moved is being moved by *something*. The role of vii is to secure the conclusion that what is being moved and what moves it are distinct; that is, that whatever is being moved is being moved by *something else*. Given the analysis of motion, a moved thing must be in potentiality in the relevant respect and, given the principle of sufficient reason, what moves it must be in actuality in that respect. Hence, the moved thing must be distinct from what moves it; a moved thing cannot be a self-moved thing.

So the argument in support of premise 1, with the analysis of motion on which it relies, constitutes Aquinas's reply to the first two sorts of objections raised above. Suppose, with the first objector, that at t an animal is being moved (*movetur*) toward S and is being moved by itself and not by something else. On Aquinas's account, if at t it is moved toward S, the animal must be (at t) in potentiality with respect to S; and if at t it moves something (namely, itself) toward S, it must be (at t) in actuality with respect to S. So the animal that is moved and moves itself is in potentiality and actuality in the same respect at the same time, which is impossible. Hence, there cannot be a case of the sort imagined. Aquinas thinks that self-moving animals in fact have parts, one of which (the soul) is the mover and the others the moved things. So Aquinas would be justified in rejecting alleged counterexamples involving self-moving moved things.[21]

Kenny objects, however, that even if Aquinas can rule out the possibility that what is moved is moved by itself, it still does not follow that it is moved by something else.

> If a thing cannot be moved by itself, it does not follow that it must be moved by something else. Why cannot it just be in motion, without *being moved* by anything, whether by itself or anything else? Does not the

---

21. But notice that this is an argument only against self-moving moved things. It shows only that something that is moved (*movetur*) cannot be the mover of itself. It does not show that animals, or rather animal souls, cannot be *unmoved* movers. But Aquinas need not rule out the possibility that animal souls are unmoved movers in order to defend premise 1, since it is a claim only about moved things.

argument need completing with a proof that whatever is in motion is being moved?[22]

Kenny directs this objection toward the general principle expressed in premise 1. Construed in this way, the objection misses the mark. According to Aquinas, whatever is moved is in potentiality, and whatever is in potentiality with respect to some state is brought to actuality only by what is in actuality with respect to that state. Something's being in motion entails that it is being moved. But perhaps Kenny's point can be reformulated so that it is not an objection to premise 1 but to Aquinas's principle of sufficient reason—premise ii of this subargument. We need, then, to look more closely at ii.

When directed toward premise ii—the claim that something can be brought from being in potentiality in some respect to being in actuality in that respect only by what is in actuality in that respect—Kenny's objection appears to ask for a defense of Aquinas's version of the principle of sufficient reason. As far as I can see, Aquinas has no argument to prove the principle. He undoubtedly thinks it self-evident; and if it needs defense, I cannot give it here. Nevertheless it is useful to see precisely to what version of the principle of sufficient reason Aquinas appeals and what role it plays in the proof from motion.

The principle stated in premise ii both asserts that certain sorts of phenomena require a cause (or explanation) and specifies the sort of cause (or explanation) that is required. Anything brought from potentiality to actuality with respect to state S must have a cause of its being brought from potentiality to actuality in that respect; the process of actualizing potentiality requires a cause. According to ii the sort of cause that can account for a phenomenon of this sort is one that is itself in actuality with respect to S. The actualizing of a potentiality requires explanation, and a sufficient explanation will cite the cause of the actualization, which must itself be in actuality in the relevant respect.

This version of the principle of sufficient reason is relatively weak. It does not require an explanation of every state whatever or even of every moving (*movere*). It requires an explanation only of changes

---

22. Kenny, *Five Ways*, pp. 18–19.

from potentiality with respect to some state to actuality with respect to that state.[23] The weaker the principle of sufficient reason on which an argument relies, the better; so it is a virtue of Aquinas's argument for premise 1 that it relies on a weak version of the principle. But that principle has work to do in support of other premises of the proof from *motus* as well and, as will emerge in section 6, it is doubtful that this weak version will bear all the weight imposed by a proof for God's existence. It is strong enough, however, to fulfill its role in support of premise 1. If we are willing to grant it, it seems to me that Aquinas's opening moves succeed: everything that is moved must be moved by something else.

Recent commentators, however, have offered reasons other than general worries about any such principle for thinking Aquinas's version of it false. Kenny, for instance, thinks that there are clear counterexamples to it. He has suggested taking Aquinas's principle as the claim that something can be brought from being potentially F to being actually F only by something that is actually F.[24] There certainly are cases of change in which what is actually F brings something else from being potentially F to being actually F. The oven's actually being 350 degrees, for example, brings the cake from being 350 degrees merely in potentiality to being actually 350 degrees. But the principle does not fit other cases: a farmer who fattens oxen need not himself be fat, and murders are not committed by dead men.[25]

Aquinas, however, has two reasons for rejecting these putative counterexamples. First, he denies that a cause must have the same actuality or form as its effect. On his view there are two ways in which a cause and its effect might fail to have the same actuality. First, the effect might have the same nature as the cause but have it to a lesser degree. The heat acquired by the cake in the oven is of the same nature as the heat possessed by the oven, though the oven may be at

---

23. Rowe has distinguished between two versions of the principle of sufficient reason. A strong version maintains that the existence of anything whatsoever requires an explanation; a weaker version maintains that only the coming into existence of things needs explanation (see Rowe, *Cosmological Argument*, chapter 2). The principle at work in premise ii is neither of these, since Aquinas is concerned about potentialities being brought to actuality rather than about things coming into existence, but it is in the same spirit as the second, weaker version.

24. Kenny, *Five Ways*, p. 21.

25. The counterexamples are Kenny's in *Five Ways*, pp. 21–22.

350 degrees and the cake only at 300 degrees.[26] Second, the effect might have, not the same nature as its cause, but a nature with less actuality. Aquinas calls causes that have a different nature from their effects "equivocal" causes.[27] God is an equivocal cause of the things he makes. God is the cause of inanimate objects but is not himself an inanimate object; God's nature is such that he has greater actuality than inanimate objects.[28]

Now, if we draw a distinction between being in actuality with respect to S and being actually in S, we can understand premise ii in such a way as to leave room for the sorts of cases Aquinas has in mind. We might say that a thing is in actuality with respect to S if it is either actually in S or in a state S* where S* is a state of greater actuality than S. Thus, if we let C be the cause of some object's coming to be in state S (where S admits of degrees), then C can be in actuality with respect to S to degree n in at least three ways: either by being actually in S to degree n, by being actually in S to some degree greater than n, or by being in some state S* with greater actuality than S.[29]

---

26. In light of cases of this sort, Kenny suggests altering the principle to "A can make B become F-er, only if A is itself F-er than B" (*Five Ways*, p. 22).

27. "Effects that fall short of their causes do not agree with them in name and nature. Yet some likeness must be found between them since it belongs to the nature of action that an agent produces its like (since each thing acts according as it is in actuality). Therefore, the form of an effect is certainly found in some measure in a transcending cause. . . . For this reason the cause is called an equivocal cause" (SCG 1.29). See also ST 1.4.3.

28. This requires us to understand Aquinas's notion of a hierarchy of natures, which I cannot develop here.

29. Patricia Matthews has objected that once one grants my distinction between a thing's being in actuality with respect to some state and its being actually in that state, premise vii no longer seems to be a logical truth and in fact seems false. On that distinction, a thing that is not actually in S might be in actuality with respect to S *and* potentially in S at the same time. At time t an oven might be at 350 degrees, and so in actuality with respect to being 300 degrees and also in potentially with respect to being 300 degrees (since the oven can cool to 300 degrees). There seem to me to be two different ways of replying to this objection. First, one might restrict the concepts of actuality and potentiality in such a way that one can say that at t, x is in potentiality with respect to S only if it is the case that x is not in S at t and can come to be in S after t and that x can come to be in S only by virtue of acquiring real or positive properties. On this line, the oven at 350 degrees could not be said to be in potentiality with respect to being 300 degrees because the oven can come to be at 300 degrees only by virtue of losing heat or energy. (The oven that is cooling, then, is not being moved

So premise ii must be read in light of Aquinas's doctrine of equivocal causes. Second, its application must be restricted to cases of immediate causation. Aquinas can reply to the case of the fattened oxen, for example, by denying that the farmer is the proper and immediate cause of the oxen's growing fat; the nutritive faculties of an ox's soul are the cause of its growing fat—an animal's soul has sufficient actuality to cause (equivocally) certain effects in the animal's body. (Of course the farmer is a remote cause by virtue of his providing hay for his oxen, for example.) Similarly, a murderer is not the proper and immediate cause of his victim's death, though he may be the immediate cause of an alteration in the body of the victim, an alteration he has sufficient actuality to bring about.[30]

Cases of local motion, however, are more difficult to accommodate. Premise ii appears to commit Aquinas to holding that something that is being moved from position A to position B (and so is in potentiality with respect to being at position B) must be moved by something else that is in actuality with respect to position B, i.e., that is actually at position B. But this seems clearly wrong. This objection to premise ii is closely related to the third objection to premise 1 that I raised in the second section, so I will discuss them together.

The argument for premise 1 that was laid out in the previous section requires us to take the premise as the claim that whatever is being moved is (now) being moved by something else. But cases of projectile motion seem to be cases of things that need not be moved by something else during the whole interval in which they are in motion. Something may be required initially to impart motion to a projectile, but after having been moved initially the projectile con-

---

[*moveri*] though it is moving [*movere*]; the surrounding environment is being moved.) Second, one might allow that the oven that is cooling from 350 to 300 degrees is being moved, but maintain that what counts as being in actuality with respect to some state depends on the direction of the motion toward that state. When the state of being at 300 degrees is the end-state of a process of cooling, things that are 300 degrees or cooler will count as being in actuality with respect to that state; when that state is the end-state of a process of heating, things that are 300 degrees or hotter will count as being in actuality with respect to it. On this line, the oven that is cooling will not count as being in actuality with respect to being at 300 degrees.

30. I am grateful to Alfred Freddoso for suggestions along these lines.

tinues in motion without continually being moved. So projectile motion constitutes a counterexample to premise 1.

Aquinas apparently mistakenly believed that the medium through which a projectile moves—for example, the air through which a ball is thrown—continues to move it.[31] This belief would explain why he did not see projectile motion as a difficulty for premise 1 (the air continues to move the ball after it has been released by the thrower) or local motion in general as a difficulty for premise ii (the medium stretches all the way to the end-point of the motion, and so is actually at the end-point). But of course, this explanation of local and projectile motion essentially depends on archaic physical theory.

I think these are genuine counterexamples to the respective principles, understood as Aquinas understood them, but it seems to me quite easy nevertheless to salvage Aquinas's argument. We can simply restrict premises 1 and 2 of the proof to a narrower range of cases than Aquinas intended, a range that excludes cases of local motion (and projectile motion as a subclass of local motion). The observation premise, then, would appeal not to *motus* generally but only to certain sorts of *motus*; premise 1 would claim that things that are now being moved in these particular ways are now being moved by something else. By restricting the range of the observation premise and the principle expressed in premise 1 we would be sacrificing generality. Still, provided there are *some* members of the domain to which we appeal, premises 1 and 2 will be true and the argument can proceed. Aquinas was misled by a false physical theory to overstate his case, but it seems easy enough to restrict his claim in relevant respects.

In fact, there are good reasons, ones that Aquinas acknowledges, for distinguishing local motion, on the one hand, from alteration and increase and decrease, on the other. Once that distinction is made we will have grounds for restricting the proof from motion to the latter sorts of *motus*, and we will be able to see how the principle expressed by Aquinas's premise 1 can be brought into line with modern physics.

Local motion involves change in place, and a thing subject to local motion changes in virtue of changes in characteristics that belong to the category of place. Characteristics in the category of place, however, characterize their subjects only extrinsically; that is, a subject is characterized by a predicate in the category of place in virtue of its

---

31. See Kenny, *Five Ways*, p. 16.

spatial location, and its spatial location is wholly extrinsic to the subject considered in itself.[32] Alteration and increase and decrease, on the other hand, involve changes grounded in characteristics from the categories of quality and quantity (respectively), and these sorts of characteristics characterize their subjects intrinsically.[33] So alteration and increase and decrease require an ontological ground in the subject considered in itself, whereas local motion does not. This can serve as the basis for a distinction between the former two species of motion and the latter. I will call instances of motion grounded in changes of intrinsic characteristics "*motion**" (*motus**).[34] Motion* is a species of motion but not a lowest species, since it is the genus for alteration and increase and decrease. By restricting the proof from motion to motion*, we will be able to rule out counterexamples involving local and projectile motion.

Having excluded local motion from the scope of the argument, however, it is worth noticing that cases involving projectile motion typically do involve elements that are genuine instances of motion*. When I throw a ball through the air, my arm imparts momentum to the ball. The ball's acquisition of momentum is a case of motion* (provided the acquisition is a process satisfying conditions a–c of the analysis of motion) since it involves a change in the ball's intrinsic characteristics.[35] Moreover, when I release the ball its momentum is

---

32. As Alfred Freddoso has pointed out to me, not all scholastic philosophers were in agreement on this point.

33. Aquinas distinguishes between types of change based on an intrinsic change (alteration, increase and decrease, and generation and corruption) and types of change based on extrinsic change (local motion) in his commentary on Aristotle's *Metaphysics* 12.7 (Cathala-Spiazzi no. 2530). Following Aristotle, he takes local motion to be the primary sort of change precisely because a thing that changes only in place does not suffer intrinsic change. (I take it that local motion is the primary sort of change because it requires the least change.) For more detailed discussion of the distinction between intrinsic and extrinsic characteristics and intrinsic and extrinsic change, see "The Metaphysics of Goodness and the Doctrine of the Transcendentals," in *Being and Goodness: The Concept of the Good in Metaphysics and Philosophical Theology* (Ithaca: Cornell University Press, 1991), pp. 31–55.

34. In terms of the analysis of motion in section 1 above, we can state this restriction as a restriction to cases of motion satisfying conditions a–c in which the states in question (S_{pr}, S_i, and S_{po}) are either qualitative or quantitative states of M.

35. Presumably an adherent of medieval impetus theory, and perhaps Aquinas, could accept an account along these lines.

gradually reduced by the friction of the air through which it travels, and that gradual change in the ball's momentum might also be a case of motion*.[36] The observation premise of the proof from motion*, then, might appeal to the ball's acquisition or loss of momentum, but not to the ball's local motion, as a starting point for the proof.

So the critics are right to point out that some of the grounds on which Aquinas holds premises 1 and ii do not support them, but they are wrong to suppose that these principles are thereby undermined. In the rest of this paper I will leave local motion out of consideration and assume that any objections based on features peculiar to it are irrelevant. As long as there are some cases of *motus** to which Aquinas's analysis applies—the fire heating the water in the kettle, for instance—the argument can proceed. (From now on when I use the terms "motion" and "being moved," I understand them as restricted to what I have just now been calling motion*.)

Aquinas's denial that there can be an infinite series of moved movers—premise 8—is the other premise besides 1 that Aquinas argues for in some detail and that commentators have found most objectionable. In the statement of the first way in ST Aquinas says:

> But this [series of moved movers] cannot proceed to infinity because then there would be no primary mover [*primum movens*]. Consequently, there would be no other mover [*movens*] either, because secondary movers [*moventia secunda*] move [*movent*] only in virtue of the fact that they are moved [*sunt mota*] by a primary mover. For example, a stick moves [*movet*] only in virtue of the fact that it is moved [*est motus*] by a hand. (ST 1.2.3)

It has been objected that this argument is fallacious since it does not follow from the denial of a primary (or first) mover in a series that no other things in the series can move or be moved. Of course, if one denies that there is a first mover in a *finite* series of movers, the motion cannot get started, as it were, and any potential secondary movers will remain merely potential movers. One way of denying that there is a first mover, however, is by maintaining that the series in question is infinite, in which case there will be no first mover, but an infinite number of movers nevertheless. Aquinas is not entitled to assume that

---

36. But see note 29, above, for a reason for denying that the loss of momentum is a case of motion*.

the series in question is finite. Hence the argument either begs the question or turns on an equivocation regarding "denying that there is a first mover."[37]

I think that this objection is misguided. Aquinas cannot intend the argument to rule out the possibility of an infinite series of causes or movers of just any sort, since he thinks that certain sorts of infinite series are at least possible. He admits, for example, that an infinite line of human ancestors extending back in time is at least a possibility. What sort of infinite regress, then, is Aquinas's argument supposed to block?

In ST Aquinas distinguishes between causal series ordered *per se* and causal series ordered *per accidens*, and it is clear that he means to claim that an infinite series is impossible only in series ordered *per se*:[38]

> It must be said that as regards efficient causes it is impossible to go on *ad infinitum per se*. For example, if causes that are required *per se* for some effect were multiplied *ad infinitum*, such as if a stone were moved by a stick, the stick by a hand, and so on *ad infinitum*. But it is not thought to be impossible to go on *ad infinitum* in the case of *per accidens* efficient causes. For example, if each of the causes that are multiplied *ad infinitum* possesses an order with respect to [only] one [other] cause, their multiplication is *per accidens*. The smith, for example, works by means of many hammers *per accidens* because one after another breaks. Therefore, it is accidental to this hammer that it works after the action of another hammer. Similarly, it is accidental to this man, insofar as he generates another, that he has been generated by another; for he generates insofar as he is a man and not insofar as he is the son of another man. . . . Thus, it is

---

37. This objection has been raised or discussed by Paul Edwards, "The Cosmological Argument," *The Rationalist Annual 1959*, reprinted in *Readings in Philosophy of Religion*, edited by Baruch Brody (Englewood Cliffs, N.J.: Prentice-Hall, 1974), pp. 71–83; C. J. F. Williams, "Hic autem non est procedere in infinitum," *Mind* 69 (1960): 403–405; Patterson Brown, "Infinite Causal Regression," *The Philosophical Review* 75 (1966): 510–525; Kenny, *Five Ways*, p. 26; and Rowe, *Cosmological Argument*, pp. 18–37.

38. Commentators who have recognized that Aquinas's argument against an infinite causal regress depends on this distinction have appealed to Scotus for an explicit account of the distinction. See, for example, Brown, "Infinite Causal Regression," pp. 218–227; and, following him, R. G. Wengert, "The Logic of Essentially Ordered Causes," *Notre Dame Journal of Formal Logic* 12 (1971): 406–422; as well as Rowe, *Cosmological Argument*, pp. 23–29. It seems to me, however, that there is plenty of evidence in Aquinas for constructing such an account, as will emerge.

not impossible that a man be generated by [another] man *ad infinitum*. But it would be impossible if the generation of this man depended on that man and on an elementary body and on the sun and so on *ad infinitum*. (*ST* 1.46.2.ad 7)

In order to evaluate premise 8, then, we will need to be clear about the distinction between these two kinds of causal series.

In this passage and in many other places, Aquinas takes over Aristotle's example of a man's being generated by a man and by the sun. The example has led some commentators to suppose that the distinction between two sorts of causal series rests on ancient astrology, according to which the heavenly bodies are causes of events in the sublunary world.[39] But the distinction seems to me not to depend crucially on astrology and to be defensible apart from such examples.

Aquinas draws the distinction in different ways in different passages. In the passage quoted just above, the distinction is between causal series in which prior causes are ordered to only one other posterior cause (or effect) and those in which the prior causes are ordered to all the posterior causes (and effects). Imagine the causal series D-causes-C-causes-B-causes-A. In a series of this sort D is ordered to C, C is ordered to B, and B is ordered to A. Now, Aquinas suggests that causal series ordered *per se* are ones in which some prior cause is ordered to all the other causes (and effects) posterior to it. Thus, if our imagined causal series is ordered *per se*, it will be the case, not only that D causes C, C causes B, and B causes A, but also that D causes B and D causes A. Consider a case in which a fire heats a kettle, which in turn heats the water contained in it.[40] In this case the fire moves (heats) the kettle and also the water (by means of the kettle), and so the fire is ordered to both the kettle and the water.

Causal series ordered *per accidens*, on the other hand, are such that each cause is ordered to *only* one other posterior cause (or effect). Thus, if our causal series is such that D causes C, C causes B, and B causes A, but it is not the case that D causes B and D causes A, then it

---

39. See Kenny, *Five Ways*, pp. 43–44; J. L. Mackie repeats Kenny's appraisal in *The Miracle of Theism* (Oxford: Clarendon Press, 1982), p. 87.

40. Aquinas's own example—a hand moving a stick, which moves a stone—involves local motion. For the reasons given in the fourth section, I am restricting the discussion to cases of alteration and increase and decrease. I think my example involving alteration captures what Aquinas takes to be essential in his.

will be a series in which each cause is ordered to only one other cause (or effect); hence, it will be a causal series ordered *per accidens*. Aquinas offers a genealogical series as an example of a causal series ordered *per accidens*. He thinks that if Abraham causes Isaac, who causes Jacob, it is not the case that Abraham causes Jacob; Abraham is ordered to only one other cause (or effect) in the series—to Isaac.

Of course there is at least some sense in which Abraham can be said to be one (if not the only) cause of Jacob, as well as of Isaac, so it might seem as if Aquinas's distinction collapses.[41] But Aquinas's characterization of the distinction in other passages helps to clarify his view. Elsewhere he characterizes the distinction as being between causal series in which the posterior causes exercise their causal power solely in virtue of the power of a prior cause (those ordered *per se*) and those in which the posterior causes exercise their own proper causal power (those ordered *per accidens*).[42] One might think of the kettle that heats the water as being under the (causal) control of the fire that moves it; it is not exercising a causal power it has independently of the fire. Isaac, on the other hand, possesses his own causal power and can exercise it of his own accord. He is an independently existing human

---

41. For commentators who have taken Aquinas's characterization of causal series ordered *per se* to depend on taking prior causes as antecedent necessary conditions, see Kenny, *Five Ways*, p. 43; and Anthony Flew, *God and Philosophy* (New York: Delta Books, 1967), paragraph 4.26. I claim that we might be willing to say that Abraham causes Jacob since Abraham's causal activity is a necessary condition of Isaac's causing Jacob. Brown, however, argues in support of the intransitivity of causal series ordered *per accidens* by claiming that we cannot say that Abraham begets Jacob, but only that Abraham begets Isaac; thus, "begetting" is an intransitive causal relation ("Infinite Causal Regression," pp. 226–227). But Brown's argument depends on the (irrelevant) fact that some ways of describing a particular causal relation may yield intransitivity, while other ways of describing the same causal relation may yield transitivity. For example, suppose my hand is pushing a stick to which is attached a string with a stone tied on the other end. When I push the stick, the stone is pulled along by the string that trails along behind the end of the stick. Aquinas would clearly take the case I have just described as a causal series ordered *per se*: the hand moves the stick and also moves the string and the stone. Hence, the causal relation (described as "moves") is transitive. But if I say not that the hand *moves* the stick, but that it *pushes* the stick, the relation is no longer transitive because the hand does not push the string or the stone—which are being pulled by the stick.

42. For example, "secondary movers move only in virtue of the fact that they are moved by a primary mover" (*ST* 1.2.3); "a secondary mover cannot move apart from a primary [mover]" (*In libros Physicorum* 8.9).

being possessing his own causal powers, and he begets Jacob by exercising those causal powers.

Aquinas often characterizes the secondary causes in causal series ordered *per se* as instruments, as in this passage from his commentary on the *Physics*.

> Further, [Aristotle] claimed above that the last mover does not move without the primary [mover]. . . . In this passage he says instead that it is impossible that that by means of which something moves [something else], as by an instrument, move anything without the principal mover which moved it; for example, the stick without the hand. (*In libros Physicorum* 8.9)

He tells us what he means by "instrument" in the following passage:

> Now a thing works for the production of an effect in two ways. In one way, as a *per se* agent, where that which acts by means of some form inhering in it in the manner of a complete nature (whether it has that form from itself or from something else, whether naturally or violently) is said to act *per se*. . . . In another way, a thing is said to work for the production of an effect instrumentally, where that thing does not work for the production of the effect by means of a form inhering in it, but only insofar as it is moved [*motum*] by a *per se* agent.
>
> For it is the nature [*ratio*] of an instrument insofar as it is an instrument that, having been moved, it moves [*moveat motum*]. Thus, the motion [*motus*] by which [the instrument] is moved by the principal agent is related to the instrument as the complete form is related to the *per se* agent. (*De veritate* 27.4)

In some causal series, then, the posterior causes are mere instruments by which a prior cause produces an effect. In such series the causal power of a prior cause—say D—is carried all the way through the other, posterior causes in the series to the final effect—A—so that one can say that D (*per se* and immediately) causes A. And, although each of the posterior causes can be said to be a cause, none exerts a causal power of its own but merely transmits the causal power of the prior cause. Because it is D's causal power that causes A, the causal series is ordered *per se*; one and the same causal power is at work through all the links in the series.[43] So when Aquinas says that sec-

---

43. In his commentary on the *Liber de causis*, Aquinas says that a causal series ordered *per se* is one in which the intention (*intentio*) of the primary cause is referred (*respicit*) all the way to the last effect through all the intermediate causes. Though he uses the word "intention" in this description, he seems not to mean that the primary

ondary causes (in causal series ordered *per se*) act only in virtue of the power of a primary cause, he does not mean only that the activity of a prior cause is some sort of necessary condition of the activity of the posterior causes. He means further that the posterior causes are exercising no independent causal power in the causing of the relevant effect.

In other causal series, by contrast, a different causal power is at work at each link in the series. Abraham's causal power is at work in the production of Isaac, but it is Isaac's causal power and not Abraham's that is at work in the production of Jacob. Causal series of this latter sort are ordered *per accidens* because there is no single causal power uniting the series. Isaac is not the instrument by which Abraham causes Jacob, but an independent cause with independent causal power.[44]

Given that causal series ordered *per se* are series in which a primary cause causes some effect by means of purely instrumental secondary causes, and given Aquinas's conception of purely instrumental causes, we can see why Aquinas claims that causal series ordered *per se* cannot go on to infinity. The instrumental secondary causes in series of this sort exercise no independent causal power, and so they cannot in themselves adequately account for the effect.

It might seem, however, that once all this is granted, our paradigm case of a causal series ordered *per se* (the fire heating the kettle, which

---

causes in such series must be beings capable of having intentions and that they must in fact intend the last effect in the series. He holds rather that the causal power of the primary cause is directed towards the final effect, whether by intention or nature or whatever.

44. Brown has focused on the transitivity of the causal relation as the key to identifying and understanding causal series ordered *per se*, but I think transitivity is not a sufficient condition of a causal series's being ordered *per se*. A man who lights a match which lights a fuse which ignites explosives which demolish a building can himself be said to cause the demolition of the building, but this is not a causal series ordered *per se* on Aquinas's account. Aquinas's view seems to be that a causal series ordered *per se* is a series in which the only independent causal power at work is the causal power of the primary cause. In the case of the hand moving the stick that moves the stone, the stick exercises no independent power; it is merely an instrument or a vehicle through which the hand exercises its causal power. In the case of the demolition of the building, however, the match, the fuse, and the explosives exercise their own causal powers. The match, the fuse, and the explosives, of course, would not exercise their causal powers were it not for the man's causality, but they are not merely instruments for his causal power.

heats the water) fails to satisfy the conditions for being a causal series of that sort. In our paradigm case the kettle appears not to be a purely instrumental cause since, according to the passage from *De veritate*, an instrumental cause causes not by means of a form inhering in it but only insofar as it is moved by an agent that acts *per se*. But the kettle has a temperature of its own (even if it was caused by the fire to have that specific temperature), and so it has a form of heat inhering in it and heats the water by means of that form. It seems, then, that the kettle in the paradigm case is not a purely instrumental cause, and the causal series described in that case seems not to be ordered *per se*. Indeed, we might wonder whether there are any genuine examples of causal series ordered *per se*.

If we look more closely at the paradigm case, keeping in mind Aquinas's analysis of motion, we can see how Aquinas's account of secondary, instrumental causes avoids this difficulty. Suppose that the water in the kettle is being brought to a boil by the fire, and suppose that S_e designates that end-state. Given that the case is an instance of a causal series ordered *per se*, the water (the last effect) is being moved toward S_e, and so it is in potentiality with respect to S_e. The kettle (a secondary, instrumental cause) is moving the water, but it also is being moved toward S_e, and so is in potentiality with respect to S_e. The fire (the primary cause) is only moving and is not also being moved toward S_e, and so it is in actuality with respect to S_e. Now, so long as the kettle is being moved toward S_e (even if it also moves the water), it cannot be the explanation of the water's being moved *toward* S_e. This is because only what is in actuality with respect to S_e can bring the water from being potentially in S_e to being actually in S_e, and *ex hypothesi* the kettle is not in actuality with respect to S_e. If it is in fact true that the water is being moved to S_e, and if Aquinas's principle of sufficient reason is true, then only the fire, which is in actuality with respect to S_e, can account for the water's being moved in this way.

To see this more clearly, imagine that at time t during the process of the water's being heated continuously from 0 to 100 degrees the kettle is at 50 degrees. At t the water will have a temperature less than or equal to that of the kettle. The kettle and its states at t explain the water's having (or having come to have) the temperature it does at t. They can explain this because the kettle is in actuality with respect to the relevant state of the water at t. But the kettle and its states at t

cannot account for its being the case that the water is being heated to 100 degrees. The kettle's being at 50 degrees is not the cause of the fact that the water at *t* is ordered toward that further actuality. Only the fire, which at *t* is in actuality with respect to the further actuality, being at 100 degrees, can account for that fact.

So even if the kettle in our paradigm case possesses an inhering form (its temperature), and moves the water by means of that form, it is not in virtue of the kettle and its inhering forms that the water is being moved to 100 degrees. What is essential to the kettle's being an instrumental cause in this particular case of motion is its lacking, at some time during the interval of motion, the form or actuality necessary to bring the motion to its end-state. The kettle is a mover that is itself being moved toward the end-state. So the kettle, like the water, is in potentiality with respect to the end-state, and hence lacks the actuality required of an explanation of the water's being moved to that end-state.[45] This is what Aquinas means, I think, when he says that an instrumental cause "does not work for the production of the effect by means of a form inhering in it, but only insofar as it is moved by a *per se* agent" (*De veritate* 27.4).[46]

It is clear, then, that Aquinas thinks that causal series in which at least one effect is something that is being moved (*movetur*) are causal series ordered *per se*.[47] The observation premise 2 is meant to call our

---

45. When the kettle itself reaches 100 degrees it will no longer be the case that it is being moved toward that state; it will have already been moved to it. So it will be in actuality in the respect necessary for bringing the water to that temperature.

46. In *ST* 1.45.5 Aquinas makes it clear that instrumental secondary causes may possess an inhering form that gives them certain causal powers. These powers may play a role in the production of the final effect but are not of the right sort to account for its realization. The example there is of a saw that cuts wood by virtue of its own form, thereby producing the form of a bench, which is nevertheless the proper effect of the craftsman, who is the primary cause. I am grateful to Alfred Freddoso for pointing this passage out to me.

47. "One finds three things in [cases of] motion [*motu*]: (1) the movable thing that is moved [*movetur*], (2) something else that is the mover [*movens*]; and (3) an instrument by which the mover moves [*movet*]" (*In libros Physicorum*, 8.9). See also *In libros Metaphysicorum* 12.6 (Cathala-Spiazzi no. 2517). In *In libros Physicorum* 8.9, and in the passage from *ST* 1.46.2 ad 7 that I quoted above, Aquinas points out that in a given series ordered *per se* there might be no secondary causes or an infinite number of secondary causes. In either case there must be a primary cause on the causal power of which each secondary cause (if there are any) depends.

attention to an effect in a causal series ordered *per se*, and the two main theoretical premises 1 and 8 are meant (respectively) to show that there must be at least one mover in a series of this sort and that not all movers in such a series can be secondary, purely instrumental movers.

It is important to see that this argument against an infinite regress differs from two superficially similar kinds of argument that appear in cosmological proofs. One sort of argument claims that a secondary cause can serve as a sufficient explanation of a thing's being moved, but that the motion of the secondary cause itself must be explained. Thus, in one's explanation of the first phenomenon one introduces a second phenomenon that needs explaining. Hence, even though the first case is explained, we are left with something else to explain. If there is no primary cause, there will be an infinite number of things to explain; and where there is no end to the explaining, there is no adequate explanation. The second sort of argument claims that there may be an infinite series of secondary, dependent causes, each explaining the next, but that one will still need an explanation of the series as a whole, and any such explanation must appeal to some primary cause outside the series itself.[48]

Aquinas's argument against an infinite regress as I have just sketched it is of neither of these kinds. He thinks that citing a secondary mover is not an adequate explanation of some thing's being moved. It is not that an explanation of this sort explains, but at the cost of introducing something *further* to be explained; it is that it does not explain. One must find a primary mover in order to explain some thing's being moved.

It seems to me, then, that the most common objections to premises 1 and 8 of Aquinas's proof from motion can be met. There is, however, another problem for the proof. Assuming that Aquinas can block a regress in the case of movers and things moved, why must the primary mover be not just unmoved, but unmovable? Aquinas thinks that if the mover of some moved thing is not itself moved, it is an unmovable mover (premises 5 and 7). What justification does he have for supposing that an unmoved mover is unmovable?

The sort of causal series he has in mind in the proof from mo-

---

48. Blair mistakenly takes Aquinas's first way to be an argument of this sort ("Another Look," pp. 303–304).

tion has as a member something, M, that is being moved. M's going from being in potentiality with respect to some state S to being in actuality with respect to S needs to be explained by some primary mover, P. All that is required of P is that it be in actuality with respect to S; P's being in actuality with respect to S is what makes P the primary mover in this causal series ordered *per se*. So in order to count as a primary mover, as the stopping point in a causal series ordered *per se*, P must be unmoved (because it is in actuality) in the relevant respect. But it does not follow from this that P must be unmoved (and hence in actuality) in *all* respects. If P were in actuality in all respects, P would be absolutely unmoved and unmovable, but the fact that P is unmoved with respect to some state S does not entail that P is unmovable.[49]

Given that Aquinas's argument so far has shown only that there must be some primary mover that is in actuality in the respect relevant to the particular case of motion at hand, it seems likely that there will be very many relatively uninteresting primary movers. The fire in our paradigm case seems to be a suitable primary mover, animals (or their souls) might be unmoved movers, and some of Aquinas's own examples of causal series ordered *per se* apparently have human beings filling the role of primary mover, at least as Aquinas describes them.[50] We might call fire, animals, human beings, and other natural unmoved movers (if there are any) mundane primary movers. The problem, then, is that the proof from motion gives us no reason to suppose there are any primary movers other than mundane primary movers.[51]

In at least some contexts, Aquinas seems to be aware of the problem of mundane primary movers. In stating the second of the two "Aristotelian" proofs in SCG, he takes up the possibility that animals or human beings are unmoved movers. The second "Aristotelian" proof proceeds in two stages. Aquinas argues first that there is a primary mover, and then that this mover is absolutely unmovable and separate. Aquinas begins the second stage of the argument: "But

---

49. Kenny raises an objection of this sort in *Five Ways*, p. 23.
50. See *In libros Physicorum* 8.9: "Therefore, the man of himself is the primary mover, and he moves the stone through several intermediaries."
51. See Blair, "Another Look," pp. 310–311.
52. See *In libros Physicorum* 8.12, where Aquinas makes the same claim about Aristotle's strategy.

Aristotle proceeds further . . . because from the conclusion that there is a primary mover that is not moved [*non movetur*] by anything exterior to it it does not follow that it is completely unmovable" (SCG 1.13.21).[52] He repeats the arguments from the first "Aristotelian" proof against the position that the primary mover is a self-moved moved thing and then offers four arguments to show that the primary mover must be absolutely unmovable. The first three of these four arguments closely follow the text of *Physics* 8 (258b23 ff.);[53] the last is drawn from *Metaphysics* 12.

The general strategy of the first three arguments is to show that the existence of primary movers that are movable in some respect (mundane primary movers) entails the existence of a primary mover movable in no respect. The first of these arguments, for example, argues that mundane primary movers are corruptible (or contingent), and so must be explained by appeal to something incorruptible, which will be an unmovable mover.[54] The third argues that there must be some eternal (beginningless) mover, since motion is eternal, but no mundane primary mover can be an eternal mover (each mundane primary mover's moving begins). Mundane movers cannot be eternal movers because even if they are not moved *per se* and so do not depend on another mover for the very causal power by which they move, they are moved *per accidens* and so depend on other things in order to move, though not for the very causal power by which they move. Animals that are primary movers with respect to some local motion, for instance, are moved *per accidens* in that they depend on nutritive processes such as digestion and breathing in order to initiate local motion.[55]

I cannot evaluate these arguments from contingency here. I want only to point out that they are themselves cosmological proofs essentially *different* from the proof from motion. Their starting points are the existence of corruptible beings of a certain sort or the beginninglessness of motion, not the fact that some particular thing—the sun in the sky or the log on the fire—is moved. It appears that the

---

53. See *In libros Physicorum* 8.12–13.

54. SCG 1.13.24; see *In libros Physicorum* 8.12. Compare *In libros Metaphysicorum* 12.6 (Cathala-Spiazzi no. 2501).

55. SCG 1.13.26; see *In libros Physicorum* 8.13. In *In libros Metaphysicorum* 12.5 (Cathala-Spiazzi no. 2494), Aquinas connects the argument from corruptibility with the argument from the eternity of motion.

proof starting from an instance of *motus* and relying on the weak version of the principle of sufficient reason I have discussed can get us only as far as mundane primary movers. The proof for an absolutely unmovable mover must take a different phenomenon as its starting point and will require a different version of the principle of sufficient reason.[56] If these arguments from contingency are the only bridges Aquinas has from mundane primary movers to an unmovable primary mover, then the proof from motion must contain another cosmological argument—perhaps the third way—as an integral part. These other cosmological arguments might stand on their own, but the proof from motion is invalid without one of them. Of course, this is not to say that the proof from motion fails; it is just to say that it is parasitic on another version of the cosmological argument.

Of the four arguments for an absolutely unmovable mover that are offered in *SCG*, however, the last suggests another argument that might be construed as an attempt to bridge the gap between mundane primary movers and the unmovable primary mover. Following Aristotle, Aquinas takes animals and human beings to be composed of an unmoved moving part, the soul, and a moved part, the body. Aquinas denies, however, that this unmoved moving part—the soul—is absolutely unmovable:

> For since every mover [*movens*] is itself moved [*moveatur*] by appetite, it must be that the mover [*movor*] that is a part of what moves itself moves on account of appetite for some appetible object that is superior to it in moving [*in movendo*]. For what has an appetite [*appetens*] is a kind of moved mover [*movens motum*], but what is appetible is an altogether unmoved mover [*movens omnino non motum*]. Therefore, there must be a

---

56. Salamucha has pointed out that the second "Aristotelian" proof in *SCG* is linked with the proof from the contingency of the world. But he claims that it is for this reason that Aquinas found it unsatisfactory and abandoned it in favor of the third way when he wrote *ST*. See J. Salamucha, "The Proof Ex Motu for the Existence of God," *New Scholasticism* 32 (1958), reprinted in *Aquinas: A Collection of Critical Essays*, edited by Anthony Kenny (New York: Anchor Books, 1969), reprint ed. (Notre Dame: University of Notre Dame Press, 1976), pp. 175–213, p. 117. But I see no evidence that Aquinas found it unsatisfactory. His statement, "But two [objections] seem to count against the arguments given above," does not, as Salamucha supposes, indicate his dissatisfaction with the second proof. It is merely a way of raising possible objections that he goes on to rebut. On the link between the proof from motion and the proof from contingency, see section 7, below.

primary, separate, altogether unmovable mover [*primum motorem separatum omnino immobilem*], which is God. (SCG 1.13.28)[57]

This argument purports to show that souls cannot be absolutely unmovable movers: souls are moved by the objects of their appetites. If there is an absolutely unmovable mover, it cannot be a soul, but must be an appetible object. But must there be an absolutely unmovable mover?

Aquinas might be suggesting the following line of reasoning. A soul cannot after all be a primary mover in a causal series ordered *per se*, because it moves with respect to some state S only by virtue of some appetible object. For example, the hand would not be using the stick as a lever to pry the stone out of the field if the farmer's soul were not moving it; the farmer would not be willing that the stone be moved from his field, however, if he did not desire to grow crops. So it is after all the farmer's desire to grow crops that accounts for the farmer's willing and the stone's being moved. If this is what Aquinas has in mind, then the argument seems intended to show that one has to move farther along in the causal series to reach a primary mover than one might have thought. One has to get to an appetible object.

If this is the argument, it is a striking move.[58] It is striking because it is a move from explanation in terms of efficient causality to explanation in terms of final causality. The proof from *motus* has invoked efficient causes at each stage until now—the stick that moves the stone, the hand that moves the stick, and the soul that moves the hand are all efficient causes of motion. But the appetible object that moves a soul is a final cause of the soul's motion. Apparently, that is why Aquinas says "for what has an appetite is a kind of moved mover" (*quodammodo movens motum*). It is a "kind of" moved mover because it is moved by a different sort of causality from that by which the hand or the stick is moved.[59]

---

57. Aquinas attributes this argument to Aristotle in the *Metaphysics*. See *In libros Metaphysicorum* 12.7 for Aquinas's commentary on the relevant text.

58. I am not sure, however, that Aquinas does intend this argument. In his commentary on the *Metaphysics*, at least, Aquinas takes it as established (at the end of 12.6 [Cathala-Spiazzi nos. 2517–2518]), on the basis of the arguments from the *Physics* I have just sketched, that there is an absolutely unmovable mover whose substance is actuality. He then argues (in 12.7) that an absolutely unmovable substance must be an appetible object.

59. Aquinas frequently asserts the principle that the final cause is the cause of all

Still this argument does not succeed in bridging the gap between mundane primary movers and the unmovable mover; it simply replaces one sort of mundane primary mover (souls) with another (appetible objects). The argument gives us no reason to suppose that the appetible objects that will count as the primary movers are absolutely unmovable movers.

Of course, final causes as well as efficient causes can be ordered *per se*.[60] The farmer may desire to grow crops only because he desires to eat, and so on. Some ends, then, will be purely instrumental, but it seems we will never get to an unmovable mover that is God. The farthest we can go, even on Aquinas's account, is the farmer's happiness, and then only the farmer's conception of happiness.[61] The farmer's conception of happiness (whatever that is) will be the primary mover in any causal series ordered *per se* in which the farmer's will figures as a moved mover. So there is still a gap between the conceived ultimate good and God. Moreover, the conceived ultimate good need not exist at all (except in the conceiver's mind) in order to play its role as primary mover. The argument from souls to appetible objects, then, is not sufficient to bridge the gap between mundane primary movers and the primary mover that is God.

Perhaps Aquinas intends the move from souls to appetible objects to lead in another direction. In the fourth way (*ST* 1.2.3), he argues to the existence of God from the existence of things that are good or noble to some degree or in some respect. If that proof works, then we have a way of getting from appetible objects to the existence of God: appetible objects are good to some degree, and so they constitute a

---

the other causes. See, for instance, his *In Posteriorum Analyticorum* 1.16: "But causes are arranged in a definite order to one another: for the account of one [cause] depends on another. Thus an account of the matter depends on the form. . . . Moreover, an agent accounts for the form. . . . Finally, it is on the end that the account of the agent depends." This general principle squares with the line of reasoning I am suggesting.

60. See, e.g., *ST* 1–2.1.4.

61. For discussion of Aquinas's views on the role of final causes in human intention and action, see my "Egoistic Rationalism: Aquinas's Basis for Christian Morality," in *Christian Theism and the Problems of Philosophy*, edited by Michael Beaty (Notre Dame: University of Notre Dame Press, 1990), pp. 327–354; and "Ultimate Ends in Practical Reasoning: Aquinas's Aristotelian Moral Psychology and Anscombe's Fallacy," *The Philosophical Review* 100 (1991).

starting point for the fourth way. But if the proof from motion must be completed by appeal to the fourth way, it will be invalid on its own.

It seems, then, that the proof from motion is incomplete. It may be that the third or fourth way will fill the lacuna in the proof, but in any case it is essentially parasitic on some other proof for God's existence.

I have suggested that there is evidence in SCG 1.13 indicating that Aquinas was aware of the problem of mundane primary movers. In his presentation of the second "Aristotelian" proof, he acknowledges that the claim that there is a primary mover that is not moved by anything exterior to it does not entail that there is a primary mover that is completely unmovable. He proceeds to offer supplementary considerations that do, in his view, imply the latter claim. Now this development in the discussion of the second "Aristotelian" proof occurs only after the presentation of the first proof has been completed with the explicit conclusion that there is a primary unmovable mover, and so it might seem that Aquinas does not see the lacuna in the first proof.[62] It seems to me plausible, however, to suppose that he was aware of the parasitic nature of the first "Aristotelian" proof and that he left it unremarked in view of the forthcoming supplementary discussion.

There is some interesting evidence in *ST* 1.2.3 that supports this assumption. As I have said, the presentation of the first way in *ST* differs in only two respects from the presentation of the first "Aristotelian" proof in *SCG*. The first of these—the fact that in *ST* Aquinas incorporates two of the subarguments from *SCG* into the main body of the proof—is relatively unimportant. But the second difference—the fact that Aquinas states the conclusion of the proof differently in the two presentations—seems to me significant. In *ST* he concludes, not that there is some primary unmovable mover, but only that there is some primary mover that is not moved by anything.[63] This latter

---

62. There is a question, of course, about how the second stage of the second Aristotelian proof might relate to the first Aristotelian proof. These arguments are for the most part taken from *Physics* 8 (257a35 ff.), from the text immediately following that which provides the proof from motion. See Aquinas's *In libros Physicorum* 8.9–12.

63. This way of stating the conclusion is quite close to that at the end of the first stage of the second Aristotelian proof in *SCG* 1.13. *ST*: "Ergo necesse est devenire ad

statement of the conclusion is weaker than the former, and in just the way we would expect if Aquinas were aware of the problem of mundane primary movers.

If I am right that Aquinas saw the problem of mundane primary movers and that his drawing only the weak conclusion to the first way shows his awareness of it, then we are left with two other exegetical questions. First, why does Aquinas suppose, later in *ST*, that he has established the strong, modal conclusion that the primary mover is unmovable? In texts just following the presentation of the five ways, for instance, he claims that he has shown that there is some primary unmovable principle (*ST* 1.2.3 ad 2) and that there is some primary unmovable mover (*ST* 1.3.1). It might seem that Aquinas thinks that the first way warrants this stronger claim even if he did not state it as the first way's explicit conclusion.

I think this explanation is incorrect, and I think the context of Aquinas's later claims in fact supports my thesis. I have argued that Aquinas would be entitled to the stronger, modal version of the conclusion only after the proof from motion has been supplemented by other proofs, perhaps the third or the fourth way. The fact that in *ST* Aquinas makes the modal claim only after the presentation of the five ways (and so after the presentation of the third and fourth ways) shows, I think, that he takes the first way to be parasitic on these other proofs in just the way I have suggested. He draws only the weak version of the conclusion at the end of the first way because he sees that it is all he is entitled to. Then, after he has filled the lacuna in the

---

aliquod primum movens quod a nullo movetur." Second Aristotelian proof: "Ergo relinquitur quod oportet ponere aliquod primum quod non movetur aliquo exteriori." In *SCG* Aquinas explicitly acknowledges that this conclusion is an inadequate stopping point for a proof for God's existence. See my discussion in the sixth section, above. Notice that the conclusion given in *ST* is ambiguous. Given my analysis of the proof from motion, I think it should be read as the claim that there is some primary mover that is not being moved by anything with respect to S, where S is the end-state of the motion identified in the proof's observation premise. It might alternatively be read as the stronger claim that there is some primary mover that is not moved by anything in any respect. Taken in the latter way, I think the conclusion is unwarranted by the proof (for the reasons given in the sixth section, above). Even if we read it this way, however, it is still weaker than the modal version of the conclusion stated in *SCG*. It does not follow from the fact that something is unmoved that it is unmovable.

proof with the third or fourth way, he goes on to state and use the stronger, modal conclusion.

This interpretation of Aquinas's procedure seems to me to be clearly supported by a close look at the first appearance of the modal claim in *ST*. It occurs in his reply to the second objection in *ST* 1.2.3. The objection argues that it is unnecessary to suppose that God exists since all features of the world can be explained by appealing either to nature or human reason and will—in effect, by appealing only to mundane primary movers. Aquinas replies that nature must be directed by a higher agent, God, and that human reason and will must be explained by a higher cause, too. This is because human reason and will "are changeable and corruptible [*mutabilia et defectabilia*]. But all things that are changeable and susceptible to corruption [*deficere possibilia*] must be traced back to some primary principle that is unmovable and of itself necessary, as has been shown" (*ST* 1.2.3. ad 2). In my view the striking feature of this part of Aquinas's reply is his conjoining the starting points and conclusions of two of the five ways, the proof from motion and the proof from contingency.[64] The starting point of this little argument is that human reason and will are both changeable and corruptible, and its conclusion is that there must be something that is both unmovable and of itself necessary. Aquinas has run together the first and the third ways, and it is here—with the first and third ways simultaneously called to mind—that he first claims that the primary mover must be unmovable. I think this is not inadvertent but, rather, shows that Aquinas knows that the first way is parasitic on the third.

The second exegetical question raised by my claim that Aquinas knew that the first way is a parasitic cosmological argument is why he chose to include it in *ST* among his proofs for God's existence. If it is essentially parasitic on the third or fourth ways, why not simply present these latter proofs, leaving the former aside altogether? Moreover, why would he present it as the clearest of the five ways when he knows that it is not a complete way at all?

---

64. To call a thing *defectabile* might be to say that it is corruptible either in the sense that it can go out of existence or in the sense that it can be flawed or suffer imperfection. The latter sense might call to mind the possibility of degrees of goodness or nobility, in which case the reply to the second objection would connect the first way with the fourth.

The answer, I think, is that he takes the proof from motion to be the clearest of the five ways not in the sense that it is the easiest way of proving God's existence but in the sense that it begins from the most readily accessible phenomena. Ordinary processes of change are ready to hand, immediately obvious to the senses, in a way that the contingency of things, their degrees of nobility, and their being related in a providential world order are not. A plainer starting point cannot be had.

So Aquinas would have straightforward strategic reasons for opening his discussion of the proofs for God's existence with a proof that begins from phenomena that are obvious to anyone.[65] He also has theoretical reasons for starting with a proof that begins from what is obvious to the senses. Aquinas's empirically based theological methodology requires us to proceed toward knowledge of God on the basis of God's sensible effects; Aquinas's Aristotelian empiricism requires us to proceed toward what is knowable in itself on the basis of what is better known to us, namely, what is obvious to the senses. Each of the five ways starts from God's sensible effects, and it would be natural for Aquinas to begin the five ways as a whole with a proof that starts from the most obvious of those effects.

Aquinas must have thought that these strategic and theoretical considerations in favor of the first way outweighed the difficulty presented by the parasitical nature of the proof. The first way by itself could not resolve the issue raised in *ST* 1.2.3 ("Does God exist?"), but it can contribute to the discussion by preparing the way for the independent proofs that follow it. After all, the proof is not seriously flawed, only incomplete. Aquinas intended his readers to find the completion of the proof in the immediately succeeding paragraphs of *ST*.[66]

University of Iowa

---

65. These strategic reasons would be all the stronger if his intention in *ST* is to provide a manual for the teaching of theology.

66. I am grateful to Evan Fales, Alfred Freddoso, and Norman Kretzmann for comments on earlier versions of this paper.

Peter of Candia's Hundred-Year "History" of the Theologian's Role

STEPHEN F. BROWN

Pitros Philargis (Petrus Philaretus) was born of Greek parents on the island of Crete (Candia) around 1340. Left an orphan at an early age, he was cared for by Italian Franciscans. After joining the Franciscan order on Crete in 1357, he was sent to Padua for his studies in the Arts. He attended the Franciscan *studium generale* at Norwich and also that at Oxford, where he received his baccalaureate in theology. From 1378–1380, he lectured *ordinarie* on the Sentences at Paris, obtaining his doctorate in theology in the fall of 1381. Quite likely he became a lecturer in Lombardy, for we know he was lecturing on theology at the convent of St. Francis in Pavia during the school year of 1384–1385.

Ioannes Galeatus, the duke of Milan, saw great promise in Peter's oratorical and administrative abilities and made him one of his counselors. His talents were also noted by Pope Urban VI, who named him bishop of Placenza in 1386. Early in 1388 Peter became bishop of Vicenza; a year later, of Novara; and within three years, of Milan, where he became cardinal in 1405.

These episcopal offices did not interfere with his temporal duties in the service of Ioannes Galeatus. Peter was the prime minister to

Galeatus and his son for more than a decade. He was also a "Father of letters" in the literary circle of the duke of Pavia from the time he arrived to teach there. He was a close friend of Hubertus Decembris, the leading representative of humanism in Lombardy, and of Antonius Lusco, the learned humanist who was chancellor to the duke of Milan. Peter's sermons and poems show a man deeply learned in humanistic sources, a man of lofty literary style. His *collationes*, or principal sermons, presented as introductions to each of his commentaries on the four books of Lombard's *Sentences*, reveal a striking literary power and a vast knowledge of patristic sources. His commentaries on the *Sentences* offer a clear academic style and show him to be a well-balanced scholar rather than a deep, creative thinker.

During the last half of Peter's life, the Christian world was in great disarray. In 1278, Clement VII claimed for himself the papal authority held legitimately, but not clearly, by Urban VI. The great schism that ensued in the Western religious world led over the years to a growing number of advocates of conciliarism. Along with many other cardinals, Peter saw a general council as the solution to this ecclesiastical conflict. On 25 March 1409, a general council was called at Pisa with the hope of putting an end to the schism. The council, after many stormy sessions, declared both popes deposed, and in the nineteenth session it elected Peter as pope. Taking the name of Alexander V, Peter did not settle the papal conflict. In fact, his election only confused things more, by increasing the number of popes to three. He set up his residence at Bologna in January 1410 but died there, in the convent of St. Francis, on 3 May of the same year.[1]

---

1. For the best general introductions to the life and works of Peter of Candia, see F. Ehrle, *Die Sentenzenkommentar Peters von Candia*, Franziskanische Studien 9 (Münster in Westf.: Aschendorff, 1925); as well as L. Salembier, "Alexandre V," *DTC* 1 (1923), cols. 722–724; and A. Emmen, "Petrus de Candia, O.F.M. *De immaculata Deiparae conceptione*," in *Tractatus quatuor de immaculata conceptione B. Mariae Virginis*, Bibliotheca Franciscana Scholastica 16 (Quaracchi: Collegium S. Bonaventurae, 1954), pp. 235–259. The only parts of his *Sentences*-commentary edited so far are the convocation sermons that he delivered each term on the four books of Lombard and the *De immaculata Deiparae conceptione* (an excerpt from book 3 of the *Sentences*). See S. F. Brown, "Peter of Candia's Sermons in Praise of Peter Lombard," in *Studies Honoring Ignatius Charles Brady, Friar Minor*, Franciscan Institute Publications, theology series 6 (St. Bonaventure, N.Y., 1976), pp. 141–176; and Emmen, "Petrus de Candia."

As we have mentioned, Peter of Candia delivered his lectures on Lombard's *Sentences* at Paris over the two-year period 1378–1380. He opened the prologue to his *Commentary* on book I, where theology teachers usually asked what kind of habit or developed ability is fostered by study in the theology faculty, with the question: "Does the intellect of human beings here in this world acquire through theological study evident knowledge of revealed truths?"[2]

In formulating his response Peter provided a brief introduction to the positions of the great thirteenth- and fourteenth-century thinkers who influenced him both negatively and positively: Thomas Aquinas, John of Naples, Peter Aureoli, John Duns Scotus, William of Ockham, and Gregory of Rimini.

AQUINAS'S POSITION

Peter of Candia notes only two things concerning Aquinas's position: Thomas held that the ability developed by theological study is science in the proper Aristotelian sense of the term; and, more specifically, that theological study has the character of a subaltern science.[3] Interpretations of what exactly the Angelic Doctor was trying to say in the first question of his *Summa theologiae* provoke divisions not only among his modern-day interpreters or such famed commentators as Cajetan and John of St. Thomas but also among his contemporaries in the schools of theology.[4]

Following the detailed critique of Godfrey of Fontaines, the four-

---

2. Peter of Candia *Sent.* 1.pro (lines 6–8). The edition is given below, in the appendix.

3. Peter of Candia *Sent.* 1.pro.1 (lines 163–164, 188–189, 197–198, 444–445). Cf. Thomas Aquinas *Summa theol.* 1.1.2.

4. For the interpretations of the classical commentators, see the references given by J. A. Weisheipl, "The Meaning of *Sacra Doctrina* in *Summa theologiae* I, q. 1," *The Thomist* 28 (1974): 56–60, where he presents the views of Cajetan, Bañez, Sylvius, John of St. Thomas, Billuart, Buonpensiere, and Garrigou-Lagrange. For the more recent understandings of Thomas, some starting points would be J. Beumer, "Thomas von Aquin zum Wesen der Theologie," *Scholastik* 32 (1955): 195–214; J. F. Bonnefoy, "La théologie comme science et l'explication de la foi selon saint Thomas d'Aquin," in *Ephemerides Theologicae Lovanienses* 14 (1937): 421–446, 600–631, and 15 (1938): 491–516; M. D. Chenu, *La théologie comme science au XIIIe siècle* (Paris: J. Vrin, 1957); M. Grabmann, "Il concetto di scienza secondo s. Tommaso d'Aquino e le relazioni della fede e della teologia con la filosofia et le scienze profane," *Rivista filosofia neoscolastica* 26 (1934): 127–155; G. F. Van Ackeren, *Sacra Doctrina: The*

teenth-century theologians Scotus, Aureoli, Ockham, and Rimini took Aquinas to mean what he said in the passage in its proper and strict sense.[5] Godfrey, for example, in his *Quodlibet* 4 of 1287, represents Thomas as holding that the theologian, while proceeding from principles that are held by divine faith, arrives at conclusions concerning which he truly has science.[6] The plausibility of such a position is founded on the parallel that Aquinas saw between Aristotle's view of the relation of a subalternating and subaltern science and the case of theology. Just as a subaltern science, such as optics, borrows principles from a subalternating science, such as geometry, and still is a true, if subaltern, science, so theology borrows its principles from the knowledge that God and the blessed in heaven have of the divine mysteries. Using such truths as premises, theology arrives at conclusions that are true, though subaltern, science.[7]

Godfrey, however, accepted neither the logic of the main argument nor the simile. For him science carries a twofold certitude: the certitude of evidence and the certitude of adherence, i.e., holding to the truth of something without any doubt. Faith has the latter type of certitude, but not the certitude of evidence. Faith, then, resembles knowledge to the extent that it has certainty but differs from knowledge because it lacks the certitude of evidence. Faith also is like opinion insofar as both faith and opinion lack the certitude given by evidence; but faith differs from opinion since it has the certitude of adherence, which opinion lacks.

Subject of the First Question of the Summa Theologica of St. Thomas Aquinas (Rome: Catholic Book Agency, 1952); and the article of Weisheipl mentioned above. C. Dumont provides helpful leads to early attemps to interpret Thomas in a more favorable light than Godfrey of Fontaines in his article "La réflexion sur la méthode théologique (II)," *Nouvelle revue théologique* 84 (1962): 26–32.

5. Scotus *Sent.* 3.24.1.2–3 (ed. Vivès, 15:36–37); William Ockham *Scriptum in I Sent.* pro. 7 (ed. G. Gál and S. F. Brown, 184); Peter Aureoli *Scriptum* 1.pro.1.2–8 (ed. E. M. Buytaert, 1:132–133); Gregory of Rimini *Sent.* 1.pro.1.3 (ed. Venice, 1521, a6vL–Q).

6. Godfrey of Fontaines *Quodl.* 4.10 (ed. M. DeWulf and J. Hoffmans, *Les philosophes belges* 2:261). Cf. P. Tihon, *Foi et théologie selon Godefroid de Fontaines* (Paris and Bruges: Desclée De Brouwer, 1966), pp. 120–131. Henry of Ghent likewise criticizes the subalternation theory of Aquinas in his *Summa quaestionum ordinariarum* 7.5 (Paris, 1520, ff. 53r–54v).

7. Thomas Aquinas *Summa theol.* 1.1.2.

Basing his argument on the foundation of these distinctions, Godfrey argued:

> Therefore, to say that the principles of theology or of any science whatsoever within theology are only believed and not known or understood, and thus while only having the certitude of adherence that they produce the certitude of science in the conclusions drawn from them, is to say that conclusions are better known than the principles, namely, that the conclusions have both types of certitude whereas the principles have only the one. Now this is to say contradictory things, and it harms on a large scale theology and its teachers to propose such fictitious claims concerning it to those entering upon its study.[8]

> Neither is the simile that is introduced into the argument worthwhile, because no one with a balanced mind understands that subaltern science is truly science if it only has opinion about its principles, for it gets them from a higher science and awards to them purely human faith due to the fact that they are known and handed down by an expert in a higher science. For whatever is drawn from principles that are handed down or held on faith—since they could not have certitude unless they went back and established it in those principles—would only be believed or accepted as opinion. Whatever is drawn from such principles might even be weaker than the principles themselves. So, then, is it the case with theology: although the principles of theology may be most certain in themselves and evident to God and the blessed, yet insofar as they are revealed by God, they are believed. Just as human authority begets opinion, a state of mind lacking both types of certitude, so divine authority produces faith, a state of mind having the certitude of adhering without fear of error. Of what advantage is it for a person using such principles accepted on authority and only believed by him and deriving conclusions from them, that the blessed have the certitude of evidence in regard to the principles and that the principles in themselves are evident and certain? The certitude of the blessed does not bring him evidence. Therefore, it is necessary that the principles of subaltern science be certain with the certitude of evidence in order that one may have science of the conclusion derived from them.[9]

---

8. Godfrey of Fontaines *Quodl.* 4.10 (ed. DeWulf and Hoffmans, *Les philosophes belges*, 2:261).

9. Godfrey *Quodl.* 4.10 (262).

Early reaction to Godfrey's presentation of the subaltern approach to theology gave rise to a different reading of Thomas's text by James of Metz,[10] Hervaeus Natalis,[11] and Bernard of Auvergne.[12] By the time we come to Duns Scotus, the arguments defending the subaltern science position are not strictly speaking Thomas's but those of these followers.[13] In Peter Aureoli's *Scriptum*, the supports for Aquinas's theory are sevenfold and subtle, but Aureoli admits frankly that they may not really represent Thomas's own position ("quamvis non ponantur ab eis").[14] In fact they come from Godfrey and Scotus, at least in their direct formulation, though in turn they may well represent earlier attempts to clarify Thomas's position itself.[15] When we come to our author, Peter of Candia, any real historical connection with Aquinas is gone. Candia gives Aquinas's name, but the position is not meant to be a historical portrait of the Angelic Doctor's theory. Thomas's position represents the limit position of evidence: the study of theology never brings the student to such evidence that he in this life has the certitude of evidence for his conclusions. To expect such is to ask too much of theology.[16]

THE THEOLOGY OF CONSEQUENCES

If there is an outer limit of expectation for Candia, so is there an inner limit of expectation—when one allows no evidence at all in regard to the contents of theological discussion and reduces theology to a knowledge of consequences. In this view the theologian is considered a believer who has the ability to lead theological conclusions back to the basic principles or truths of faith. Already in the

---

10. Cf. C. Dumont, "La réflexion," p. 26, n. 64.

11. See E. Krebs, *Theologie und Wissenschaft nach der Lehre der Hochscholastik an der Hand der bisher ungedruckten Defensa doctrinae D. Thomae des Hervaeus Natalis*, BGPM 11/3–4 (Münster, 1912), p. 37*.

12. See P. Stella, "Teologi e teologia nelle 'Reprobationes' di Bernardo d'Auvergne ai Quodlibeti di Goffredo di Fontaines," *Salesianum* 19 (1957): 187–189.

13. Scotus *Sent.* 3.24.1.2–3 (ed. Vivès, 15:36–37).

14. Aureoli *Scriptum* 1.pro.1.1.23 (ed. Buytaert, 1:139). For the arguments themselves, see nos. 2–8 (1:132–133).

15. See S. R. Streuer, *Die theologische Einleitungslehre des Petrus Aureoli* (Werl in Westf.: Dietrich-Coelde Verlag, 1968), pp. 64–65.

16. Peter of Candia *Sent.* 1.pro.1 (lines 162–166).

1230s Odo Rigaud defended a place for theology among the sciences, defined according to the new Aristotelian ideal, by showing that sacred science uses scientific procedures. The theologian truly arrives at *conclusiones causaliter demonstratae*, since he follows the demonstrative process of Aristotelian science.[17]

Though theology may imitate the Aristotelian method of argumentation, still the perception of consequences is not, in Godfrey of Fontaines's eyes, for example, a sufficient definition of the goal of theological study.[18] "This is to attribute too little to the theologian's task." Theological study should also deepen our knowledge of the mysteries of our faith.[19]

In truth, and despite the rhetoric of their opponents, neither Odo Rigaud nor John of Naples—to whom the position is also often attributed—nor any other theologian held that the sole goal of theological study was the perception of consequences.[20] Logical ability plays an important role in theological study, but it is not the only, nor even the most important, role. By the time we come to Peter of Candia, however, the intensity of earlier debate concerning the theology of consequences is gone. For him this is, once again, a limit position. That is why he represents it in its absolute and exclusive form: "others have said that theology is *only* a knowledge of consequences."[21]

THE POSITION OF PETER AUREOLI

Candia's format so far reveals not only the framework of his own treatment, but also the cadres of many fourteenth-century conceptions of theology. Theological study never attains evidence the way a strict Aristotelian science does—that would claim so much evidence that it would take away faith. Nor is it limited to the study of formal logical relationships between theological principles and conclusions drawn from them—that gives no evidence at all to truths of

---

17. C. Dumont, "La réflexion," pp. 20–22.
18. Godfrey of Fontaines *Quodl.* 9.20 (ed. DeWulf and Hoffmans, 4:285).
19. Ibid.
20. Cf. R. Guelluy, *Philosophie et théologie chez Guillaume d'Ockham* (Louvain and Paris: E. Nauwelaerts–J. Vrin, 1947), p. 55, n. 1.
21. Peter of Candia *Sent.* 1.pro.1 (lines 191–192).

the faith but shows at best only a logical acumen regarding the interconnection of theological truths. These dimensions are the general limits within which Peter of Candia asks the question: "Does the intellect of human beings here in this world acquire through theological study evident knowledge of revealed truths?" In formulating his response within the framework just described, his theological companions now are Scotus, Aureoli, Ockham, and Rimini.

Within the borders of these two limit positions, Candia presented two approaches to theology with which he disagreed on certain points. They were the declarative theology of the French Franciscan Peter Aureoli, who commented on the *Sentences* at Paris in 1316–1318,[22] and the deductive theology of the Augustinian hermit Gregory of Rimini, who began his *Sentences*-commentary, also at Paris, in 1343.[23]

Aureoli realized that many different types of intellectual activities legitimately go on in theology and that one could not reasonably limit the study to what is properly theological discourse.[24] Sometimes, for example, theologians are no different from metaphysicians. When they argue for the unicity or infinity of God, they do so demonstratively from necessary and naturally known propositions that could force the intellectual assent of a pagan or a philosopher. When theologians argue in this way frequently, they develop a certain intellectual facility. Yet such a habit is metaphysical rather than properly theological.[25]

At other times theologians are quite different from metaphysicians. They argue from premises that have their origin and ground in faith. In arguing correctly from premises rooted in revelation, they can produce conclusions that are not evident in the way metaphysical conclusions are, but that are nonetheless certain, provided the argument

---

22. Aureoli *Scriptum* I, intro. by E. M. Buytaert (1:xv). For the latest appreciation of Aureoli, see K. H. Tachau, *Vision and Certitude in the Age of Ockham* (Leiden and New York: E. J. Brill, 1988).

23. O. Grassi, "La questione della teologia come scienza in Gregorio da Rimini," *Rivista di filosofia neoscolastica* 68/1 (1976): 610, n. 1.

24. Aureoli *Scriptum* 1.pro.1 (ed. Buytaert, 1:132–175). Aureoli's position on the nature of theology is explained in detail by Streuer, *Einleitungslehre*, pp. 20–78. For Candia's summary, see Peter of Candia *Sent.* 1.pro.1 (lines 91–115).

25. Aureoli *Scriptum* 1.1.2.77–79 (ed. Buytaert, 1:154–155; hereafter, citations of Aureoli *Scriptum* 1 shorten the parenthetical reference to the first volume of Buytaert's edition to page numbers only).

consists of two revealed premises or one revealed and one necessary premise. An example of the latter type could be: (1) In Christ there are two intellectual natures, a divine one and a human one. (2) Now every intellectual nature has its own will. (3) Therefore, in Christ there are two wills, a divine one and a human one. Such a conclusion is held by faith, and Aureoli asserted that by arguments of this kind one does not acquire any habit distinct from faith. One holds to the conclusion by faith unhesitatingly, not because of the deduction *per se*, but because one believes the faith-premise from which the conclusion is inferred by necessity. What takes place here is a specification or a making explicit of faith.[26]

Sometimes, furthermore, theologians may begin with premises that are premises of faith and join to them in their arguments premises that are probable. The result is a conclusion that is opinion. The same result occurs if they work completely with unrevealed, probable premises of natural reason. In many questions within theological treatises, this procedure is the type of argument in play. It provides us with the opinions of theologians.[27]

Godfrey of Fontaines, we might recall, distinguished three types of knowledge: science (having both the certitude of evidence and the certitude of adherence); faith (having only the certitude of adherence); and opinion (having neither certitude). In his critique of Thomas he focused on the knowledge of conclusions. Aureoli continues to this point along the same line: he analyzes the different types of arguments and the premises involved and gives the knowledge-value of the conclusions in terms of the weight of their varying premises. Some of the arguments in theology do give us conclusions that are truly scientific. Others present conclusions lacking the certitude of evidence but possessing the certitude of conviction. Finally, many others offer conclusions that are plainly the opinions of theologians. Granting the precision of such detailed analysis of the knowledge-value of various conclusions, and realizing that a great deal of effort in theology is given to such deductive activity, Aureoli thought that he had not yet come to what theology is properly about. In carrying out their proper role, theologians do not focus on conclusions drawn from articles of faith. Rather, they center themselves on what such deduc-

26. Aureoli *Scriptum* 1.1.2.80–88 (155–158).
27. Aureoli *Scriptum* 1.1.2.89–90 (158–159).

tive theology would call premises or principles, certain revealed propositions whose truth has been determined by the Church—namely, the articles of faith. They do not start with them as principles and unfold new conclusions of varying worth depending on the other premises they use; rather, they focus on these very articles of faith and attempt to bring clarity to them (*declarare eas*).[28] For Aureoli, this is the discipline of the theologian that is most properly theological. It is not science, since theologians do not demonstrate such truths. Neither is it faith, since they already believe them. Nor is it opinion, since they bring forth arguments from other sciences that give support for the articles of faith, or explain the meaning of the terms of these articles, or respond to doubts raised against them. All of this is not opinion, for such operations do not bring with them any hesitancy regarding the truths of faith. Indeed, it would be foolish to spend so much effort in explaining, supporting, and defending the articles of faith if the end result were to weaken one's faith by reducing it to hesitant opinion. In developing such skills of support, clarification, and defense, the theologian does not produce conviction such that he can now affirm these truths without fear of error. He was already convinced through faith. Rather, he develops a habit distinct from faith—allowing him to make more clear what he already unhesitatingly believed. It was this type of developed ability that the *quaestiones* of the theologians, the *Books of the Sentences*, the writings of the Fathers, and the readings and expositions of Scripture were intended to foster. A theologian in the proper sense of the term, in contrast to the ordinary believer, is said to understand to some degree what he believes and is "ready to give an account concerning those things which are in him by faith."[29] He knows how "to defend the faith against the impious and strengthen it in the minds of the pious."[30]

Surely such a declarative theology carries on argumentation to support or illumine in some way the articles of faith. It borrows from other sciences premises of all different weights and employs them to support or illustrate as well as possible the truth of these beliefs. But it never demonstrates them in a strictly philosophical sense. Aureoli borrows an expression from Averroes to help him say what such *rationes proba-*

---

28. Aureoli *Scriptum* 1.1.2.92–128 (159–170).
29. 1 Peter 3.15.
30. Augustine *De Trinit.* 14.1 (PL 42:1037; CCL 50A:421–422).

biles accomplish. They help us to "imagine more clearly with our intellect" the revealed truths that we hold because of faith.[31]

Both the simple believer and the theologian believe the truths most firmly. But there is a difference between the two. The simple believer does not "intellectually imagine" or grasp his faith in any clear way, and this for a number of reasons. He does not understand the meaning of the terms, or he encounters objections to the faith which so entangle and confuse his mind that he cannot formulate exactly what he believes, or he doesn't have examples or analogies or any kind of parallels for what he believes, or he has no "probable reasons" to support him in his belief. A theologian surpasses a simple believer in just these respects: he has developed an ability to explain terms; he can consider and respond to objections; he is able to offer apt examples and supply probable arguments for the truths of faith.[32]

If one wishes to classify what a theologian does properly as theologian according to the Aristotelian division of intellectual virtues in book 6 of the *Nicomachean Ethics*, then it would be best not to call it science. For science gives evidence that forces our assent, whereas we already believe and do so on the authority of God revealing. What the theologian does should rather be called *wisdom*, for Aristotle describes wisdom as "the science of and insight into the things that are noblest by nature."[33] Now if Aristotle considers anything to have the character of wisdom, then surely it is metaphysics. He gives it that title in book 1 of his *Metaphysics*.[34] At least in some parts of the *Metaphysics*, namely, in book 4, where he defends its principles, and in book 5, where he explains its terms, Aristotle simply clarifies and defends the principles and terms. He does not demonstrate them or make them evident through syllogistic reasoning.[35]

A theologian performs a number of acts that show that he has developed many intellectual virtues or habits. He does at times demonstrate certain truths, not *qua* theologian, but *qua* metaphysician. In this activity he does produce science in regard to some truths about God. Furthermore, he makes many other deductions that render the

31. Aureoli *Scriptum* 1.1.3.112 (164).
32. Aureoli *Scriptum* 1.1.3.94 (160).
33. Aureoli *Scriptum* 1.1.3.117–129 (166–170).
34. Cf. Aureoli *Scriptum* 1.1.3.118–125 (166–168).
35. Aureoli *Scriptum* 1.1.3.126 (168–169).

content of the faith more explicit. Similarly he provides suitable theological opinion regarding the truths of faith. But in a more special and proper way a theologian *qua* theologian clarifies, defends, and offers probable arguments for the mysteries of faith, just as he explains the terms expressing these mysteries. Most properly, however, he provides insight. So declarative theology is wisdom, "the science of and insight into things which are the noblest by nature." It is not wisdom under the scientific aspect of wisdom but, rather, under the aspect of *understanding* or *insight*, for it brings light, understanding, or "insight into the noblest things by nature," i.e., the divine mysteries of our faith.[36]

It is no wonder that Augustine also gave this study the title of *wisdom*. He counts it the form of knowledge "by which that most wholesome faith is begotten, nourished, defended, strengthened"; and it knows how our faith "helps the pious and may be defended against the impious."[37] He has also called it "understanding," as in book 9 of the *De Trinitate*, where he locates this type of knowledge between simple faith and that certain knowledge which will be made perfect only after this life. In the same book he urges us "to seek to understand this mystery [of the Trinity], praying for help from God himself, whom we desire to understand; and as much as he grants, attempting to explain what we understand."[38] Augustine also calls this knowledge "the light of wisdom," as in his first homily *On John's Gospel*, where he informs us that God illumines the little ones in the Church with the light of faith, and the lofty souls, who are the mountains, with the light of wisdom.[39]

Richard of St. Victor, too, in the opening pages of his *De Trinitate*, urges us "to strive, insofar as we are able that we may understand [*intelligamus*] what we believe."[40] The opening chapter of the same work is his meditation on the text of Isaiah: "Unless you believe, you shall not understand [*intelligetis*]."[41]

For Aureoli, in sum, the habit that is most properly acquired by the theologian is a habit distinct from faith. It does not cause our assent to

---

36. Aureoli *Scriptum* 1.1.3.129 (170).
37. Aureoli *Scriptum* 1.1.3.127 (169).
38. Ibid.
39. Ibid.
40. Aureoli *Scriptum* 1.1.3.128 (169–170).
41. Ibid.

the articles of faith but presupposes such assent. Positively, it brings some understanding to our faith, makes it somewhat clearer, provides us with some imaginative understanding of the divine truths. Within the Aristotelian division of the intellectual virtues this properly theological habit should be considered wisdom, under the aspect of wisdom as insight or understanding, for it brings understanding, the light of wisdom, or "insight into the noblest things by nature."[42]

Although Peter of Candia knew the detailed criticisms that both William of Ockham[43] and Gregory of Rimini[44] brought against Aureoli, he limits his own evaluation of Aureoli's position to two points. First, no matter what arguments the theologian in his most proper work as a theologian might use in seeking to support the articles of faith, they will be probable reasons. On Aureoli's own admission they do not force our assent. What this means is that such arguments do not beget science or faith, otherwise they would command our assent; so they must beget opinion. Yet Aureoli himself argues that the most properly theological habit is not opinion, since if it were it would bring the hesitancy which is characteristic of opinion. In short, he seems to contradict himself.[45]

Second, when Aureoli gives declarative theology the Aristotelian title *wisdom* he seems off the mark. If he takes *wisdom* in a metaphorical sense in view of some similarity between declarative theology and the Aristotelian view of wisdom, he would just as well be justified in calling declarative theology a jackass, since both a jackass and declarative theology have some similarity: they are both beings. If, on the other hand, he means that declarative theology is wisdom in the proper Aristotelian sense of the word, then he is deceived. For Aristotle wisdom is linked to evidence. It is even more directly linked to evidence than science is. Science is distinct from insight and gets its evidence from insight, whereas wisdom is not distinct from insight, at least in the sense that insight is one of its components: wisdom is "the science of and insight into the most noble things by nature." So, if Aureoli rejects Aquinas's theory of theology as a subaltern science because a subaltern science gives evidence, then *a fortiori* he ought to

---

42. Aureoli *Scriptum* 1.1.3.129 (170).
43. William Ockham *Scriptum In I Sent.* pro.7 (ed. Gál and Brown, 195–196).
44. Gregory of Rimini *Sent.* 1.pro.1.2 (ed. Venice, 1521, a2vK–a3vK).
45. Peter of Candia *Sent.* 1.pro.1 (lines 117–147).

reject *wisdom* as a proper title for his declarative theology, since wisdom all the more gives evidence.[46] In short, theology is neither science nor wisdom in the strict Aristotelian senses of the terms.

Candia allows these observations to suffice as his direct criticisms of Aureoli's view. The overall weakness of Aureoli's position will appear more fully as our author argues for his own conception of theology.[47]

THE DEDUCTIVE THEOLOGY OF GREGORY OF RIMINI

Peter Aureoli's declarative theology was also the main target of Gregory of Rimini's treatise. If an unbeliever uses what a Christian theologian like Aureoli calls *probable reasons*, he arrives at conclusions that are opinion. Since opinion is distinct from a properly theological habit, our fictive unbeliever would not develop a theological habit. Imagine for a moment that he becomes a believer. Automatically now he has a theological habit, and therefore a new *habitus* or developed ability, without developing through any further study anything he had not already developed within himself before. What wonderful magic![48]

With this and similar arguments Gregory attempted to dismantle the *theologia declarativa* of Aureoli. In no way, however, did he think that he was undermining the theological procedures of Augustine or Richard of St. Victor, on whom he depended, as he attacked Aureoli's presentation:

> I ask that Reverend Master whose opinion of what is proper theological discourse I have disproved to go back to the *De Trinitate* and find anywhere in that or in Augustine's other books places where he proves from probable propositions that God is three in one. I think he could not find any. But he'll only find what Augustine proved from the authorities of Scripture. . . . Let him go back and reread what he has read inattentively.[49]

Rimini's own attentive reading of Augustine, Dionysius the Areopagite, Hugh of St. Victor, and Peter Lombard led him to differ-

---

46. Peter of Candia *Sent.* 1.pro.1 (lines 148–169).
47. See the last section, below.
48. Gregory of Rimini *Sent.* 1.pro.1.2 (ed. Venice, 1521, a2vMN).
49. Gregory of Rimini *Sent.* 1.pro.1.2 (ed. Venice, 1521, a3rB).

ent conclusions regarding the nature of theology and the role of the theologian.[50]

First off, he agreed with Aureoli that theology was not *science* in the strict Aristotelian sense of the term. Like Aureoli, Rimini follows Godfrey of Fontaines and Duns Scotus in their critique of the subaltern science theory of Aquinas and his followers.[51] Theological study does not bring believers to evident knowledge of the truths of the faith, whereas science in both its subaltern and nonsubaltern forms produces evident knowledge.[52]

Properly, theology extends the content of belief, and thus is not a habit distinct from faith. If a person accepts the truth of Sacred Scripture and furthermore is strong in intellectual habits, then reflection on Sacred Scripture will bring him to new conclusions. This is the situation with a theologian. He sees many truths that are not formally contained as such in Sacred Scripture but that follow necessarily from what is contained there. Now whether they are articles of faith or not, whether they are knowable through other sciences or not, and whether they are determined as revealed truths by the Church or not, he sees that they necessarily flow from what is formally revealed as such in Sacred Scripture. These are what Rimini means by theological conclusions.[53]

The theologian in his proper role sees that these truths demanded by intellectual reflection on the faith must be assented to with the same force of assent as the truths found in Sacred Scripture and that they must be admitted as unhesitatingly as the principles or premises found formally in Sacred Scripture itself. Theology thus extends the content of faith: it is a certain acquired faith. It is a *habitus creditivus*, a developed ability that extends our faith to its further logical and intelligible implications.[54]

Peter of Candia has no strong objection to this position of Rimini except for the exclusion that seems hidden in Rimini's attack on Aureoli.[55] As we shall see in Candia's own conclusions concerning the

---

50. Gregory of Rimini *Sent.* 1.pro.1.2 (ed. Venice, 1521, a2vQ–a3vK).
51. Gregory of Rimini *Sent.* 1.pro.1.2 (ed. Venice, 1521, a6vL–Q).
52. Ibid.
53. Gregory of Rimini *Sent.* 1.pro.1.2 (ed. Venice, 1521, a3rC, a2vQ–a3rD).
54. Peter of Candia *Sent.* 1.pro.1 (lines 171–179).
55. Peter of Candia *Sent.* 1.pro.1 (lines 182–186).

nature of theology, he agrees with Rimini's affirmative tendency.[56] Rimini's fault, in Candia's eyes, is found in what he omits—in his imbalance.

CANDIA'S OWN VISION OF THE NATURE OF THEOLOGY

Peter of Candia laid no claim to originality. He simply wished to steer a clear middle course between those who argue for too much, as with Aquinas's contention that theology is *science* in Aristotle's proper sense of that term, and those who argue for too little, as with those who might hold a theology of consequences. Even more specifically he wished to avoid the extreme of Aureoli's declarative theology, which denied that the proper role of the theologian was to extend the content of the faith ("nec habitus creditivus sed tantum declarativus"), and the extreme of Rimini's deductive theology, which considered the proper, and seemingly the only, role of the theologian was to extend the content of faith ("tantum creditivus").[57]

In choosing his middle road between these various extremes he chose as his guides those who led the way down the middle ("inter omnes mediando"): John Duns Scotus and William of Ockham.[58] Following their principles, Candia chose a mediating role and presented a view of theology that avoided the excessive and exclusive accents in the positions of Aureoli and Rimini by fostering a marriage of declarative and deductive theology.[59]

This marriage, in Candia's presentation, is not precisely a union of equal partners. Aureoli's declarative theology seems to have the upper hand. Three of Candia's first four conclusions are slanted in the direc-

---

56. See his fifth and sixth conclusions (lines 377–406).
57. Peter of Candia *Sent.* 1.pro.1 (lines 198–200).
58. Peter of Candia *Sent.* 1.pro.1 (lines 205–208). Cf. Scotus *Sent.* 3.24.1 (ed. Vivès, 15:36–49); William Ockham *Scriptum in I Sent.* pro.7 (ed. Gál and Brown, 183–206). For a general presentation of Scotus's position, see A. Magrini, *Ioannis Duns Scoti Doctrina de Scientifica Theologiae Natura*, Studia Antoniana 5 (Rome: Collegium Antonianum, 1952). A detailed analysis of *Sent.* 3.24 is given by L. Walter, *Das Glaubensverständnis bei Johannes Duns Scotus* (Paderborn: Schöningh, 1968), pp. 59–92. Ockham's prologue, q. 7, is given an excellent treatment by R. Guelluy, *Philosophie et théologie*, pp. 221–258.
59. Peter of Candia *Sent.* 1.pro.1 (lines 209–535).

tion of declarative theology. In fact the first conclusion, that through theological study the student acquires a habit distinct from faith, is one of Aureoli's basic theses.[60] Quite suitably, then, Candia's arguments supporting this conclusion are taken, *fere verbotenus*, from Aureoli's text.[61] Furthermore, Candia's attack on Rimini in the first conclusion would appear to make deductive theology a lesser partner in the marriage.[62] It is a very real partner even so, as Candia's fifth and sixth conclusions show.[63]

For Candia there are two basic ways in which a theologian may approach the truths of revelation, and this is the ground for the union or marriage. He may either approach them as a unified message or else focus on the individual truths. Declarative theology favors the first approach, whereas deductive theology leans toward the second.[64]

Declarative theology does not aim at extending the content of faith. It takes that content as it is and, following the urging of 1 Peter, it prepares the theologian to account for this faith. It makes him, in Augustine's phrase, able to show "in what way this belief itself may both help the pious and be defended against the impious." It also clarifies the meaning of the terms in the propositions expressing the truths of revelation and argues with probable reasons for these truths. Still, one of its principal tasks, Candia argues, makes it especially different from deductive theology: declarative theology focuses on the unified message. Accepting on faith the whole revelation with equal immediacy, the declarative theologian links together one truth within the revelation with another and shows how these mysteries hang together, how one implies the other, and how all are interrelated. Such collation of the mysteries of faith does not bring out or deduce new beliefs but shows the coherence of the mysteries.[65]

This developed ability permitting the theologian to account for this interrelation of the mysteries is distinct from faith itself, since the simple believer does not have the same facility. There is yet another sense in which such an ability is distinct from faith. None of the

60. Peter of Candia *Sent.* 1.pro.1 (lines 209–264). Cf. Aureoli *Scriptum* 1.pro.1.96–111 (ed. Buytaert, 160–164).
61. Peter of Candia *Sent.* 1.pro.1 (lines 209–264).
62. Peter of Candia *Sent.* 1.pro.1 (lines 243–264).
63. Peter of Candia *Sent.* 1.pro.1 (lines 377–406).
64. Peter of Candia *Sent.* 1.pro.1 (lines 252–264, 350–367).
65. Peter of Candia *Sent.* 1.pro.1 (lines 350–376).

declarative activities of a theologian brings about faith or makes him believe more firmly. He assents to the whole revelation because of his trust in the revealing God, not because of the harmony of the mysteries or the power of probable reasons.[66]

If deductive theology seems slighted in Candia's early conclusions, then it receives a real legitimacy in his fifth conclusion. Although one way to look at the truths of the faith is to focus on the whole revelation with equal immediacy, there is another legitimate way of looking at the truths of faith. This second way is the procedure accented by Rimini's deductive theology. It takes the truths individually and looks at them as premises for deducing further truths of faith. In such a procedure the theologian abandons the equal immediacy of revelation and rather centers his attention on new truths in relation to the ones which are prior. The new ones are held through the medium of the prior ones. Our adherence to the derived truths is due to our adherence to the principles or premises.[67]

For Candia both of these approaches are legitimate ways of considering the truths of faith. We can consider the divine revelation as truths of faith in themselves or as principles or premises for deriving further contents of our faith. Since both are legitimate ways of looking at divine revelation, it is false to speak of a declarative or deductive theology as though there were two distinct opposed theologies. We should rather speak of them as two legitimate and necessary theological habits or matured abilities that should be developed by all theologians.[68]

Both these developed abilities are the properly theological habits that theologians develop through study in the theology faculty. They may also develop in their studies many other habits, such as the ones developed by metaphysicians or natural philosophers. Through these latter abilities theologians may acquire evidence of the truths they examine, but not *qua* theologians.[69] Theologians, as theologians, through their declarative or deductive activities which are properly theological, do not acquire evidence.[70] As Candia's formal answer to

---

66. Peter of Candia *Sent.* 1.pro.1 (lines 282–299).
67. Peter of Candia *Sent.* 1.pro.1 (lines 376–388).
68. Peter of Candia *Sent.* 1.pro.1 (lines 391–406).
69. Peter of Candia *Sent.* 1.pro.1 (lines 407–442).
70. Peter of Candia *Sent.* 1.pro.1 (lines 483–494).

the original question phrases it at the end of the prologue: "Through theological study only declarative and faith-extending habits are developed, and through these developed abilities no evident knowledge of the articles of faith is acquired."[71]

Boston College

---

71. Peter of Candia *Sent.* 1.pro.3 (Bibl. Apostolica Vaticana lat. 1081, f. 20ra): "Per exercitium theologicum non adquiritur nisi habitus creditivus vel declarativus per quos de articulis fidei nulla notitia evidens adquiritur."

Appendix

The *Sentences*-commentary of Peter of Candia exists in whole or in part in thirty-seven manuscripts.[1] In the judgment of Ehrle the best manuscript is that contained in the Bibl. Apostolica Vaticana, cod. lat. 1081.[2] Emmen also used the same manuscript as the base for his edition of Peter's question on the Immaculate Conception and demonstrated its undeniable superiority.[3] We have used this manuscript for our present edition of the first question of Peter's prologue to book 1 of the *Sentences*. Any alterations that we have made to the text are found between angle brackets, ⟨ ⟩. The text we have edited is found on ff. 9ra–12rb.

⟨PETRI DE CANDIA   1
PROLOGUS LIBRI SENTENTIARUM⟩
    Super materiam prologi totius Sententiarum libri generalis incipit quaestio. Circa prologum in quo communiter quaerunt doctores de habitu per studium theologicum ad-   5
quisito, quaero istam quaestionem: utrum intellectus viatoris per exercitium theologicum adquirat evidentem notitiam de credibilibus revelatis.
    Et arguo quod non tribus mediis, et primo sic: ex nullis propositionibus probabilibus vel simpliciter creditis adquiritur   10
evidens notitia; sed totum theologicum exercitium est circa probabilia vel simpliciter credita; ergo quaestio falsa. Consequentia patet. Et maior declaratur, quoniam ex probabilibus causatur opinio et ex credibilibus fides; sed tam fides quam opinio sunt habitus inevidentes, aliter habentes opiniones   15
vel credulitates de conclusionibus contradictoriis haberent notitias evidentes, quod videtur falsum. Sed minor probatur

---

1. Emmen, "Petrus de Candia," pp. 247–250.
2. Ehrle, *Der Sentenzenkommentar*, p. 21.
3. Emmen, "Petrus de Candia," pp. 261–266.

sic: omne intellectuale exercitium vel est commune elenchum, vel topicum, sive demonstrativum, vel sophisticum, ut patet per Philosophum sufficienter dividentem intellectuale exercitium in libris logicae disciplinae.[4] Sed constat quod theologicum exercitium non est commune ⟨elenchum⟩, nec demonstrativum vel sophisticum: ergo per sufficientem divisionem quadrimembrem et remotionem trium partium sequitur quod est topicum vel probabile sive creditivum, quod erat probandum.

Praeterea, et secundo arguo sic: quodlibet statui viae incompossibile repugnat intellectui viatoris; sed evidens notitia de credibilibus revelatis est huiusmodi; ergo quaestio falsa. Consequentia et maior patent. Sed minor probatur sic: quorum rationes formales contradicunt et ipsa sunt ad invicem incompossibilia; sed ratio formalis fidei evidenti notitiae contradicit, ut patet per Apostolum, Ad Heb. 11,[5] fidem taliter describentem: *Fides est substantia rerum sperandarum, argumentum non apparentium*; ergo fides et notitia evidens sunt ad invicem incompossibiles. Nunc vero fides est statui viae annexa, ut patet per Apostolum, I Ad Cor. 13:[6] *Videmus nunc per speculum et in aenigmate; tunc autem facie ad faciem.* Ergo notitia evidens veritatum credibilium est statui viae incompossibilis, quod erat probandum.

Praeterea, et tertio, arguo sic: quaelibet notitia ponens viatorem in termino repugnat viatori; sed evidens notitia veritatum credibilium est huiusmodi; ergo quaestio falsa. Consequentia et maior patent. Et minor probatur: quodlibet statui patriae annexum de necessitate ponit habentem illud in patria; sed evidens notitia ⟨veritatum credibilium⟩ est de necessitate statui patriae annexa, iuxta illud *Ioan* 17:[7] *Haec est vita aeterna, ut cognoscant te, solum Deum verum.* Quae auctoritas non potest intelligi nisi de notitia evidente, cum ⟨nulla⟩ alia sit nobis pro statu viae possibilis. Ergo evidens notitia veritatum credibilium ponit habentem illam in termino.

---

4. Aristotle *Topics* 1.1.100a18–b24; cf. *On Sophist. Refut.* 2.165a34–b12.
5. Hebrews 11.1.
6. Corinthians 13.12.
7. John 17.3.

Ad oppositum, et pro veritate quaestionis, arguo tantum unico medio: omnis habitus intellectualis est sapientia, vel intellectus, scientia vel prudentia, ars, fides vel opinio. Sed constat quod per exercitium theologicum aliquis habitus adquiritur, aliter esset studium otiosum. Et non fides, quia aeque bene habetur sine tali studio sicut cum tali, ut patet de vetulis et simplicibus Christianis. Nec opinio, cum includat formidem, et est contra statum fidelis, nam ut dicitur *Extravagantes, 'De haereticis'*:[8] "Dubius in fide infidelis est." Nec ars, cum sit respectu factibilium, ut dicitur VI *Ethicorum*.[9] Nec prudentia, quia tunc maiores theologi essent prudentiores, cuius oppositum experimur. Ergo adquiritur vel sapientia, ⟨vel⟩ intellectus, vel scientia; quorum si aliquod detur, habetur propositum, cum quilibet praemissorum habituum sit habitus evidens, ut ex ipsorum definitionibus potest clarius apparere.

⟨DIVISIO PROLOGI⟩

Pro decisione quaestionis istius iuxta materiam trium argumentorum ad quaestionis oppositum adductorum tres erunt articuli pertractandi, quorum primus, iuxta materiam primi argumenti: Utrum habitus theologiae sit tantum creditivus seu probabilis in studente, vel sic: Utrum habitus per exercitium theologicum adquisitus sit evidentis notitiae portio substantiva. Secundus, iuxta secundi argumenti materiam: Utrum in intellectu studentis theologiam fides et scientia possint simul exsistere subiective, vel sic: Utrum in eadem mente respectu eiusdem obiecti fides et evidens notitia possint simul exsistere subiective. Tertius, iuxta materiam tertii argumenti: Utrum studenti theologiae, ut viator est, repugnet cognitio scientifica credibilium veritatum, vel sic: Utrum veritatum credibilium evidens notitia viatorum statui formaliter sit repugnans.

---

8. In 'Extravagantibus primis,' that is, in Compilatione I (= *Breviarium extravagantium* Bernardi Papiensis, c. 1187–1191), ed. A. Augustini, *Antiquae decretalium collectiones* (Paris, 1621), 123; following *Decretales Greg. IX*, lib. V, tit. 7 "De hereticis," cap. 1 (ed. A. Friedberg, *Corpus Iuris Canonici*, 2:778).

9. Aristotle *Nic. Ethics* 6.4.1140a1–23.

⟨ARTICULUS PRIMUS⟩

Pro declaratione primi articuli sic procedam: primo quorundam doctorum opiniones praemittam; secundo eliciam seu conflabo positionem meam per certas conclusiones; ex quibus patebit quid sentio de materia quaestionis.

⟨I. OPINIONES ALIQUORUM DOCTORUM: OPINIO PETRI AUREOLI⟩

Quantum ad primum est advertendum quod dominus frater Petrus Aureoli, *Scripto suo primo super Sententias*, prima questione prologi, articulo secundo,[10] sententialiter sic imaginatur, dicens quod in sacra scriptura est multiplex processus: quandoque ad propositionem scitam, quandoque ad creditam, quandoque ad credendam. Et secundum hoc potest imaginari septuplex processus, videlicet triplex simplex et quadruplex compositus. Simplex ⟨est⟩ vel ex propositionibus necessariis tantum vel ex probabilibus tantum, vel ex simpliciter creditis tantum. Compositus seu mixtus est vel ex omnibus simul, vel ex una necessaria et altera probabili, vel ex una necessaria et altera credita, vel ex una credita et altera probabili. Ex quibus dicit quattuor theologica documenta: primum, quod in primo processu adquiritur habitus scientificus. Secundum, quod in secundo processu adquiritur habitus dumtaxat probabilis. Tertium, quod in tertio processu adquiritur habitus tantummodo creditivus. Quartum quod in quarto processu, quo videlicet proceditur ex omnibus simul, et cum hoc adducuntur rationes et dubia persolvuntur, adquiritur proprie habitus theologicus. Quod qualis sit quattuor ponit conclusiones. Prima, quod habitus huiusmodi est alius a fide. Secunda, quod non est habitus adhaesivus. Tertia, quod est habitus dumtaxat declarativus. Quarta, quod est huiusmodi habitus habet vere rationem sapientiae virtutis intellectualis.

⟨CONTRA OPINIONEM PETRI AUREOLI⟩

Licet illa positio videatur probabilis quoad multa, tamen quoad duo ipsius dicta quae mihi in hac parte

---

10. Aureoli *Scriptum* 1.pro.1 (ed. E. M. Buytaert, 1:132–175).

non videntur vera arguam contra ipsam. Primum, in hoc quod dicit quod ex omnibus propositionibus, videlicet probabilibus, necessariis et creditis, generatur habitus theologicus. Contra hoc arguo sic: quilibet habitus discursive causatus ex habitibus vel propositionibus differentibus secundum perfectionem semper sequitur naturam minus perfecti. Sed habitus discursive causatus ex propositionibus necessariis, probabilibus et simpliciter creditis simul est habitus discursive causatus ex habitibus vel propositionibus differentibus secundum perfectionem; ergo huiusmodi habitus sequitur naturam habitus minus perfecti. Cum igitur inter omnes habitus probabilis sive creditivus sit minus perfectus, sequitur quod habitus huiusmodi erit aut creditivus aut probabilis et per consequens non theologicus iuxta suam imaginationem. Maior huius rationis patet ex hoc quia in omni discursiva mixtione semper conclusio sequitur naturam minus perfectae aut debilioris praemissae, ut vult Philosophus,[11] et omnes logicae tractatores. Et minor est de se nota; ergo etc.

Confirmatur exemplariter, nam formata copulativa cuius una pars sit necessaria et altera contingens in forma syllogistica, conclusio sequens de necessitate erit contingens. Verbi gratia: omne ens est substantia; Sortes est ens; ergo Sortes est substantia. Constat manifeste quod conclusio quae contingens dinoscitur, videlicet 'Sortes est substantia', non naturam imitatur propositionis necessariae sed potius contingentis, et ita regulariter in omni syllogistica mixtione reperies; ergo ad praedicta conformiter habitus discursive causatus ex omnibus praemissis simpliciter sequitur naturam habitus minus perfecti, quod erat probandum.

Secundum dictum suum quod mihi non placet ⟨est hoc⟩ quod est eius quarta conclusio, videlicet habitus theologicus habet vere rationem sapientiae virtutis intellectualis. Contra hoc arguo sic: vel accipit sapientiam proprie vel metaphorice. Si metaphorice, nihil ad propositum, ⟨quia⟩ sic posset vocare habitum theologicum asinum, propter quandam similitudinem quam habet cum asino, quia quilibet eorum est ens. Si autem accipit proprie; contra: omnis habitus sapientialis est ad-

---

11. Aristotle *Prior Analytics* 1.27.43b37.

haesivus, cum sit evidens; sed per ipsum ex sua conclusione secunda habitus theologicus non est adhaesivus, ergo per consequens nec sapientialis. Praeterea, si habitus theologicus esset sapientia proprie, tunc esset evidentior habitu scientifico, quia scientia capit evidentiam ab intellectu; nunc autem sapientia est intellectus et scientia simul, ut vult Philosophus, VI *Ethicorum*.[12] Consequens est falsum, etiam secundum eum, nam in pugnando dicta Sancti Thomae qui tenet quod habitus theologicus habet rationem scientiae subalternae dicit quod hoc non potest esse per hoc quod omnis scientia causat evidentiam, cuiusmodi non facit habitus theologicus.[13] Ergo, si loquatur proprie, sibi ipsi contradicit; si vero improprie, nihil ad propositum. Et ⟨haec⟩ tantum de ista positione, quia improbando dicta mea etiam improbabuntur haec dicta.

⟨OPINIO GREGORII DE ARIMINO⟩

Ulterius est Gregorius de Arimino qui dicit quattuor circa propositam quaestionem, prima quaestione prologi, articulo quarto.[14] Primum, quod ex discursu theologico non adquiritur scientia. Secundum, quod adquiritur adhaesio. Tertium, quod adquiritur adhaesio sine formidine. Quartum, quod adquiritur ⟨habitus creditivus⟩ sive fides. Ex quo patebit[15] quod huiusmodi habitus theologicus qui communiter adquiritur est quidam habitus creditivus et fides quaedam adquisita.

⟨CONTRA OPINIONEM
GREGORII DE ARIMINO⟩

Haec positio quoad ultimam suam conclusionem, si intelligatur cum exclusione, ut ipse videtur dicere arguendo etiam contra positionem domini Petri Aureoli, non videtur vera. Cuius improbatio apparebit ex probatione conclusionum mearum.

12. Aristotle *Nic. Ethics* 6.7.1141b2–3.
13. Aureoli *Scriptum* 1.pro.1.30 (ed. Buytaert, 1:140).
14. Gregory of Rimini *Sent.* 1.pro.1.2 (ed. Venice, 1521, a2vK–A3vK).
15. patebit] dicit *add. cod.*

⟨OPINIO BEATI THOMAE AQUINATIS⟩
Alii dixerunt quod habebat rationem scientiae subalternae, ut beatus Thomas.¹⁶

⟨OPINIO IOANNI DE NEAPOLI ATTRIBUTA⟩ 190
Alii¹⁷ ⟨vero dixerunt⟩ quod est tantum notitia consequentiarum.

⟨OPINIONES IN GENERALI⟩
Unde generaliter quidam¹⁸ tenent quod habitus theologiae est scientia; et quidam¹⁹ quod non. Tenentes 195
negativam ⟨aliqui⟩²⁰ dicunt quod non est creditivus; alii²¹ quod sic. Vult igitur beatus Thomas quod theologia sit scientia proprie dicta. Vult dominus Petrus Aureoli quod non sit scientia, nec habitus creditivus sed tantum declarativus. Vult Gregorius quod sit tantum creditivus. 200

⟨II. RESPONSIO AUCTORIS⟩
Omissis igitur positionibus istorum doctorum quae mihi in certis suis dictis non placent, venio ad illud quod mihi videtur magis consonum veritati et prout potest colligi ex dictis Doctoris Subtilis, III Sententiarum, distinctione 24,²² 205

16. Thomas Aquinas *Summa theologiae* 1.1.2.
17. John of Naples *Quaestiones variae Parisiis disputatae* 18.3.5 (ed. Naples, 1618, 154): "Si vero loquamur de hac doctrina quantum ad suas conclusiones, sic etiam dicendum est quod est scientia proprie et stricte. Scimus enim quod conclusiones huius doctrinae necessario sequuntur ex suis principiis. Sic ergo patet quod haec doctrina potest dici scientia quinque modis. . . . Quinto potest dici scientia consequentiarum; scit enim theologus quod conclusiones theologiae necessario sequuntur ex suis principiis."
18. Thomas Aquinas *Summa theologiae* 1.1.2.
19. Averroes *In Aristot. Metaph.* 2.1 (ed. Juntas 8:14rb–va); *In Aristot. De anima* 3.36 (ed. F. S. Crawford, 494–495). This opinion is attributed to Averroes by Henry of Ghent *Summa* 4.5 (ed. Paris, 1520, 1:32B–33E).
20. Aureoli *Scriptum* 1.pro.1.96–111 (ed. Buytaert, 1:160–164).
21. Gregory of Rimini *Sent.* 1.pro.1.2 (ed. Venice, 1521, a2vK–a3vK).
22. John Duns Scotus *Sent.* 3.24.1 (ed. Vivès, 15:36–49).

et Venerabilis Inceptoris Ockham, quaestione septima prologi,[23] inter omnes mediando, pro cuius[24] declarationes septem pono conclusiones.

Prima conclusio: intellectus viatoris per exercitium theologicum adquirit habitum ultra fidem. Haec conclusio sic probatur: positis causis sufficientibus et non impeditis ad productionem alicuius effectus ⟨necessario⟩ ponitur ille effectus; sed propositiones in sacra scriptura contentae cum propositionibus aliis naturaliter adquisitis et lumen naturale intellectus agentis quo intellectus exercitatur in declarando et exponendo sacram scripturam sunt causae sufficientes ad productionem certi habitus; ergo his positis in intellectu studentis theologiae necessario causabunt aliquem habitum, et non fidem, quia, ut suppono, illam prius habebat; ergo aliquem alium, quod est propositum. Si dicatur quod licet non adquirat fidem, tamen augmenta est; contra: omnis habitus adhaesivus per aliquod tempus augmentatus in fine illius temporis firmius adhaeret per illum habitum habens eum quam prius; patet de se. Sed in fine exercitii theologici non firmius quis adhaeret quam ante, ut experientia docet; ergo propositum.

Praeterea, quicumque habet aliquem actum intellectus in sua potestate ab actu assentiendi distinctum respectu creditae veritatis habet alium habitum a fide. Sed exercitatus in theologia habet actum huiusmodi, ergo conclusio vera. Consequentia patet, et maior est Philosophi, II *De anima*,[25] dicentis quod habitibus operamur cum volumus. Et minor declaratur, quoniam iste sic exercitatus novit reddere rationem et fidem defensare et infirmos roborare. Sed constat quod isti actus sunt valde distincti ab actu assentiendi, aliter hos actus haberent similiter simplices fideles, quod non videtur verum; ergo conclusio vera.

Praeterea, frustra fit per plura quod potest fieri per pauciora.[26] Sed si per exercitium theologicum nullum alium habitum a fide adquirit studens in theologia, sequitur quod

---

23. William Ockham *Scriptum in I Sent.* pro.7 (ed. Gál and Brown, 195–196).
24. cuius *corr. cod. ex* quaestione *interl. (al. man.).*
25. Aristotle *On the Soul* 2.5.417b23–24.
26. Aristotle *Physics* 1.4.188a17–18.

huiusmodi exercitium est frustra, cum sine tali potest adquirere talem habitum, ut simplices fideles faciunt; ergo praeter habitum fidei oportet ponere alium habitum in studente.

Ex hac conclusione apparet falsitas opinionis Gregorii, si intelligat conclusionem suam universaliter, ut apparet. Unde advertendum est quod opinantem decipit hoc, quia omnis propositio vel est necessaria et evidens vel probabilis vel credita, ideo imaginatur quod ex his simul non potest sequi nisi credita vel probabilis, et quod propositionum quae in theologico exercitio sumuntur communiter altera illarum est credita. Ideo dicit quod ex his simul non potest adquiri aliud quam habitus creditivus.

Propterea dico quod ex propositionibus aliquem habitum causari contingit dupliciter: vel illative vel collative. Verbi gratia, nunc adhaereo certae conclusioni in sacra pagina contentae, et postea per aliquam propositionem sacrae scripturae infero illam. Tunc de illa propositione causatur in me, si actus fuerit frequentatus, habitus quo adhaereo, et iste est causatus illative. Secundo modo possum adhaerere omnibus propositionibus contentis in sacra scriptura, non uni propter aliam sed omnibus aeque immediate; tunc conferendo unam cum alia, ex isto frequenti actu causatur in me unus habitus, qui non est fides, quo reddo rationem de his quae continentur in sacra pagina, et istum modum forsan non viderunt oppositum affirmantes.

Secunda conclusio: habitus huiusmodi taliter adquisitus sub evidenti notitia minime continetur. Haec conclusio sic probatur: nullus habitus qui potest stare cum errore est evidens notitia; sed habitus huiusmodi taliter adquisitus potest stare cum errore; ergo conclusio vera. Consequentia patet; et maior probatur ex hoc, quoniam omnis notitia evidens vel est necessaria vel contingens; sed nulla notitia evidens necessaria potest stare cum errore, cum illa sit vel sapientia, ⟨vel⟩ intellectus, vel scientia, qui sunt habitus de necessitate veridici. Nec etiam contingens, quia licet talis posset non esse, non tamen staret quod esset evidens et erronea, igitur simpliciter maior vera. Minor vero declaratur, nam signo certum magnum theologum qui postmodum efficiatur hereticus; certum est quod licet iste perdat habitum creditivum, non tamen illum per quem sciebat sacram scripturam exponere. Ergo ille habitus ita stat cum errore sicut sine errore; et per consequens conclusio vera.

Praeterea, omnem habitum quem potest naturaliter adquirere fidelis potest et infidelis; sed huiusmodi habitum potest naturaliter adquirere fidelis; ergo et infidelis. Maior patet, quoniam individua eiusdem speciei aeque naturaliter possunt. Minor vero apparet, quia omnis talis habitus potest adquiri a parvulo ⟨infideli⟩ inter fideles nutrito. Et tunc ultra ab infideli potest adquiri talis habitus respectu credibilium ⟨veritatum⟩, et non evidens notitia, quia sic firmissime adhaereret, et ita non esset infidelis, quod est contra suppositum.

Praeterea, omnis habitus evidens inducit certitudinem ultra fidem; sed talis habitus ⟨theologicus⟩ non inducit certitudinem ultra fidem; ergo conclusio vera. Consequentia et maior patent; et minor declaratur, quoniam habens talem habitum non firmius adhaeret per talem habitum et fidem quam per solam fidem; ergo propositum. Consequentia patet; et antecedens est notum de studentibus in theologia qui non experiuntur se firmius adhaerere huic 'Deus est trinus et unus' post exercitium theologicum quam ante; ergo propositum.

Tertia conclusio: habitus huiusmodi taliter adquisitus non exsistit habitus adhaesivus. Haec conclusio sic probatur: omnis habitus adhaesivus est sapientia, intellectus, scientia, fides vel opinio. Sed habitus huiusmodi non est sapientia, intellectus vel scientia, nec fides nec opinio; ergo conclusio vera. Consequentia patet; et maior declaratur, quoniam omnis adhaerens alicui aut adhaeret propter evidentiam necessariam aut contingentem. Si primo modo, aut illa est evidentia principiorum, et sic est intellectus, aut conclusionum, et sic est scientia, aut tam principiorum quam conclusionum, et sic est sapientia, ut vult Philosophus, VI *Ethicorum*.[27] Si secundo modo aut adhaeret ex notitia intuitiva singularium, et sic habetur communis notitia contingentium, ut videndo Sortem et albedinem adhaereo ⟨huic⟩: quod Sortes est albus. Aut ex auctoritate dicentis, et sic est fides. Aut adhaereo ex aliquali rerum apparentia, et sic opinio causatur. Sed minor de-

---

27. Aristotle *Nic. Ethics* 6.7.1141b2–3.

claratur, nam iste habitus ex quo per secundam conclusionem non est evidens sequitur quod nec sapientia, intellectus, vel scientia. Nec est fides, ut dicit prima conclusio. Nec est opinio, quia huiusmodi habitus includit formidem et per consequens repugnat fidei. Sed iste habitus stat cum fide; ergo minor vera et per consequens conclusio.

Praeterea, omnis habitus adhaesivus causatur illative vel ex propositionibus necessariis vel probabilibus vel simpliciter creditis vel ex experientia rerum. Sed huiusmodi habitus non causatur ex aliquo istorum ⟨modorum⟩ illative, nec ex experientia rerum; ergo conclusio vera. Consequentia et maior patent. Et minor declaratur, quoniam, ut dictum est in declaratione primae conclusionis, huiusmodi habitus causatur collative potius quam illative. Nec etiam habetur ex experientia, proprie loquendo de experientia qua quis certificatur ut apparet; ergo propositum.

Praeterea, si habitus huiusmodi esset adhaesivus, aut convertibiliter, aut disparate, aut secundum superius et inferius, aut per accidens. Sed nullum illorum modorum est verum; ergo conclusio vera. Consequentia et maior patent.

Et minor probatur: non primo modo, quia tunc omnis habitus adhaesivus esset huiusmodi habitus; quod est falsum. Nec secundo modo, quia sic nullo modo possunt convenire. Nec tertio modo, quia quandocumque aliqua se habent secundum superius et inferius, quidquid potest praedicari de superiori universaliter potest et de inferiori; sed de habitu adhaesivo universaliter sumpto praedicatur sufficienter hoc disiunctum: sapientia, vel intellectus, vel scientia, vel fides vel opinio; ergo et posset praedicari de habitu huiusmodi; quod est falsum, ut in prima ratione ostensum est. Nec quarto modo, quia tunc accidens esset subiectum accidentis, quod non communiter est concessum, nam si iste habitus est adhaesivus per accidens huic habitui inhaereret adhaesio qua formaliter est adhaesivus, et sic accidens est subiectum accidentis; patet igitur conclusio.

Quarta conclusio: habitus huiusmodi taliter adquisitus est theologicus proprie, qui potest declarativus merito nuncupari. Haec conclusio sic probatur, et primo quoad primam partem, videlicet quod sit theologicus: quilibet habitus causatus ex exercitio alicuius facultatis dicitur pertinere ad illam facultatem, sicut habitus causatus ex exercitio geometrae dicitur esse geometricus et ex exercitio logicae logicus, et sic de similibus. Sed iste habitus, ut prius apparuit, causatur ex collatione propositionum contentarum in sacra scriptura; ergo est vere theologicus. Quoad secundam partem similiter probatur conclusio, videlicet quod sit declarativus: omnis habitus inducens explicationes terminorum, solutiones dubiorum, exempla et manuductiones est vere declarativus; sed habitus huiusmodi est talis; ergo conclusio vera. Consequentia et maior patent. Et minor declaratur, quoniam exercitatus in theologia hoc habet ultra simplicem fidelem: quod novit rationem reddere de his quae continentur in sacra scriptura, et similiter defensare; quare propositum.

Haec conclusio expresse est de mente beati Augustini, XIV *De Trinitate*, cap. primo,[28] ubi hunc habitum vocat scientiam, large tamen sumendo scientiae nomen, ubi sic dicit: "Hac scientia non pollent fideles plurimi, quamvis polleant ipsa fide plurimum. Aliud est enim scire tantummodo quid homo credere debeat propter adipiscendam vitam beatam quae nonnisi aeterna est; aliud autem, scire quemadmodum hoc ipsum et piis opituletur et contra impios defendatur." Haec ille. Ex quibus apparet veritas conclusionis.

Quinta conclusio: praeter habitum superius nominatum per theologicum exercitium adquiritur creditivus habitus qui theologicus potest similiter nominari. Haec conclusio sic probatur: omnis habitus causatus ex propositionibus in sacra scriptura contentis est theologicus; sed habitus creditivus est huiusmodi; ergo conclusio vera. Minor vero probatur, quoniam ex propositionibus in sacra scriptura contentis discursive infero unam propositionem cui per prius non adhaerebam et nunc adhaereo; sed constat quod huiusmodi adhaesio non excedit fidem, cum adhaesio conclusionis non excedat adhaesionem illius unde causatur; ergo simpliciter ex tali discursu adquiritur habitus creditivus.

Ista conclusio expresse videtur de mente Salvatoris, *Ioan* 20:[29] *Haec scripta sunt ut credatis, et ut credentes vitam habeatis.*

---

28. Augustine *De Trinitate* 14.1 (PL 42:1037; CCL 50A:421–422).
29. John 20.31.

Sexta conclusio: habitus theologicus per creditivum et declarativum habitus dividitur adaequate. Volo dicere quod omnis habitus theologicus ⟨vel⟩ est creditivus vel declarativus. Haec conclusio sic probatur: omnis habitus causatus ex propositionibus in sacra scriptura contentis vel causatur discursive vel illative—seu collative; sed omnis habitus theologicus est habitus causatus ex propositionibus in sacra scriptura contentis; ergo omnis habitus theologicus vel causatur discursive vel collative. Ergo est creditivus vel declarativus. Probo istam consequentiam, quia omnes propositiones in sacra scriptura contentae vel sunt necessariae et evidentes vel creditae. Sed constat quod ex his discursive nihil aliud adquiritur quam habitus creditivus; ergo propositum. Si vero sit inter eas collatio, non adhaerendo uni propter aliam sed ipsas dumtaxat ad invicem conferendo, tunc certum est quod adquiritur habitus tantum declarativus; ex quibus patet conclusionis veritas.

Septima et ultima conclusio est haec: praeter habitus superius nominatos per exercitium theologicum adquisitos possunt de veritatibus theologiae adquiri plures habitus non theologici ad diversas scientias pertinentes. Haec conclusio sic probatur: in sacra scriptura continentur non solum veritates speculativae sed etiam practicae, non solum necessariae sed etiam probabiles et contingentes. Sed constat quod de primis, videlicet speculabilibus et necessariis, utpote "Deus est actus purus," "Deus est summum bonum" habetur notitia evidens et scientifica causata ex propositionibus necessariis evidenter notis lumine naturali, ut patet per argumenta philosophantium quae fiunt ab effectu ad causam demonstratione quia; ergo de ipsis causatur habitus scientificus. Et sicut ex veritatibus speculativis scientificus habitus ⟨habetur⟩, ita ex moralibus practicus. Et sic de aliis habitus varii causantur, et per consequens conclusio quoad primam partem ⟨est⟩ vera.

Quod autem huiusmodi habitus non sint theologici patet ex praedictis, quoniam habitus ⟨proprie⟩ theologicus viatoris secundum communem cursum naturae non est evidens. Et dico signanter 'habitus viatoris secundum cursum naturae' ad differentiam habituum comprehensorum qui sunt evidentes—similiter, ad differentiam habituum qui possunt alicui infideli praeter cursum naturae ex omnipotentis imperio voluntatis:

430 quales fuerunt infusi beato Paulo in raptu, qui secundum communem doctorum opinionem fuerunt evidentes; de quarum notitiarum differentia loquitur Apostolus, I Ad Corinthios 13:[30] *Videmus nunc per speculum et in aenigmate*—quoad viatores; *tunc autem facie ad faciem*—quoad comprehensores. Est
435 ergo conclusionis intentio ⟨loqui⟩ de habitu adquisito per exercitium theologicum a viatore secundum cursum naturae; qui habitus est proprie theologicus cum sit causatus ex propositionibus revelatis et necessariis ad aeternam beatitudinem consequendam, et iste non alius in genere quam creditivus vel
440 declarativus dinoscitur, ut superius est expressum. Constat autem quod praemissi habitus sunt evidentes, ergo non theologici, et per consequens tota conclusio vera.

Ex qua positione apparet facillime, et sequitur correlarie, quod habitus theologiae non est scientia proprie dicta: contra
445 positionem beati Thomae. Similiter, quod praeter habitum creditivum adquiritur habitus alius a fide: contra opinionem Gregorii. Similiter, quod adquiritur habitus adhaesivus: contra opinionem domini Petri Aureoli. Sequitur quarto quod non est opinio—contra aestimationem philosophorum
450 communiter opinatam.

⟨DUBITATIONES ET SOLUTIONES EARUM⟩

Quamvis autem istae conclusiones videantur verae, tamen est dubium de duabus conclusionibus ultimis, videlicet sexta et septima. Primum dubium est circa sextam
455 conclusionem, quod non videtur verum quod habitus theologicus sit sufficienter divisus in creditivum et declarativum, cum omnis ille habitus sit theologicus qui causatur ex propositionibus theologicis. Nunc vero multae sunt veritates theologicae naturaliter cognoscibiles, ut 'Deus est sapiens,' et sic
460 de multis aliis; ergo habitus adquisitus non est creditivus sed evidens in lumine naturali. Quod autem tales veritates sint theologicae apparet, quia sunt necessariae ad aeternam beatitudinem consequendam, et tales vocat theologicas beatus Augustinus, XIV *De Trinitate*, cap. 1.[31]

30. 1 Corinthians 13.12.
31. Augustine *De Trinitate* 14.1 (PL 42:1037; CCL 50A:421–422).

Secundum dubium est quia si multi habitus de veritatibus theologiae adquirerentur ad diversas scientias pertinentes, ut innuit conclusio septima, tunc idem habitus esset theologicus et metaphysicus, quod non videtur verum.

Ad primum istorum dico quod licet multae veritates theologicae sint naturaliter cognoscibiles, non tamen ut theologicae theologia viatoris. Unde habens utrumque habitum, tam videlicet creditivum quam declarativum, etiam si nullam talem veritatem cognosceret in lumine naturali, non minus adhaereret eidem. Dico igitur quod licet eandem veritatem possimus cognoscere diversis viis, non tamen sequitur quod habitus theologicus sit evidens, sed sequitur quod respectu eiusdem veritatis possunt esse diversi habitus per diversos discursus generati.

Unde pro maiori praedictorum declaratione advertendum est quod multae sunt veritates theologicae quarum notitia non habetur per exercitium theologicum. Verbi gratia, hae sunt veritates theologicae: 'Deus est supremum ens,' 'Deus est id quo melius excogitari non potest.' Et tamen per exercitium quod quis habet in sacra scriptura non adquirit illarum veritatum notitiam, quoniam absque tali exercitio habetur talium veritatum notitia, ut patet in viris scientificis qui aliunde talium veritatum notitiam sunt adepti. Si autem quis per exercitium sacrae scripturae primo caperet praedictarum veritatum notitiam, tunc talis notitia esset theologica et non evidens, tamen ipsius notitia ex propositionibus dumtaxat creditis causaretur. Unde si postea se in aliis scientiis exercitaret, utpote philosophiae naturalis aut metaphysicae, tunc adquireret illarum veritatum notitiam evidentem, et priorem amitteret, theologicam videlicet creditivam. Sicut tenens per fidem quod triangulus habet tres angulos aequales duobus rectis, si postea se exercitet in geometria adquiret habitum evidentem de illa conclusione, per cuius adquisitionem desinet prima notitia tantummodo creditiva. Et si non subito quoad substantiam habitus tamen quoad potentiam perceptivam totaliter immutat, prout in sequenti dicetur articulo.[32] Similiter, viator nunc tenet per fidem quod Deus est trinus et unus.

---

32. Peter of Candia Sent. 1.pro.2 (cod. Vat. lat 1081, ff. 12rb–15ra).

Cum autem pervenerit ad patriam habebit praemissae veritatis notitiam evidentem, et tunc evacuatur notitia creditiva iuxta illud Apostoli, *I Ad Cor.* 14:[33] *Cum autem venerit quod perfectum est evacuabitur quod ex parte est.* Non ergo habeo pro aliquo inconvenienti quod aliquae veritates theologicae sint viatoribus evidenter notae. Sed bene haberem pro inconvenienti quod veritates huiusmodi, naturaliter videlicet cognoscibiles, essent viatoribus evidenter notae theologia viatoris secundum cursum naturae. Unde non sequitur: haec veritas est theologica, ergo eius notitia est theologica, theologia videlicet viatoris secundum cursum naturae. Propter quod concedendae sunt istae propositiones: 'aliqua notitia de veritatibus theologiae non est theologica,' 'aliqua est veritas theologica cuius notitia non adquiritur per exercitium theologicum viatoris,' 'alicuius veritatis naturaliter cognoscibilis adhaesio est viatori necessaria ad aeternam beatitudinem consequendam.'

Et per praedicta patet responsio ad **secundum dubium**: quod nullum est inconveniens eandem veritatem ad diversas facultates vel scientias, sumendo nomen scientiae largo modo, pertinere. Verbi gratia, simplex fidelis habet istam 'Deus est unus' ex fide, ut dicitur in symbolo 'Credo in unum Deum,' et sic dicitur theologica. Metaphysicus vero demonstrat eandem, ut patet, XII *Metaphysicae*:[34] "Entia neque volunt male disponi, unus ergo princeps." Et sic respectu eiusdem veritatis sunt metaphysicus habitus et theologicus, et ita eadem veritas ad diversas reducitur facultates. Et si **dicatur**: quomodo respectu eiusdem habetur habitus evidens et inevidens, metaphysicus videlicet et theologicus; dicitur quod hoc pervenit ex varietate subiectorum, nam unitas obiectiva varietati non obviat subiectivae. Sed utrum stante unitate tam ex parte obiecti quam subiecti sit possibilitas, de hoc nihil ad praesens, quia in sequenti articulo ista materia declarabitur. Ex quibus luculenter apparet quid de isto primo articulo sit tenendum.

---

33. 1 Corinthians 13.10.
34. Aristotle *Metaphysics* 12.10.1076a3–4.

062165

DATE DUE

DE1 4 '99			

```
B                    62165
56
.M4      Medieval philosophy and
v.1          theology.
```

HIEBERT LIBRARY
Fresno Pacific College - M.B. Seminary
Fresno, CA 93702

DEMCO